W9-BQY-552

THE LEARNED PRESIDENCY

Other books by David H. Burton:

American History—British Historians
Edwin Arlington Robinson
Holmes-Sheehan Correspondence
Oliver Wendell Holmes, Jr.
Oliver Wendell Holmes, Jr.: What Manner of Liberal?
Progressive Masks
Theodore Roosevelt
Theodore Roosevelt and His English Correspondents
Theodore Roosevelt—Confident Imperialist
William Howard Taft in the Public Service

THE LEARNED PRESIDENCY

*Theodore Roosevelt, William Howard Taft,
Woodrow Wilson*

David H. Burton

Rutherford • Madison • Teaneck
Fairleigh Dickinson University Press
London and Toronto: Associated University Presses

Associated University Presses
440 Forsgate Drive
Cranbury, NJ 08512

Associated University Presses
25 Sicilian Avenue
London WC1A 2QH, England

Associated University Presses
2133 Royal Windsor Drive
Unit 1
Mississauga, Ontario
Canada L5J 1K5

The paper used in this publication meets the requirements
of the American National Standard for Permanence of Paper
for Printed Library Materials Z39.48-1984.

Library of Congress Cataloging-in-Publication Data

Burton, David Henry, 1925–
    The learned presidency.

    Bibliography: p.
    Includes index.
    1. Presidents—United States—Intellectual life.
2.. Roosevelt, Theodore, 1858–1919—Knowledge and
learning.   3. Taft, William H. (William Howard),
1857–1930—Knowledge and learning.   4. Wilson, Woodrow,
1856–1924—Knowledge and learning.   5. Presidents—
United States—Biography. I. Title.
E176.1.B935   1988   973.91′092′2 [B]   86-46327
ISBN 0-8386-3313-7 (alk. paper)

Second Printing, 1989

PRINTED IN THE UNITED STATES OF AMERICA

For
Mom and Dad
Extraordinary Parents and Grandparents

CONTENTS

ACKNOWLEDGMENTS

As do most authors, I owe debts of support and encouragement. I especially want to acknowledge the generosity of the Earhart Foundation, which awarded a Fellowship that gave me time to write and a Grant for readying the manuscript for publication. Saint Joseph's University's Faculty Research and Faculty Development Programs also extended financial aid. A. E. Campbell gave the manuscript a thorough reading, much to its improvement. Antoinette M. Burton aided me in some aspects of my research. Others whose encouragement I value included colleagues James E. Dougherty, Frank Gerrity, Anthony J. Joes, Graham Lee, Randall Miller, as well as friends, John S. Monagan and John Lukacs. Stephanie Auer's dedication to the task of typing various drafts of the manuscript deserves special thanks.

PREFACE

The American presidency may appear a strange if not an unnatural place to seek men of learning, and when they have been found, it is equally likely that a judgment will be made that they do not belong there after all. This is a popular misconception and, it may be said, a scholarly misconception from which the popular impression arises. The best of the presidents, by common consent, have been men who *did* things, as commanders in chief in time of war, civil or foreign, and as statesmen in the face of a variety of other serious challenges. The worst of them have been corrupt, incompetent, or indolent, characteristics exhibited singly or in some combination. As a powerful office, from the chief magistracy of George Washington to the imperial presidency of our time, it has tended to enjoy extremes of reputation. A president should be great in the estimation of most Americans, and if he is not, he is criticized insofar as his accomplishments fail to meet the high standards of anticipation that come with the high office itself. There have been mediocre or ordinary men as president, and these are thought of as poor or weak or bad because they were not great. Such judgments, in any event, are made on the basis of measurable achievements. The learning of the office holder, whether extensive or limited, makes no immediate or discernible difference to those who pass judgments. Overviewing the presidency and presidents shows that knowledge of a theoretical kind and erudition of any sort, if recognized at all, are factors quickly discounted as irrelevant to the game of rating the presidents. Morton Borden summed it up in *America's Eleven Greatest Presidents,* when he wrote "the fact seems to be that America's greatest presidents have been chosen on the basis of success," and "the majority of scholars think much along the same lines as most Americans. . . . the ultimate criterion is still success." The success referred to is the product of actions taken rather than ideas conceived, even though the ideas may have enjoyed a significant role in shaping policy.

Ralph Waldo Emerson spoke of the ramifications of the conflict between thought and action in "The American Scholar," his Phi Beta Kappa address at Harvard in 1837. "There goes the notion in the world," he complained, "that the scholar should be a recluse, a valetudinarian,—as unfit for any handiwork or public labor, as a penknife to an axe. The so-called 'practical men' sneer at speculative men, as if, because they specu-late or *see,* they could do nothing." But Emerson found that "Action with the scholar is subordinate, but it is essential. Without it, he is not yet a man. Without it, thought can never ripen into truth." Emerson's special concern was for the scholar. But there is wisdom in the reverse of his judgment when applied to the presidency. The man of action who does not think is not yet a man. Without thought, action may never ripen into truth. And truth is a crucial ingredient in a great president.

The image of the typical president, devoid of intellectual distinction, persists nonetheless, and it has worked to perpetuate certain charac-teristics found in successive chief executives. The developing standard made few concessions to the life of the mind. A procession of nonintellec-tual presidents has reinforced the image over a period of almost two hundred years. The more recent occupants of the White House have not been learned, whether viewed by friend or foe. The presidential mold has fully hardened.

It is a mistake, however, to agree altogether with this stereotype of American presidents. At least a half-dozen of the forty or so presidents have substantial claims to being men of intellect, without forfeiting the right to being deemed men of action. John Adams, Thomas Jefferson, and James Madison at the onset of the Republic, and Theodore Roosevelt, William Howard Taft, and Woodrow Wilson at the beginning of this cen-tury were all men of marked intellectual attainment. Each in his own way demonstrated that thought and action could mingle naturally and con-structively. Of the first group, Adams was a political thinker, Jefferson a universal genius, and Madison, "the philosopher of the Constitution." Of the presidents in the twentieth century Roosevelt was a historian and naturalist, Taft a serious legal mind, and Wilson a scholar and political theorist. Drawing upon what these particular presidents reveal of them-selves, it is apparent that historians, philosophers, and scientists have been presidents at one time or another. With the exception of Jefferson, no claim is made that these individuals were necessarily great thinkers, but just as surely their learned achievements were of high caliber. For exam-ple, no American commentator of the period down to the Civil War, apart from Jefferson, would rank above either Adams or Madison as a political philosopher, which means they stand favorably compared with Calhoun and John Taylor of Caroline. By the twentieth century learning had be-come much more specialized and less conveniently accessible, so that it is not as likely Roosevelt could have been a first-rate historian while remain-ing an active public man, or that Wilson's political writings would be placed ahead of those of James Bryce. But one may today still read with profit Roosevelt's *The Winning of the West,* while Americans continue to wrestle with the problem of presidential-legislative interaction explored in seminal fashion by Woodrow Wilson in *Congressional Government.*

The present book is concerned primarily with an examination of the intellectual background, the minds, and the learning that describe the first three twentieth-century American presidents. Its leading purpose is to analyze what they thought and what they wrote and how ideas shaped them as individuals prior to high office—and to look at them in the context of the totality of their mental lives. Of secondary relevance, this study seeks to suggest the influence of the ideas of Roosevelt, Taft, and Wilson on their presidencies. The circumstances they encountered while in the White House doubtlessly helped to direct their translation of thought into action, but as a refinement of a philosophy already matured, one largely defined before entering upon the presidency.

Roosevelt, Taft, and Wilson should be linked to the three remarkable men who came to the presidency after the retirement of Washington. Adams, Jefferson, and Madison are a necessary reference point in any consideration of the learned presidents who introduced the high office to the twentieth century. The three latter-day chief executives were themselves deeply aware of the power of the office. As close students of the American past they appreciated the promise inherent in the minds of Adams, Jefferson, and Madison, and they deplored the nineteenth-century developments by reason of which that promise went unfulfilled. They consciously proposed to continue to exercise the great powers of the office, while at the same time restoring it to the level of honor and respect that had obtained one hundred years before their time. Their personal ambitions and sense of national purpose combined to return an intellectual dimension to a position that had become, at various times, a prize, a sectional pawn, a political football, and a martyr's seat. Given their achievement, it becomes necessary to add that the promise they ably renewed met rejection, as it had in the preceding century. While they did not stand out as individuals of exceptional intellectual habit, as John Quincy Adams and Abraham Lincoln did during the long hiatus of the nineteenth century, it is still reassuring to record Herbert Hoover's literary accomplishments as well as his technological expertise, or Harry Truman's mastery of the facts and no small part of the meaning of the American past. If such efforts failed to sustain the intellectualism of the country's early decades, at least one or more of these men come through to us as perhaps touched by the fire of their predecessors.

For those skeptical of the intellectual as president, it is worth noting that the office never stood in higher repute than it did in the early nineteenth century and again in the first years of the present century, periods in which

American chief executives were republican variants of the philosopher-kings celebrated by the Enlightenment and scholarly witnesses to the very history they were working to make. In this respect it is also appropriate to stress that as the passive conception of the presidency common to the last century gave way to the dynamic executive leadership, the transition was shaped and directed by men of the mind, Theodore Roosevelt and Woodrow Wilson in particular. The character of the office did not change simply because of necessity breeding opportunity. Conditions at home and abroad will always have a part to play in momentous institutional changes, but Roosevelt and Wilson, thoroughly schooled in the historical past and especially concerned with the uses of power, had carefully gauged the possibilities of the presidency as a place of national leadership. Furthermore, they deliberately brought the office through the first, critical stages of its new life. In all this, learning preceded thought as thought preceded action in a fashion best described as spontaneous and unaffected. The presidency in consequence became something other than a bully pulpit and the president someone other than a schoolmaster scolding the Senate into taking its medicine. Such representations are honest enough, having more than a grain of truth about them, yet they hardly portray the nature of the energetic presidency that, grounded in history and theory combined, was the handiwork of men of exceptional intellect and learning.

What part of learning subsumes intellectualism? What is meant by "learned" or "intellectual"? How, for example, is intellectual distinguished in meaning from "an intellectual"? Is "learning" in the eye of the subject alone, or also in that of the beholder? What proportions of thought and action may be deemed appropriate for the word intellectual to be used at all? These and similar queries that arise in the course of this book can not be answered simply or all at once. What may appear applicable to Taft may be less pertinent to Wilson. The legal mind works in different ways from one steeped in the study of political institutions. Some propositions, however, may be stated at the outset that will serve as guidelines. Serious study and wide reading place a person within the orbit of the intellectual world. A recognition that action calls for a reference to past modes of thought no less than to past policies, that what one does should be influenced by an awareness of the functions of that action in a larger context, is a second consideration. The imperialism of Theodore Roosevelt may serve as a plain example. TR consciously treated his advocacy of American expansion overseas as part of the extension of the superior peoples (which he defined in terms of political stability, technological proficiency, and the "fighting edge") across the backward spaces of the world. It was a process begun in the sixteenth century, as he judged the matter. Roosevelt was a student of imperialism before he developed as an imperialist president.

Roosevelt, Taft, and Wilson all respected learning and knowledge for their own sake, the pursuit of which was integral to their personalities and not a mere appendage or decoration. This is the third guideline for estimating intellectual presidents. They were honestly intellectual in their outlook, occasionally to their disadvantage. Woodrow Wilson and the misfortune of the Versailles treaty come readily to mind. Had Wilson been less arrogant, or less adamant, traits due to an intellectually and morally inspired overconfidence, he might have been able to achieve his goals in 1919. But then, had he been less intellectual, he might not have been elected president in 1912 or reelected in 1916. The lesson is clear. Not only was learning integral to these men, it was an inescapable element in their destiny.

THE LEARNED PRESIDENCY

PROLOGUE

An office desired "by an enlightened and reasonable people"

The presidency of the United States was intended from the outset as an office to command attention and respect. Writing in *The Federalist,* the papers by Alexander Hamilton, James Madison, and John Jay expounding the Constitution and of which Jefferson once remarked there was "no better book" respecting the practice of constitutional government, Hamilton defended so powerful an office in a republic. The basis of his argument was that it should and would be occupied by "characters pre-eminent for ability and virtue."[1] Even in anticipation, the quality of the men in the presidency was thought critical to the success of the position. In certain ways the inclusion of a single magistrate designed to exercise a wide range of executive power was a daring proposal. Memories of "the royal brute and tyrant," "the sullen hardfisted pharoah," as Tom Paine described George III in *Common Sense,* were vivid and troubling.[2] Patriot indictments of the king had gone a long way toward making Americans suspicious of monarchs or those who might be made to look like them. It was against "the images of Asiatic despotism and voluptuousness" conjured by opponents of the Constitution that Hamilton was moved to write of what his countrymen might expect in their president.[3] In the various *Federalist* essays dealing with the presidency that appeared over the signature of Publius in the *New York Packet* during March and April 1788, Hamilton both destroyed the charges levied at Article Two of the Constitution, the Executive Article, and explained in reassuring fashion the nature, powers, and purpose of the presidency. In his judgment "well directed men," those of "understanding," would grace the presidency, men "disposed to view human nature as it is, without either flattering its virtues or exaggerating its vices." Finally, Hamilton envisioned the presidency as an office that would be desired "by an enlightened and reasonable people," exhibiting in their choice the attributes that were to be the distinctions of a responsible chief executive.[4]

Reading *The Federalist* papers that treat the presidency, thoughts of the philosopher-king—virtuous, intelligent, just, and wise—come almost immediately to mind. What Hamilton described was, of course, his conception of a model chief executive, but the model tended to set a tone for the presidency. Nor did the first occupants of the office fail to meet the standards that had been laid down, beginning with George Washington. As the Philadelphia convention came to a close in September 1787, Washington, its presiding officer, spoke simply but earnestly of the Constitution. "Let us," he urged, "raise a standard to set a tone for the whole of government under the Constitution." When the time came for the choice of the first chief magistrate, Washington had no rival.

Evaluating George Washington as president has been a problem for historians and biographers alike, without the intention of denying his greatness. Did he do too much or too little while chief executive? Was he too formal or too open to special pleading? Was he the president of the nation or of the Federalist party? Such questions aside, there can be no doubt that he gave to the presidential office, during the uncertain months of its infancy, the dignity and respect it deserved and that the young republic required of it. Indeed, Washington by reason of his character may have helped to shape the presidency in a special way. As it became obvious in the deliberations of the convention that the executive was to be entrusted to one person, some of the delegates, expecting Washington to be the first president, were content to leave certain features of the office vague or to give it more strength than it might otherwise have received.

Whatever his limitations as a man of formal learning, Washington possessed, in the estimate of Jefferson, a mind "great and powerful, without being of the very first order;" and, he added, "his penetration [was] strong, though not so acute as that of Newton, Bacon, or Locke."[5] Despite its apparent caution this was perhaps an overdrawn assessment of Washington, though Jefferson knew his subject well and his judgment can not be altogether discounted. Washington's contribution to the development of the presidency lay in another direction, in any case. He had so dignified the office that men of the mind openly desired to succeed him and because of his precedence felt called to a high responsibility. Rather than having defined the presidency and thereby possibly circumscribing its character as well as its functions, he had conducted public affairs in a manner to ennoble it. Hostile critics were not lacking during the eight years he was in power, yet Washington's composure remained part of his style and his legacy. And because the spirit of that age looked upon learning as one of man's proper endeavors, the learned presidents who followed, far from being incongruous, received an inheritance they proceeded to use and enrich according to their talents. The first of these was John Adams.

As a man of intellect John Adams's reputation stood high with contemporaries, as it has with later commentators. The Jeffersonian *Philadelphia*

Aurora at the time of his presidential inauguration found "that the resources of his mind are equal to the duties of his station." Jefferson himself thought Adams "profound in his views." Many years after, Theodore Parker wrote: "With the exception of Dr. Franklin, I think of no American politician in the eighteenth century who was his intellectual superior. For though Hamilton and Jefferson, nay, Jay and Madison and Marshall surpassed him in some high qualities, yet no one of them seems to have been quite his equal on the whole." His daughter-in-law, Louisa Johnson Adams, the wife of John Quincy Adams, wrote warmly of him. "I have never met with a mind of such varied power, such acute discrimination . . . so intrinsically *sound*. Everything in his mind was rich, racy and true." Vernon Louis Parrington held that John Adams was "the most notable political thinker—with the possible exception of John C. Calhoun—among American Statesmen," an assessment whose impact is enhanced by Parrington's known Jeffersonian bias. Harold Laski called Adams, quite simply, the greatest American political philosopher down to mid-twentieth century.[6]

The bow must not be overstrained in the name of learning. Adams was born under the sign of Scorpio, the sign of one who is destined to strife, and he played any number of vital parts in the drama of American independence, considered from start to finish. He was not a philosopher in the closet, but a philosopher in action. Jefferson's estimate of his work in the Second Continental Congress bears this out. He recalled Adams as "the great Colossus of that Congress—the great pillar of support to the Declaration of Independence," and, Jefferson added, "its ablest advocate and champion on the floor of the House."[7] Apart from the presidency (and the vice-presidency) Adams was an attorney, legislator, financial agent, and diplomat, in which latter capacity he represented the American nation in France, Holland, and Great Britain, having been chosen the first American representative to the Court of St. James's. It is foolish to attempt to draw a line of demarcation between Adams the active public man and Adams the thinker and author. Invariably when he wrote by way of pamphlet, treatise, or book, he wrote in response to the events swirling about him and in which he was caught up. Proposing to sum him up, Parrington called him a "realist," an economical way of identifying the thinker and the man of action. Widely read, "the most widely read in political history of his generation of Americans," his life-long passion was the art and the act of republican rule.[8] In the process Adams strove to avoid extremes. Though often charged with advocacy of class government, he tended to avoid commitment either to agrarianism or capitalism, to democracy or oligarchy. "Honest John" Adams is neither a personal slogan nor a historian's label. Indicating intellectual forthrightness and political astuteness, it is a useful clue to the total man.

After graduating from Harvard College in 1755, John Adams read law with James Putnam at Worcester and then returned home to Braintree where he was admitted to the Suffolk County Bar. His first important writing, *Dissertation on the Canon and Feudal Law,* was part of the general American protest over the Stamp Act. As Anglo-American relations grew worse, Adams's pen grew more active. His *Novanglus Letters, Thoughts on Government,* and a draft of a constitution for Massachusetts all revealed a mind rich in learning and grooved to the needs of the time. Yet his greatest intellectual accomplishments lay in the future. Between October 1786 and December 1787, while serving as minister to Great Britain, Adams undertook his most extensive work, *A Defence of the Constitutions of the United States.* It was written to refute the constitutional theories of Turgot. In a letter to the English radical political commentator, Dr. Price, Turgot contended that the American state constitutions were but imitations of the British model, too lacking in centralized authority with too much emphasis on a separation of powers. Adams was not intimidated by Turgot's reputation as a leading political theorist, as his disagreement demonstrated. Apart from Turgot's strictures Adams was disturbed by Shays's Rebellion of 1786, the uprising of economic dissidents in central and western Massachusetts led by Captain Daniel Shays, late of the Continental Line. "The commotion in New England alarmed me," he wrote, "so much that I have thrown together some heavy speculations upon the subject of government." Adams feared centralized power as he feared the mob. Some Americans, Benjamin Franklin among them, appeared to favor certain centralizing features of government and Adams was impelled to make his position known. ". . . Power is always abused when unlimited or unbalanced" summed up his view simply but emphatically. Not untypically, it took him three volumes to say all that he felt needed saying on the subject. It is likely that his arguments in volume one, which was available in Philadelphia in 1787, influenced members of the Constitutional Convention. When the new government was launched John Adams was chosen vice-president, one of the host of first-administration officials who were sympathetic to the cause of the Republic under the Constitution and whose ardor and ability helped to make it a success.[9]

A second major treatise, *Discourses on Davila,* was a philosophical essay in which Adams felt free to roam over centuries of history and politics, concluding once again that man's flawed nature required power to be divided and balanced if men were to avoid tyranny and anarchy. *Discourses on Davila* revealed Adams at his most candid respecting human nature and society.

It was an easy matter for contemporaries to read his passages as antidemocratic. Adams was not the democrat Jefferson might have meant by the word, much less in the meaning it has come to have. But he was no less democratic than most of his Federalist friends. Though he owed a great deal to Adam Smith in composing the *Discourses,* he had drawn on other sources as well, especially Alexander Pope's *Essay on Man* and Samuel Johnson's *The Vanity of Human Wishes.* But the discernment of Adams in the realities of power, his grasp of history, and his common sense were also elements in his synthesis, his last important work before assuming the presidency.

John Adams came to the presidency a learned man. Because learning was the common equipment of important public figures of the day, his intellectual attainments did not make him unique. It is the history of the presidential office in the nineteenth century, displaying an almost uninterrupted series of undistinguished minds from Jackson to McKinley, that throws Adams and his writings into high relief. He was one of that remarkable generation that spun off from the conjunction of English political thought and Enlightenment teachings on the full range of man in society, a rare historical event not likely to be repeated for many generations and perhaps never to occur again in the lifetime of a civilization. The times called for thought and action combined in individuals, a prescription that Adams, Jefferson, and Madison, among others, admirably filled. The list is a long one, extending beyond these presidents and including men of lesser position though not of lesser intellect: Franklin, Hamilton, Jay, Marshall, and many others.

Adams's public career had its ups and downs. His presidency, for that matter, has been variously judged a success and a failure. Critics point to the fact that he was not reelected to a second term, one of the conventional standards for measuring success. Adams's policies, in addition, brought on divisions within the Federalist party from which it did not recover, which may help to explain his single term as chief executive. But the weight of opinion in the matter of John Adams, president, must be that he did well by his country if not his party, despite certain negative outcomes.

At first glance it may seem otherwise because he must also be judged by what he did not do. He did not go to war with France. He withstood the considerable provocation that France gave to the United States by its seizure of American commercial vessels on the high seas and the insistence of a considerable number of Federalist party members that war with France be declared officially. In pursuing a policy of neutrality Adams was fearful that civil strife might erupt in the wake of war against a major European power. Disorder and uncertainty could only harm the fortunes of the new nation. He had expressed his abhorrence of disorder throughout his political commentaries. The well-being of the Republic was uppermost in his mind. The uniqueness of America was an argument that had been put forth in his *Dissertation on the Canon and Feudal Law,* as he urged America to dissociate from Old World habits and outlook. His activities in the patriot cause leave no room to doubt where his heart lay; his writings speak equally clearly for his head. Adams was prepared to sacrifice party and personal political ambitions while president to preserve American national interest as he perceived it. What John Adams brought to the presidency from a lifetime of study and reflection was a sense of history derived from the written record, a view of mankind based in acute observation, and a devotion to country because, in a fashion somewhat different from Jefferson, he too believed that America was "the world's last best hope."

The similarity in thought and values between Adams and Thomas Jefferson is attested to by their long-standing friendship, the foundation of which was mutual respect and admiration. Having tested their common ideas in the fires of debate, war, and history, they proceeded to have their political differences in the 1790s. When the new government under the Constitution moved in directions not to Jefferson's liking, their paths diverged. Jefferson's strong taste for liberty and Adams's equally definite preference for order lay at the bedrock of the disagreements. Later, during the Adams presidency, fresh strains were placed on the friendship. The undeclared war with France and the ongoing diplomatic maneuvering offended Jefferson's French sensibilities. But the cruelest blow was struck by the Alien and Sedition Acts. Though initiated by the anti-French, anti-Jefferson faction in the Federalist-controlled Congress, Adams enforced these laws aimed at silencing political opposition by the imposition of fines and jail terms. No laws could have been more repugnant to Jefferson; they violated his basic creed as an American and as a philosopher. In concert with Madison he wrote the Virginia and Kentucky Resolutions to protest this high-handed interference with the Bill of Rights. The whole episode threatened the Jefferson-Adams relationship with a permanent rupture. Once tempers cooled and time had its chance to heal the wounds inflicted, the two found that their old camaraderie surfaced again. For the last years of their lives they were fellow patriarchs, down to the common day of their deaths. It was to be 4 July 1826, the half-century anniversary of the Declaration of Independence that Jefferson had drafted and Adams had defended in the Congress.

For all of that, the learning of Adams and Jefferson was differently wrought and differently displayed. Jefferson's thought lacked the sharp, relentless focus exhibited in the writings of John Adams. His mind was, instead, all-encompassing. It delighted in principles of gardening quite as much as in principles of government. Jefferson was inventive and reflective; he was educated in science and trained in law; he built no system of philosophy but remained an active thinker throughout a long life. The learning of Jefferson was as wide-ranging as his intellect was fertile; so that neither lends itself to a ready account. With a mind that was restless and active Jefferson was on the lookout for practical results, not cosmic designs. He helped to stir a revolution by his Declaration but had too little to do with initiating a system of national government, the only way to preserve what had been won by war and diplomacy. No educational theorist, he proceeded to found the University of Virginia on the common sense of the matter, claiming it as one of his finest achievements. The great champion of human rights was a slave owner who could not escape history when it came to a universal application of his beliefs in the rights of man. To indicate some of the paradoxes of Jefferson's thought is only to imply its complexity, which continues to defy the most painstaking and astute Jeffersonian scholars. Neither Dumas Malone nor Merrill Peterson, for example, both of whom have spent their lives in pursuit of Jefferson, claims to have isolated the inner man. Peterson concluded simply that Jefferson was, for him, "impenetrable."

Like Adams at Harvard, Jefferson enjoyed the fruits of a classical education at The College of William and Mary and read law with George Wythe, Virginia's most erudite lawyer. And as with that of Adams, Jefferson's pen came alive in response to events that led to American independence. When news of the Boston Tea Party reached London in 1773, the stage was set for a confrontation with Massachusetts and with such other colonies as would stand by her. The scene at the same time darkened with forebodings. Thomas Jefferson took two parts in the drama that followed: a leader of political action and a voice of the astute propagandist, with a mind well furnished by learning to support both roles. During the turbulent decade of the 1770s he was to write three powerful statements of his political philosophy: "A Summary of the Rights of British America" (1774), the Declaration of Independence (1776), and "An Act for Establishing Religious Freedom" (1779). Learning, as was the case with Adams, preceded action as naturally as it mixed with it.

"A Summary of the Rights of British America" was a pioneering effort. It underscored, for example, the principle that the establishment of new states should be under such laws and regulations as the inhabitants deemed most likely to promote public happiness. The "Summary" was studded with historical references that lent to Jefferson's words a weight and a force appropriate to the seriousness of his purpose. Like John Adams in the *Novanglus Letters*, he saw George III "holding the balance of a great if well poised empire; who by his just leadership will establish fraternal love and harmony through the whole empire." Jefferson appealed to common sense and to reason throughout the "Summary," to sentiments as well as to precedents. Yet he remained the learned advocate of a point of view, urging men to think before they acted.[10]

So much has been written about the Declaration of Independence; it has been analyzed and dissected, celebrated and honored, so that almost anything said about its intellectual dimensions is obvious. Not that the last book on the subject necessarily has been written. Garry Wills's *Inventing America* (1978) at the very least illustrates the proposition that each generation is entitled to study and reinterpret the ultimates of the past. But whether one turns to old-time admirers, such as Carl Becker, contemporary authorities from Brodie to Schachner, or to the challenging judgments of Wills, the result must always be the same. The mind of Thomas Jefferson was that of the Enlightenment, at once narrowed to a single thinker and broad enough to illuminate the political landscape with the total candlepower of a creative and daring century. In other words, there can be no dissent from the self-evident truth that the Declaration contains a full measure of the thought of the Age of Reason. Whether Jefferson was more indebted to John Locke's *On Civil Government*—the thesis long held—or to Francis Hutcheson's *System of Moral Philosophy*—as lately suggested—Jefferson's reputation as a thinker is enlarged and enshrined when reference is made to his authorship of the Declaration. Long after the event, in writing to Richard H. Lee in 1825, he described his work simply: "Neither aiming at originality of principles or sentiment, nor yet copied from a particular or previous writing, it [the Declaration] was intended to be an expression of the American Mind."[11] Jefferson's assessment is enough.

In 1779 Thomas Jefferson gave extended meaning to his conception of natural rights with his proposal for "A Bill for Establishing Religious Freedom." A philosophical consideration of his views that he derived from reflections based on reason and history, it was enacted into law by the Virginia Assembly in 1786. His statement began with an insistence that God had created the mind free and that any attempt to coerce this freedom was a "departure from the plan of the Holy Author of our religion." Whether interference came from the church or the state, it was all the same, a judgment that Jefferson proceeded to demonstrate by repeated reference to the deleterious effects of moral indoctrination by civil magistrates and ecclesiastical officials. The evidence having been adduced, Jefferson insisted on the principle that "no man shall be compelled to frequent or support any religious worship, place or ministry whatsoever, nor shall be enforced, restrained, molested, or burthened in his body or goods, nor shall otherwise suffer on account of his religious opinions or belief; but that all men shall be free to profess, and by argument to maintain, their opinions in matters of religion, and that the same shall in nowise diminish, enlarge, or affect their civil capacities." One of the distinctive features of the American republic thus had been articulated: church and state forever separate. The important reason for this separation was made plain as Jefferson closed his resolution before the assembly: "the rights hereby asserted are of the natural rights of mankind."[12]

Though public affairs were the preoccupation of Jefferson during the revolutionary war, including service in the Virginia legislature and later as wartime governor of the state, he yet remained an individual for whom writing was a necessary outlet for intellectual curiosity. A great burst of energy had characterized the 1770s. Thereafter he studied and wrote with less passion but with a sustained inquisitiveness. *The Notes on Virginia,* Jefferson's only full-length, original book, was written in 1781–82 and published first in Paris in 1784. This limited edition of two hundred copies was soon followed by popular editions in French, German, and English, and the book was circulated in both Britain and America. *The Notes on Virginia* has been pronounced a prodigious book, as valuable for its scientific observations as for its human wisdom. In fact, Jefferson much impressed the European intellectual world on both scores. Nothing appeared to escape his notice. He speculated on the geology of Virginia, described its topography and natural resources—his account of the Natural Bridge was a compound of a naturalist's curiosity and a boy's wonder—investigated the plants and animals common to his native land, and discussed the aborigines and their folkways in colorful detail (to be hairy on the body was a disgrace to the Indian because it likened man to a hog), to provide but a short list of scientific interests.

The book also contained further disclosures of Jefferson's social and political views. His faith in liberal democracy, in which the good of the individual must always take precedence over the interests of the group and the government, was fully explored. Celebration of the independent yeoman farmer, distrust of cities and manufactures—"let our workshop remain in Europe"—his faith in government derived from common consent, the ever-present worry over freedom of conscience, especially in religious matters, his concern for public literacy and education—all these and more were discussed at length and with an intelligence of purpose that enhanced his reputation at home and abroad.

Essays on the Anglo-Saxon Language (1798) readily identified the scholarly Jefferson. He first became interested in Anglo-Saxon while studying law under Wythe, proposing to simplify grammar, make spelling consistent, and otherwise render the old language more accessible. In 1798 he sent his findings to the English philologist, Herbert Croft, with whom he had been corresponding. He urged a study of Anglo-Saxon as an important part of the training in the English language and proposed that it be taught at the University of Virginia. In his treatise Jefferson provided historical background for the alphabet and spelling, pronunciation and grammar, in which latter category he literally got down to cases. "No language can be without them [cases]," he observed, "and it is an error to say that Greek is without the ablative."[13] This concern for language continued into old age. Less than a year before he died Jefferson updated his earlier letters to Croft as required by more recent findings of working scholars, including himself.

Thomas Jefferson's election to the presidency in 1800, in which he narrowly defeated Aaron Burr, did not produce the revolution that his Federalist enemies had predicted and feared. Fisher Ames, one of the virulent New Englanders, described Jefferson and his followers as "Jacobins born in sin . . . sons of darkness . . . trumpeters of sedition."[14] Clearly nothing but evil could arise from an anti-Federalist triumph. Those who knew Jefferson realized full well he planned no coup; it was his opponents who were pleasantly surprised. As president he promoted the cause of the Constitution in ways that, while reflecting his own principles, were constructive and reassuring to all. By the close of his second term in 1809, the United States stood on a firm footing, the most significant of Jefferson's accomplishments in office having been to demonstrate that political power could pass from one party to its rival without disruption of law and order.

The Jeffersonian presidency has been viewed by some as disappointing. In his second term, especially, the president had little to show of concrete accomplishment. Admirers, for that matter, have expressed qualms about the policy of embargo that utterly failed to force either Britain or France to respect American neutral rights at sea. Whether on the whole successful or unsuccessful, Jefferson's presidency bore his stamp as a philosopher and as an American. He had wanted political freedom for his country through a representative democracy. Its foundation was to be an agrarian way of life for the majority of the people. He wanted America to remain a simple, dignified, and moral civilization; at the same time it was to continue as an experiment in government. What he did and how he conducted himself as president to achieve these objectives were symbolic, inasmuch as such objectives by their nature had to be realized as the result of an ongoing process. Jefferson might give direction to the process and encourage its development, but as a son of the Enlightenment he accepted as a truism that government was the act and art of governing, that America itself was a process of individual fulfillment by a responsible use of freedom to experiment.

By gesture as by deed Jefferson proposed to deprive the presidency of the formalities instituted by Washington and the stiffness accorded it by Adams. He walked to his inauguration, received diplomats with a relaxed etiquette, and, as in his first inaugural address, spoke words of political reconciliation. "But every difference of opinion," he pleaded, "is not a difference of principle. We are all republicans—we are all federalists."[15] Jefferson was preparing America for the blessings of the Enlightenment.

Thomas Jefferson's policies while he was president also reflected his outlook as a philosopher and an American. Some of them were negative in character, while others were altogether positive. He made no move to disturb Hamilton's pet, the Bank of the United States, despite his earlier constitutional misgivings about it, and, while he encouraged a reduction in the size of the federal judiciary, the Supreme Court remained intact. If America was meant to be an experiment, Jefferson was tolerant enough to accept the experiments of men other than himself. His determination to pursue a war against the Barbary pirates was one of his positive moves, a direct outgrowth of his conviction that a free people should not pay tribute to brigands, near or far from home. The future of that free people could be assured if the vast tracts of the Louisiana country were purchased on offer from Napoleon. A more definite example of philosophy informing policy is hard to imagine. Here was the means, unexpectedly at hand, to provide the blessings of land and liberty for generations to come. The two, land and liberty, were linked in Jefferson's mind as they were linked in Locke's political philosophy.

The centrality of the intellectual Jefferson in the presidency of the new republic is evident in his friendship with both Adams and James Madison. While the three were contemporaries, Adams was the older and Madison the younger by sixteen years. Madison combined leading traits of his two immediate predecessors in office. His love of liberty was equal to his love of order. It is fascinating to consider how these individuals, all having studied the same philosophers, historians, and poltical commentators, exhibited distinctive profiles of the mind. No doubt Jefferson and Madison were much more alike. Adrienne Koch has written of their friendship as "the great collaboration." But she divined more. "Jefferson and Madison were philosopher-statesmen," she wrote, "perhaps the best this nation has ever produced, their long careers demonstrate the real power of intellect and moral integrity in shaping the structure of a free society."[16] And no doubt she had the presidency in mind in concluding that "their habits of mind are at least as important as the outward acts of their official careers." Koch restated Emerson's insistence on idea informing action with particular reference to the two Virginia presidents. John Quincy Adams described the friendship in his "Discourse at the Jubilee of the Constitution" in 1839: Madison was "the intimate, confidential, and devoted friend" of Jefferson, he said, "and the mutual influence of their two mighty minds upon each other is a phenomenon like the invisible and mysterious movements in the physical world. . . ." Mutually influential, to be sure, but not really invisible or mysterious. Such elements were foreign to the Age of Reason, of which the mind of Madison no less than that of Jefferson, was an apt expression.[17]

Surveying the intellectual backgrounds of John Adams and Thomas

Jefferson, separating the strands of their thinking, and attempting to demonstrate the influence of this philosopher or that book on certain specific views entertained by them, often reveals a causal nexus. Adams deeply admired the moral sentiments of Adam Smith, and Smith in turn was no stranger to passages of *Discourses on Davila*. Jefferson read the Stoics at an early age and commenced to fashion a political faith that in later years showed strains of that school. Adams and Jefferson, however, and especially the latter, were too complex in their philosophies to allow consistently straightforward interpretations. The feeling arises, nonetheless, that the flow of ideas from the great minds and the great works of the past had an identifiable impact on much of their developing philosophies of man and society. Madison's thought, in contrast, does not yield to such an easy formula. There are evident reasons for this. Madison wrote relatively less of political theory or philosophy, apart from his contributions to *The Federalist* papers. These essays are of supreme importance, for they establish beyond doubt the quality of Madison's mind and the accomplishment of his learning. When compared with the output of either Adams or Jefferson, however, his work will not be understood or his intellect properly respected if judged on a straight-line model, for there is too little to connect to his learned preparations. The times of Madison's maturity did not call for the full-scale political presentations common to Adams and Jefferson. Madison's lasting work was not that of a revolutionary, however much in sympathy he was with the movement for independence. He was the father and the philosopher of the Constitution, essentially a builder of institutions as well as an explicator of them. Differing estimates of Madison may be offered in consequence. Being less prolific, he was less obviously a thinker. But, though Madison wrote less, what he did produce bore the sign of a remarkable originality.

Madison and Jefferson are conventionally thought of as partners. Because they supported many of the same causes in a friendship that might be said to have extended even beyond the grave—shortly before he died Jefferson wrote Madison asking him to "take care of me when dead"—it becomes useful also to stress the differences in their intellectual expression. Madison was more analytical, more logical, more mundane in his methods and his purposes; he was also less tender in his affections than Jefferson, less indulgent of man's weaknesses, and less confident that reason alone would hatch the egg of progress into the brightly plumed bird of happiness. Both men were gifted with vision; Madison's was fixed on the nearer horizon while Jefferson's eye roamed further but detected the future with less accuracy. With considerable justification, Garry Wills, in *Explaining America,* has called the fourth president of the republic "the Hamiltonian Madison,"[18] as though to ensure the view that Madison and Jefferson went separate ways.

Madison displayed a kinship with John Adams in a fondness for the immediate prospect. More peculiarly a child of the Enlightenment, Madison avoided the skepticism that Adams sometimes allowed to degenerate into cynicism. He was less preoccupied with self than Adams and thus less inclined to adhere rigidly to his private prejudices, and better able to find room for compromise. Workability meant more to Madison, the constitutionalist, than finely spun theories of the rights of man or Adams's lugubrious "passion for distinction." All in all, Madison appeared to combine features of Jefferson and Adams in his thought. But the mix was uniquely his, and his place in a history of the learned presidency is secure. How he arrived at that place is more a story of his mind than of any other single ingredient.

In his endeavors as a delegate to the Constitutional Convention Madison "reached the height of his career as a philosopher-statesman," according to Adrienne Koch. For those efforts she has concluded that "historians have almost unanimously dubbed him 'the father of the Constitution.'" Another view has been offered, not necessarily contrary but somewhat different. Writing to William Cogswell in 1789 Madison himself protested, "You give me credit to which I have no claim, in calling me '*the* writer of the Constitution. . . .' This was not, like the fabled Goddess of Wisdom, the offspring of a single brain. It ought to be regarded as the work of many heads and many hands."[19] One biographer, Harold S. Schultz, has concluded that Madison's "denial of fatherhood of the Constitution was good history and not false modesty."[20] The proper acclamation to resolve this difference of interpretation may be that of "the philosopher of the Constitution," the suggestion of Edward McNall Burns;[21] or the differences may be semantic. Madison's *Notes* on the convention alone would have entitled him to a special rank among the delegates who brought about the Constitution. None of the other members, including John Adams, arrived at the State House in Philadelphia better prepared for the specific task at hand. Nor was any man among them less influenced or constrained by personal economic considerations. Madison was neither debtor nor creditor. As a matter of principle he never allowed himself "to deal in public property, lands, debts, or money, while a member of the body whose proceedings might influence those transactions."[22]

Madison's work on the floor of the convention and in committee showed an astute grasp of the possible, the workable, and the valuable. Study of European confederations, reinforced by his realistic appraisal of man in society, led him to support compromises that altered the Virginia Plan, both to establish a republican form of rule by providing for popular elections to a lower house and to achieve stability of government, especially by allowing the central authority power over the states. In spite of Madison's *Notes* and the amplifications made on them by numerous historians of the convention, it remains difficult to identify specifically the impact of learning on Madison in action. Learning no doubt suffused his outlook, guided his judgment, advised him of the wisdom of compromise, and supported him when his spirits flagged. In the midst of convention deliberations and decisions, Madison was a mind in action. His movements can be carefully measured in terms of the steps he took to reject efforts to weaken the concept of a powerful central government or to gain acceptance for the three-fifths compromise for representation from the slave states. Yet the exact function of learning in all this is imprecise. The problem presented may be understood in some way by applying the Heisenberg Principle of Uncertainty to history. It may be argued then that if historical momentum is to be measured with accuracy, then historical position can be less exactly determined. Historians, depending on their methods and purpose, tend to write about either momentum or position at a given time. By choosing to examine momentum, in this case Madison's actions in the convention, the position, that is, Madison's learning, can be less carefully indicated. Fortunately for an understanding of Madison the philosopher-statesman of the Constitution, he has left us his contributions to *The Federalist*. These papers constituted the mind of Madison as it concentrated on the nature of the Constitution. They possessed a kind of motionless quality, as an object that is still—Madison's mind in a reflective posture—and from them his learning pertaining to constitutions can be appraised with a meaningful accuracy.

The learned Madison never showed to better advantage than in *The Federalist*. These papers were written to persuade as well as to explain, and if, in the event, views of how the Constitution would function were slanted, its weaknesses glossed over, and some arguments misdirected for better effect, the essays continue to be a singularly impressive array of political commentary. Among Madison's contributions, numbers eighteen, nineteen, and twenty dealt with the history of ancient and modern confederacies; number fourteen argued in favor of the suitability of a republic for a large geographic area, number thirty-nine brought out distinctions between the federal and national character of the Union under the Constitution; and number forty-four was an exposition of the "necessary and proper clause." Throughout these and other essays Madison showed a mastery of understanding and explanation that marks the essays as highly original.

Madison's most frequently quoted essay is also the most controversial, the famous number ten. Here the future president showed to what extent he was a student of Donald Robertson. His argument was woven into a fabric of logic, displaying both the power and the pretensions of logical distinctions. He began by warning of the dangers of factions in popular government, defining faction as "a number of citizens . . . who are united and actuated by some common purpose . . . adverse to the rights of other citizens." There were two methods of dealing with factions: either remove the causes or control the effects. Subdividing further, Madison found two methods for removing the causes: destroy liberty or equate all citizens by bringing them down to a common level. Objecting to both approaches, he proceeded to point out that the causes of factions were sown in the nature of man. Because a cause was not removable, the effects must be controlled. As a pure democracy can not control factions, only a republic "promises the cure for which we are seeking." Madison's key reason for faith in a republic was that representation drawn from a wide area would refine the wishes of the people and reduce the dangers of factions by making factions that much harder to form. This was especially true for a large republic, which the new nation promised to become. Once again, Madison invoked his logical formula. The same advantages that a small republic had over a democracy, a large republic had over a small republic, namely, the reduction of factionalism, and thus the protection of the general citizenry against selfish concentrations of power.[23]

The Federalist was a work of the first rank in the history of political philosophy. That Madison must share credit with Hamilton and Jay for so formidable an analysis of the Constitution is less a diminution of his reputation as a thinker than a commentary on the genius of the generation that wrote the Constitution, secured its ratification, and placed it in operation.

Madison's presidency came after he had served in the Congress of the United States and as Jefferson's secretary of state. While a member of Congress he married, in 1794, Dolly Paine Todd, an admirable life's companion. His preparation for the highest office was as nearly complete as could be wished; he had an impressive mix of learning and experience and a wife of great charm who was to be a classic first lady. During his years in the executive office, however, Madison was plagued by diplomatic problems growing out of the Anglo-French contest for hegemony, problems that eventuated in a second war for independence with England. The War of 1812 provided little opportunity for the president to display, much less utilize, his learning. Once peace was restored, Madison's outlook took on attributes of a philosopher-king. A genuine admirer of Jefferson and his philosophy of man and state, Madison nonetheless welcomed a strengthening of the national government and its enhanced prestige as expressed by the mood of the nation and in legislation such as the tariff and bank laws of 1816. He put mean party advantage aside, treating it as part of the past, and kept an eye very much on the future. It was a promising future if, as the president hoped, his fellow citizens proved wise enough to stand together. His thorough knowledge of the growth of other nation-states coupled with his keen historical sense, persuaded him that the natural tendency toward a more complex federation of states could not and should not be resisted. It should, on the contrary, be encouraged, and in the limited time he had left in office he had the vision to support American nationalism. Madison as president had acted to fulfill the prophecy of Jefferson: "We are all republicans, we are all federalists."

The promise of a learned presidency went largely unfulfilled over the course of the nineteenth century. James Monroe, the last of the Virginia dynasty, and John Quincy Adams, a worthy New England mind by any standard, were but the lingering evidence of a presidential persuasion that was to die out. The reasons for this are not hard to determine. During their formative years, Adams, Jefferson, and Madison were products of a British and a continental fermentation of ideas in which America actively partook. America was a necessary element in the new political theorizing. The New World, in the absence of the historical restraints common to Europe, could better transform theories into practice. After 1816, however, the young nation turned westward and inward, tending to cast off European intellectual ties, as it had broken the political connection in the previous century. Andrew Jackson's election to the presdency in 1828 symbolized a variety of changes, including the passing of a learned presidency. Old Hickory brought to his office authority and vigor, however, and was an imposing figure in the development of the presidency. Lincoln, of course, "belongs to the ages," but to be Lincolnesque was to be wise, patient, and compassionate as well as canny and practical. Lincoln was indigenously American in his training and outlook, and the America from whence he came was raw and unsophisticated. The kind of learning that characterized the early presidents was incongruous with the frontier law and politics familiar to Lincoln.

Lincoln's lack of formal education and his particular circumstances mark him off from the Adams-Jefferson-Madison kind of learning. Yet his use of books, his respect for literature, his grounding in Blackstone, his contemplation of scriptural passages—all this and more make him a special kind of learned president. The difficulty in establishing Lincoln's knowledge lies in the separation of fact from fiction. Some things are generally agreed upon. Lincoln acquired what learning he had on his own initiative; schools played no real part in the process. Second, except for law books that were necessary to his profession, he read what he liked and little else, whether it was the poetry of Bobby Burns, lines from which he was fond of repeating, or the Six Books of Euclid, which showed his mathematical bent. Lincoln was neither a bibliophile nor a collector. In keeping with his practical bent, his books were to be read, to be used, and then to be put aside. As one friend of his mature years put it, study for Lincoln was "a business not a pleasure."[24]

Books were an obvious attraction for an active and acquisitive mind, however. Late in his life he grew cynical about history and biography but apparently continued to read both. He concerned himself especially with the history of the Netherlands and the revolution of 1640 in England, and he studied the lives of Washington, Jefferson, Clay, and Webster. The doubts he had about biography arose from his feeling that the subject's faults were passed over with his virtues unduly enlarged, traits typical, in fact, of the biographies of the time.

Scattered references indicate that Lincoln knew Butler's *Analogy of Religion* and John Stuart Mill's *On Liberty;* of course he had read Volney and Tom Paine. He also admired the *Iliad* and the *Odyssey* of Homer in translation and quoted both Plato and Terrence on occasion. He owned a much-prized collection of Shakespeare's plays and admired Byron's *Childe Harold* and Gray's "Elegy." Oliver Wendell Holmes, James Russell Lowell, and Edgar Allan Poe were American favorites. For all the evidence of a literate Lincoln, it may be best to allow William Herndon, who knew him well, to have the last word: "The truth about the whole of the matter is that Mr. Lincoln read *less* and thought *more* than any person in his sphere in America. . . ."[25]

Well-educated men occupied the White House in the post-Lincoln years, among whom Rutherford B. Hayes and James A. Garfield were prominent. Hayes attended Kenyon College in Ohio, grew fond of the English and French classics, and worked to promote an interest in literature. Along with William Howard Taft's father he was a leading member of the Literary Club in Cincinnati, where he practiced law after 1850. Successful as a lawyer and a community leader, Hayes wore his learning as a badge of accomplishment. It was not a clue to the inner man. He turned his learning outward in such endeavors as seeking support for public libraries, worthy in itself, but typical of an impulse to translate respect for knowledge into tangible forms. After his presidency, which was ill starred from the first, Hayes occupied himself in various educational causes at the same time he enjoyed the advantages of his own extensive library.

The short time Garfield held office has obscured his scholarly side, while his conception of the presidency as a position of negative power probably would have limited his reputation even had he not been assassinated four months after his inauguration. Garfield was an intellectual as at home with ideas as with politics. Schooled at The Western Eclectic Institute in Hiram, Ohio, and at Williams College, he owed his education to his innate curiosity rather than to college instruction. His great interest was history, which he read seriously from an early age; his approach to public trust was often that of a research historian. Appointed to the House Ways and Means Committee, the young congressman, for example, made an exhaustive study of the financial histories of England and America as part of his assignment. Garfield expressed a love of learning in various ways: by reading papers to historical societies, by studying the presidency in preparation for office, and by longing to spend his postpresidential years pursuing historical research and writing. Among the projects he had in mind was a formal history of the Western Reserve, the area he had represented in Congress.

In spite of Hayes and Garfield the learned presidency languished. Knowledge was to advance on many fronts during the Gilded Age. America once more responded to an intellectual revolution that, long gathering its strength, swept across England and the Continent and burst upon America after the Civil War. Scientific ways of thinking were now regnant, and none more ubiquitous than evolution. Herbert Spencer's apostleship to Charles Darwin's evolutionary testament did much to popularize the new learning and its social corollaries based on natural selection. Its true significance lay well below the surface of events. It was to be discovered in the minds of men as diverse as William Graham Sumner, the champion of survival of the fittest; and one of the teachers of William Howard Taft at Yale; Oliver Wendell Holmes, Jr., the progenitor of sociological jurisprudence (as well as the judge Theodore Roosevelt expected to be a Progressive jurist when he appointed Holmes to the Supreme Court in 1902); and Thorstein Veblen, the daring and innovative economist whose theories challenged the conventional socioeconomic individualism embedded in the new-freedom ideas of Woodrow Wilson.

No president before Roosevelt exhibited either in his preparation for public life or in his policies while in office the effects of these new and creative modes of thought. America throughout the nineteenth century continued to be a nation preoccupied with farm and factory and frontier. Too far removed from the intellectual affairs of the Old World to be a significant participant, its involvement was peripheral. If American philosophers and scientists, with a few exceptions, were mostly onlookers in the European intellectual scene in the decades down to the Civil War, little wonder that men in public life remained unlearned and unaffected, except incidentally, until well toward the close of the century. Once the ideas of material science had had a chance to take root and to grow, to find their way into the educational and learning processes, all manner of men would be influenced by the vogue of social Darwinism and the promise of pragmatism. Future presidents would not be immune. The difference between the last of the nineteenth-century presidents, McKinley, and the first of the new breed, Theodore Roosevelt, makes an emphatic contrast. There may be a kernel of truth in the myth that McKinley, as president, was unsure within two thousand miles of where the Philippine Islands were located when he approved the order for Dewey to attack the Spanish at Manila. By the time Roosevelt was twenty-five he had written an authoritative history of *The Naval War of 1812*. Many factors account for the difference between McKinley and Roosevelt, none of them necessarily reflecting adversely on McKinley personally. But there is no mistaking the difference. When TR succeeded McKinley in September 1901, it was again appropriate to speak of learned presidents.

1
THEODORE ROOSEVELT
Learned Style

On 7 June 1910, in the Sheldonian Theatre of the University of Oxford, ex-President Theodore Roosevelt delivered the Romanes Lecture. He called it "The World Movement—Biological Analogies in History."[1] The invitation by Lord Curzon, the chancellor of the university, to give the address was recognition accorded Roosevelt as a distinguished man of letters as well as a former American president. His reputation in each regard was understood and appreciated on both sides of the Atlantic. Roosevelt found the prospect of giving the Romanes Lecture greatly attractive. It would afford him the opportunity once more of expounding his view of modern history, the leading feature of which was the world movement of the European races across the backward areas of the world. This movement, which had been in process since 1500, he had first elaborated in writings done during the 1880s. Years later as a politician and statesman he had pursued policies that fit within this frame of historical reference. In "Biological Analogies in History" he proposed to relate his understanding of history to the scientific spirit of the day for the purpose of placing man in social perspective.

During the closing months of his presidency Roosevelt took time away from pressing political concerns to make a careful preparation of the text of his address. Early drafts were read and criticized by Henry Fairfield Osborn of the American Museum of Natural History in New York, while Lord Bryce, the British ambassador to Washington and sometime Regius Professor of Civil Law at Oxford, found himself at the White House, as the President put it, "to suffer the wholly unwarrantable torments which I design to inflict . . . by going over my Romanes Lecture with me."[2] But the result was a summation of the ideas of Roosevelt himself, a major effort on his part to pronounce a view of man in history. The success of the lecture has been dimmed by the comment of Dr. Lang, the Archbishop of

York. "In the way of grading which we have at Oxford," he said, "we agreed to mark the lecture Beta-minus but the lecturer Alpha-plus. While we felt that the lecture was not a very great contribution to science, we were sure the lecturer was a very great man."[3] If anything, Roosevelt intended to illuminate not science but society, using the methods of science where they seemed applicable and rejecting them when they were not. It is on this test that the lecture should be judged.

"Biological Analogies in History" strictly qualified the role of evolution in human affairs. The address exhibited in Roosevelt a sympathy for scientific method and achievement, as he extolled the greatness of Darwin and asserted that from the biological process of birth, growth, maturation, prosperity, and death, social patterns could be better understood: "As in biology, so in human history. . . ." He also pointed up differences and the danger of deductions from facile comparisons. For example, he said that "most of the great civilizations which have developed a high civilization and have played a dominant part in the world have been, and are, artificial, not merely in social structure but in the sense of including totally different types. A great nation rarely belongs to any one race."[4] While the important ethnic divisions of mankind could not be ignored or discounted, usually they had not remained unified, and, accordingly, had not produced cultures that could be defined as purely ethnic. Civilization flowed out of a great accumulation of spiritual, moral, and intellectual principles and ideas that a particular race at some given period in history might especially express. But Roosevelt insisted that greatness came from ideals and not from blood. "We Americans and you people of the British Isles alike," he told his audience, "need ever to keep in mind that among the many qualities indispensable to the success of a great democracy, and second only to a high and clear sense of duty, of moral obligation, are self-knowledge and self-mastery." In public as in personal affairs, he declared, "though intellect stands high, character stands higher."[5] It followed that problems, whether national or international in scope, ought to be approached in the "spirit of broad humanity, of brotherly kindness, of acceptance of responsibility." Referring to Western imperialism—in effect, to the world movement—he concluded that "in the long run there can be no justification for one race managing or controlling another, unless . . . in the interest and for the benefit of that race."[6] What Roosevelt had striven to do in "Biological Analogies in History" was to identify, contemplate, and praise human purpose in social development.

Some three months later, on 31 August 1910, at Osawatomie, Kansas, in a setting very unlike the Sheldonian Theatre, the ex-president fired off one of the major political speeches in his long career, "The New Nationalism." Though a political speech, it was laced with the pragmatism of William James as transmitted to public uses by Herbert Croly and voiced by the premier public man of the time, Theodore Roosevelt. Croly, in *The Promise of American Life,* had insisted that government was but an instrument of the people, a tool to be used in bringing about socioeconomic reforms vital to the good health of the country. The Constitution as a frame of government was rejected as a limitation on what one generation could do to solve its problems. Specifically understood, constitutional government must become a living process of change and adaptation, with man's intellect the directing force for good. Croly had been much impressed by Roosevelt's conduct of the presidency and had drawn heavily upon it in writing *The Promise of American Life.* The book, in turn, helped TR crystallize his thinking as an advanced Progressive.[7]

Early in the Kansas speech Roosevelt offered a quotation: "Labor is prior to and independent of capital. Capital is only the fruit of labor and could never have existed if labor had not first existed. Labor is superior to capital and deserves much the higher consideration." Such were the words not of a radical agitator, the ex-president announced with deliberate irony, but of Abraham Lincoln.[8] He went on to define the great issue of 1910 as "the struggle of free men to gain and hold the right of self-government as against special interests."[9] This was nothing new, he said, but in a complex industrialized society it had assumed new forms and new meanings. He reminded his audience that the objective of any reform ought to be the enhancement of opportunities for individual citizens. The "square deal" did not stand for the dole but the right to work, a right ensured "free from the sinister influence or control of interests" through the agency of a powerful central government.[10] Disposed to accept combinations in industry as "the result of an imperative economic law which could not be replaced by political legislation," Roosevelt thought that the individual would be served best "in completely controlling such combinations in the interests of public welfare."[11] Control should extend over business corporations, the money system, the national natural resources—over wealth in whatever form. This must be done in the name of "national efficiency," as pragmatism itself had efficiency as a goal. The national government was thereby promoted as a popularly elected instrument of national efficiency, blending democracy and science.

"The New Nationalism" was a notable synthesis of Roosevelt's mature progressivism. At the same time it exhibited the main elements that generally describe his thought. The evolutionary component was evident in the assertion that combinations were the "result of an imperative economic law"; the pragmatic strain was revealed in a call for "national efficiency" that had to go beyond mere negative regulation of vested interests; and, finally, a traditional national purpose—"the object of government is the welfare of the people"—suffused the entire message.[12]

The whole of Roosevelt's thinking as a public man, of which "Biological

Analogies in History" and "The New Nationalism" are compacted expressions, is an instructive detail in the broad canvas of the American mind at mid passage. The decades from 1858 to 1919, years marking TR's lifetime, were times of intellectual transition in America. The changes affecting thought were substantial, influencing happenings in the counting houses, the legislative halls, and the courts of law. If it is true that the American mind would never be the same again, it is equally proper to observe that by 1919 that mind had become an amalgam of the very new and the very old. The transition had been completed in the sense that the flow of applications of the new scientific hypotheses associated with the name of Darwin had sought out every corner and contour of the national experience. No area of individual or social significance escaped scientific interpretation. However, while the traditional ideas of the colonial and early national inheritance had been altered, adapted, and attenuated, they were far from effaced. What had occurred was a truly pragmatic version of truth-reality in the making; new ideas had been wedded to older concepts, creating a more vital synthesis.

The mid-nineteenth-century American mind had possessed a strongly traditional quality. This traditionalism was not without challenge and change in the early years, but as late as the Civil War, inherited, time-honored modes of thought and attitude commanded the adherence of most men. This was especially true of religion at a time when religious beliefs were widely held by Americans. At the center of this faith was supernaturalism, buttressed by a system of philosophical absolutism. The household that Theodore Roosevelt grew up in was permeated by a religious spirit, exceptional only in the degree of its commitment, for the senior Roosevelt was a genuinely pious, churchgoing, praying Christian. The finished fixity of the systems of faith and reason enjoyed by mid-century Americans like the Roosevelts found expression both in the development of the Constitution as the great law of the nation and in capitalistic enterprise based on the certainties of private property, the operation of the two producing a mutually reinforcing effect. The Roosevelt family fortune, derived from trade and banking, rested squarely on the twin pillars of law and property, and rejoiced in heaven's approval. It was upon this traditional world of reassurance born of final answers that the new scientific hypotheses, pregnant with change, intruded. The year after Theodore Roosevelt's birth Darwin published *The Origin of Species*.

The Origin of Species has been called the most important book written in the nineteenth century. Whatever exaggeration may attach to this claim, its impact on American thought in Roosevelt's formative years was far-reaching. Darwin's book, with its principles popularized and applied to social conditions, delivered a grave blow to the supernaturalism that was central to American Protestant Christianity. As the inherited religious outlook yielded ground to new scientific teachings, much of the traditionlism of the American mind underwent a similar change. The allegiance of philosophers switched readily to evolutionary scientism and thence to pragmatism. The personalist ethic that had been part of the democratic-capitalistic impulse succumbed to the ravages of a relentless laissez-faire. The Constitution and the law, in turn, were made to do service in the working out of the nation's economic salvation.

Three ideas critical to American thought as it developed out of Darwinism fascinated Roosevelt's generation: changeability, progress, and a material order. Of the three, change and progress had formed part of American belief and experience from the first colonial foundations. No people had become more familiar with change and were more likely to accept it as a happy fact of life than were Americans. As for progress, the very word could be used to sum up national confidence in the national destiny. Progress in colonial America had become a reality even before progress was a philosophical postulate of the Enlightenment. Americans had been influenced by the fact and the philosophy of progress, their minds conditioned not merely to hope for human betterment but to demand it as their birthright. Their concept of progress, furthermore, had been keyed to individual success and to individual improvement, the social dimension being the sum of the well-being of individuals. Of all the features of America's past pointing the way to progress, none meant more to Theodore Roosevelt, or was to have greater impact on him, than the westward movement of the frontier. His zest for outdoor life and adventure had taken him to the Dakota country in the fall of 1883, and his experience there altogether enthralled him. He later was to speak of these western days as "the most important educational aspect of all my life."[13] In the West, in its history and actuality, Roosevelt was convinced he had found all that was best for America in nature and in society. To him it signified the free self-reliance of the individual and social progress for mankind, because the westward movement of superior peoples brought new lands under their dominion and their beneficence. There is something both paradoxical and sobering about Roosevelt's appreciation of the West. The very conquest would mean the eventual disappearance of the individual frontiersman and the assimilation of frontier populations into more complex social arrangements. But the two ideas: rugged individualism with its Darwinist overtones, and the welfare of mankind redolent of religious conviction, are suggestive of the persuasions that science and tradition continued to exert on him.

As social Darwinism supplied a new rationale for established ideas of change and progress, its acceptance by the American mind was hardly surprising. The stumbling block to a more complete victory for evolutionary thought was its third proposition, a material universe. Adherence to this concept, where adherence occurred, marked a dramatic break with tradition. Leading advocates of social Darwinism dismissed the claims of religion as unscientific, unverifiable, and therefore unworthy of their attention. The residue of traditional faith even of avowed evolutionaries could be considerable, nevertheless. John Fiske's advocacy of a theistic evolution in *Outlines of Cosmic Philosophy* illustrated the reluctance or the inability of some to cut loose completely from past intellectual moorings. This type of traditionalism was central to the view of Theodore Roosevelt. He saw Western man's history, especially since 1500, as an evolutionary process of the survival of the fittest and mastery by the superior races. He also believed that the mainspring of the evolutionary mechanism was character in individual men, and that the aggregate of this individual moral sense accounted for the superior race. Furthermore, the outcome of the evolutionary process was progress, invariably judged by him according to the norms of traditional ethics.

Pragmatism presupposed the same critical principles as social Darwinism. For similar historical reasons it proved congenial to the American mind. Pragmatism also encountered obstacles. The pragmatists differed from the Darwinists in their avoidance of a truculent challenge to ancient faiths, and their insistence on progress resulting from change that men could control and direct appeared more consistent with American history and the traditional spirit. While pragmatism was in fact a philosophy, it did not demand to become *the* philosophy of someone attracted to it. Pragmatism was readily utilized as an instrument of change by those who were generally satisfied with ethical values grounded in Scripture or on the rational nature of man. As instruments of reform, pragmatically inspired techniques might do yeoman service in the cause of maintaining the old moral order. For a "conservative as Progressive," for Theodore Roosevelt, this was the meaning of the Progressive movement.[14]

Pragmatism was doubtlessly a more humane expression of scientific principles than social Darwinism. If its opposition to aspects of the traditional American mind was more subtle, it was also a philosophy better constituted to accommodate traditionalism, should the latter prove viable. After all, the ultimate test of the pragmatic dispensation was workability; a workable combination of the old with the new was among the first principles of pragmatism. Roosevelt's mature public mind exhibited this distinction in "The New Nationalism." Progressive reforms, if they were better able to bring about greater individual fulfillment, were attractive applications of pragmatism. Individual fulfillment remained for Roosevelt the key to social improvement.

The public mind of Theodore Roosevelt represented a union of traditional beliefs and scientific theories. Coming together in his vibrant and aggressive personality, they constituted what may well be termed the

"Rooseveltian ethic," for Roosevelt himself added a unique and powerful ingredient. The constituents were closely related but not necessarily of equal importance. Each worked at times to qualify the others, and each at a given moment might appear dominant. All were securely part of his outlook as he came of age politically; all remained permanently in his thought. His mind was an amalgam of the old and the new, combining loyalty to traditional morality with a respect for scientific progress that was largely characteristic of the Establishment of his generation. The claims of traditional ethics were as much a part of him as his admiration for Darwin and Huxley, "seekers after truth."[15] Insofar as Roosevelt was guided by high principles, traditionalism was modified by social Darwinism. Inasmuch as his public philosophy owed some of its character to his response to a succession of actual problems, in his mature years it displayed elements properly associated with pragmatism as an intellectual instrument, as well as with political expediency.

Theodore Roosevelt was born in 1858 into a family deeply rooted in New York City's history, the place of his birth. His father, also called Theodore, was more a philanthropist than a businessman, but his considerable success in the marketplace enabled him to indulge his sense of responsibility for the less fortunate. TR's mother was Martha Bulloch, a Georgia belle who came north in 1853 after her marriage, though she remained Southern in spirit. The Civil War created some strain on the family. Once the conflict was over, the Roosevelt horizons were unclouded, and Teedie, as young Theodore was known in the family, grew up in a comfortable, regulated household presided over by his father. Later Roosevelt was to speak of his father as "the best man I ever knew," and a warm and loving relationship was part of the fact and memory of Theodore Roosevelt's growing up.

Education figured prominently in Roosevelt's youth. His father was keen to have his son instructed in the fundamentals of learning as well as in the new ideas of the scientific revolution. His education was an ongoing one; it originated at home, continued at school, and was not yet completed by the time Roosevelt became president in 1901. The formalities of that education began with Andrew Cutler on one end of the log when Cutler was hired in 1873 to prepare his young charge for the Harvard entrance examinations. Teedie was both a willing and an able student. His imagination and curiosity had been fired by the constant round of activities in his father's house, by travels to England, Europe, North Africa, and the Middle East, and by a six-month residence in Dresden, where he learned something of the German language and culture—all this by the age of fifteen. In between these experiences he had been taught to read and write, mostly by tutors drawn from the family because of the uncertainties of his health. His father had been greatly concerned about the boy's physical well-being and had sternly but compassionately advised him "to make his body." "You have the mind but you have not the body," his father told him when he was about ten years old, "and without the body the mind can not go as far as it should." The result of this fatherly advice is well known. Theodore Roosevelt, from that moment, was the practitioner and advocate of "the strenuous life." There is no comparable episode that marks the beginning of Roosevelt's equal determination to make his mind.

He read extensively as a boy because the family was devoted to books, but his reading was commonplace in character. His father, noting his son's interest in natural history and wanting to occupy him during bouts of illness, gave him volumes by J. G. Wood, the English writer of popular books on nature. In this way and from observation and a collection of specimens, Teedie acquired an extraordinary amount of information about birds, animals, and flowers. He also read history, especially American history, and tales of adventure, including the writings of Cooper and Longfellow. In all of this there was too much of what interested the youngster and too little of an organized and rigorous approach to learning. He was able to read German well, for example, and do passably in French, but he had no grounding in Greek or Latin and had received no instruction in mathematics. It fell to Andrew Cutler to inculcate a method and to encourage a discipline, habits that were to become a permanent part of his life, as well as to accomplish the more mundane objective, passing the Harvard entrance examinations. Cutler's task, from the viewpoint of the tutor, proved both easy and satisfying. Roosevelt was the ideal student at the opposite end of the log. He prepared for eight different fields of examination, doing the minimum only in Greek. Special emphasis was given to Latin, history, mathematics, and elementary science. Roosevelt had to apply himself to these subjects, but he had little difficulty with German and French. In literature he needed neither introduction nor urging, but Cutler supplied proper guidance, while in botany and zoology he struck out on his own. Under Cutler's tutelage Roosevelt acquired the intellectual confidence necessary for him to make the most of Harvard.[16]

The Harvard of the late 1870s was in the process of absorbing the initial educational reforms of President Eliot, making the school an interesting and an exciting place to be. By introducing the elective system to the undergraduate curriculum and developing graduate programs in various fields, Eliot sought to improve the educational experience of the college students and at the same time establish Harvard as an important university. Like others, Roosevelt profited directly from the elective system and indirectly from the enhanced intellectual atmosphere. Despite the liberalizing efforts of Eliot, there were prescribed courses for freshmen and some required subjects for the second year as well. In the first year Roosevelt studied Greek and Latin literature and language, German, advanced mathematics, physics, and chemistry—an arresting blend of the knowledge of antiquity and the findings of modern science. In his soph-omore year he took rhetoric, Anglo-American constitutional history, French, German, comparative anatomy and physiology, and botany. Roosevelt applied himself diligently to all these subjects and was among the best students in what was deemed a brilliant class. By his junior year he had hit full stride, taking nine subjects that totaled twenty hours of lectures and laboratory periods. Performing well in all courses, he excel-led in political economy and zoology. These two disciplines represented diverging roads, one of which he would choose to follow as a life's work, while the other would remain an avocation. Several factors dissuaded Roosevelt from a scientific career. He was an "outdoor naturalist" at a time when natural science was exclusively a matter of the laboratory. Having fallen in love with Alice Lee and become determined to marry her as soon as possible after graduation from Harvard, he recognized the value of a career of large prospects consistent with the Lee family's position. Finally, his desire to keep up his father's name as a civic leader drew him toward some form of public life. This decision is clear enough in retro-spect, but hardly so if one examines his choice of senior subjects, which included political economy and Italian, and geology and zoology. When he graduated in June 1880 he won "honorable mention" in natural science, was elected to Phi Beta Kappa, and was ranked twenty-first in a class of 177. In his autobiography, Roosevelt recalled that he "thoroughly en-joyed" Harvard but that "there was very little in way of actual studies which helped me in after life."[17] The influence of the varied curriculum may well have been too elusive to be appreciated, but his study of history and science honed his mind as surely as the regimen of physical exercise had toughened his body. It was while a senior, for example, that he commenced his research on the naval war of 1812, the background of a book that would launch his career as a writer.

Looking beyond courses and grades and prizes, other considerations must be weighed in assessing the impact of the Harvard years on Theodore Roosevelt. The death of his father in 1877—"the best man I ever knew"—forced him to become more independent. He found the social life at college immensely appealing, and he was part of the extracurricular scene at the highest levels. His passion for Alice Lee, which was to lead quickly to marriage in 1880, thrust fresh responsibilities on him, completing his passage to manhood. Yet through it all, learning remained a critical ele-ment in his outlook, and Harvard confirmed his commitment to it. Books no longer meant withdrawal from the world as they may have during his sickly childhood, but "a reaching for a growing understanding" of the world and its people. He read literally hundreds of books over the course of the years and would later write them to describe an experience (*The Wilderness Hunter*), to analyze a historical event (*The Naval War of 1812*), and to celebrate a theory of history *(The Winning of the West)*. Books about people were also to be part of Roosevelt's literary output: *Gouverneur Morris*, a founding father, *Thomas Hart Benton*, a frontier statesman, and *Oliver Cromwell*, a leader of moral purpose. According to Henry Adams, students of Roosevelt's day came to Harvard ignorant of all that men had thought and hoped, but while at Cambridge "their minds burst open like flowers at the sunlight of suggestion." Harvard had fertilized Roosevelt's mind, which burst forth in an impressive array of books and other writings over the course of the next several years. Yet his future was to involve much more than books, devoted as he was to them. His total education had served a dual purpose. In Cardinal Newman's phrase, the end of education is "fitness for the world," by which he intended neither instant social utility nor economic success. What was meant, rather, was an intellectual fitness, the mental capacity for life that alone makes a person substantially useful and successful. This was the result of Theodore Roosevelt's education, of which Harvard was a part.[18]

The image of the frenetic Teddy Roosevelt has an unquestioned validity. He had other dimensions, one of which was given a vivid rendering in his first book, published when he was only twenty-four. *The Naval War of 1812* appeared in 1882. Edward Wagenknecht, in *The Seven Worlds of Theodore Roosevelt,* tends to dismiss the book as "hardly more than the work of a boy," yet "fair and soundly researched."[19] It was a work, in fact, marked by patriotism but marred by jingoism. Some years afterward, and on the strength of this first book, Roosevelt was invited to do a study of "the naval operations between Great Britain and the United States, 1812–1815." This became volume six of William Laird Clowes's authoritative *The Royal Navy* (London, 1901). The later work is briefer than the original and, purged of much of its American bias, secured Roosevelt's place in the ranks of recognized naval historians.

The Naval War of 1812 had four editions by 1889 and was frequently reprinted thereafter. The book largely concerned naval battles. Maps were included to help the reader visualize the tactics employed, and various charts were presented, giving tonnage, armaments, and personnel attached to the ships in action. In these respects it was highly detailed if not greatly technical and a tribute to the author's respect for research. Roosevelt also proposed to use his study for larger purposes. He determined that the major disagreement between the United States and Great Britain was not so much over the neutral rights of ships and cargo as the impressment of American seamen by British captains. This problem led ultimately to the nature of citizenship, the question of *jus soli* or *jus sanguinis*. The rule of citizenship based on the choice of the individual was extremely important to the United States at the time, but it also held extensive implications in an era of increasing migrations from mother countries to colonies that eventually might achieve independence. As Roosevelt wrote: "The principles for which the United States contended in 1812 are now universally accepted and those so tenaciously maintained by Great Britain find no advocate in the civilized world."[20] In effect, the United States had vindicated an important element of international law by its naval victories.

Equally noteworthy in *The Naval War of 1812* was the germ of the idea that was to be developed by others into the new field of geopolitics, paralleling the increasing concern with the influence of global conditions on national interests. America would have its own great geopolitician in Alfred Thayer Mahan, who would take his place alongside Sir Halford John MacKinder in his time. Years later Kaiser Wilhelm II was as intrigued by Mahan's writings on sea power quite as much as by the heartland thesis. In the preface to the first edition of *The Naval War of 1812*, Roosevelt wrote of the rising awareness of the role of the American navy in world affairs. "At present people are beginning to realize that it is folly for the great English-speaking Republic to rely for defense upon a navy composed partly of antiquated hulks and partly on new vessels rather more worthless than the old. It is worthwhile to study with some care," he went on, "that period of our history during which our navy stood at the highest pitch of its fame; and to learn . . . from the past. . . ." There is a good bit of the spirit of navalism and the Navy League mentality in these thoughts, but his basic proposition was grounded in a substantive, scholarly interest in naval history.[21]

An amplified statement of Roosevelt's navalism was embedded in the reviews he wrote of three of Mahan's books. The first and the most important of these dealt with *The Influence of Sea Power on History* and appeared in the *Atlantic Monthly* in 1890. Roosevelt praised Mahan's recognition of the enduring effects that sea power had had on the development of certain of the great nations of the world, and his understanding "of the deep underlying causes and connections between political events and naval battles." Mahan's consideration of the juxtaposition of land and sea, of the extent and density of populations, and of the character of a people and their government made *The Influence of Sea Power on History* a remarkably timely book. Furthermore, just as Mahan demonstrated from history the dangers of naval improvisation, so Roosevelt voiced his renewed demands for naval preparedness.[22] In his review of Mahan's *The Influence of Sea Power on the French Revolution* (1893), Roosevelt stressed two factors in particular: the ubiquity of the Royal Navy as the soundest explanation of British victory, along with the willingness of the French to be satisfied with privateering. Privateering was simply a variation of improvisation.[23] In 1897, as war seemed more and more likely, Roosevelt used the occasion of his critique of Mahan's *Life of Nelson* to speak out for skill and bravery as essentials to victory in battle. By this time he was the assistant secretary of the navy and these were hawkish words, but TR felt more comfortable in so warlike a pose because he had founded his views on naval history.[24]

An ardent admirer and good friend of Captain Mahan, Roosevelt had an unexampled opportunity to put into practice many of the ideas he shared with Mahan when he was appointed assistant secretary of the navy in 1897. His chief was John Davis Long, a superannuated Massachusetts politician who had been given the Navy Department for services previously rendered the Republican party. Long's age and disposition virtually made TR "lord of the navy," and he was eager to introduce Mahan's thinking into navy tactics and strategy. He rightly judged Secretary Long to be "only lukewarm" about an enlarged navy and sought to enlist Mahan's help to convince the secretary of the "vital need for more battleships now." As assistant secretary he was especially the foe of improvisation. He studied reports from the French, German, and British navies, especially regarding new developments in ships and armaments, determined to improve his grasp of the technical details of his job. At the same time he insisted on viewing the navy as an instrument of a great power. What was needed, therefore, were not merely coastal defenses or torpedo boats, but battleships and lots of them to carry American greatness across the world. Reflecting his review of Mahan's study of Nelson, Roosevelt was prepared to alter one of the sacred traditions of the navy, promotion by strict seniority. Roosevelt argued that men must be promoted to command positions on their record, because they had been brave and skillful, and they had to be young enough to be creative and energetic. Mahan had argued this persuasively and Roosevelt understood him perfectly. TR wrote the Naval Personnel bill of 1898, which the Congress passed and under which there was the strong tendency for the best officers to advance rapidly while the less fit were encouraged to retire after twenty years of service. In numerous ways the navy was stamped with the distinctive brand of Roosevelt and Mahan intertwined. The remarkable consideration was, perhaps, how much Roosevelt did in the year or so he was assistant secretary. He knew what he wanted to do, what he felt had to be done, long before his actual appointment. He learned from a study of books and from discussions with knowledgeable navy people, relating his ideas on the navy to an enlarging historical rationale.

The Naval War of 1812 was a testament to Roosevelt's scholarly if somewhat ingenuous interest in the navy and its place in national history. As keen as this interest was, the fleet remained but a means to an end, which was American greatness. Over the next ten years TR devoted himself to further writings, including books about the wilderness as he encountered it, the frontier, the marvels of nature, and the conquest of the western territories by the American race. In these literary endeavors the

West as a part of the ongoing American experience held his attention fast. He was in the process of maturing his views of modern history, and while he was prepared to rely on books to inform his judgments, he insisted that personal experiences, whenever possible, should be some part of the raw material on which he drew for historical understanding.

Once while touring Egypt in 1872, a fourteen-year-old Theodore Roosevelt wrote of standing atop a pyramid: "To look out on the desert gives one somewhat the same feeling as to look over the North American Prairies."[25] He had, to be sure, not then glimpsed the Great Plains, but his remark does suggest the significance of the West to him. Roosevelt said it best when addressing an audience at Colorado Springs in 1901:

> You and your fathers who built the West did even more than you thought, for you shaped thereby the destiny of the whole republic and as a necessary corollary profoundly influenced the course of events throughout the world.[26]

Roosevelt was to go out to the Dakota country for the first time in 1883, and a romance was born. He bought a ranch, investing a goodly portion of his inheritance in the venture. When his young wife died in February 1884, within hours of his mother's passing, he instinctively sought out his Dakota ranch at Elkhorn for solace and distraction. He divided his time between eastern politics and western ranching down to the winter of 1886–87, when, because of some of the severest weather in memory, fully one-half of his cattle herd was lost. At that point he liquidated his holdings, but not before the West had left an indelible stamp.

Theodore Roosevelt included much of his experience of the West in his natural history trilogy: *Hunting Trips of a Ranchman* (1885), *Ranch Life and the Hunting Trail* (1888), and *The Wilderness Hunter* (1893). The first two of these volumes were written on the Elkhorn ranch. As much as he internalized about the West, Roosevelt, the author, was prepared to fall back on standard authorities to verify or improve his books. At Elkhorn, for example, he had seen fit to supply himself with T. S. Van Dyke's *Still Hunter,* Richard Dodge's *Plains of the Great West,* John Dean Caton's *The Antelope and Deer of America,* and Elliott Coues's *Birds of the Northwest.* Even as an outdoorsman Roosevelt was a scholar. In addition he drew from Burroughs, Parkman, and Thoreau, and especially from the journals of Lewis and Clark, of which he had made a thorough study. As he wrote Brander Matthews in 1888: "Mind you, I'm a literary feller, not a politician nowadays."[27] It must be added that in these literary endeavors are to be found a number of salient general statements that illuminate Roosevelt's theory of history, and especially demonstrate his attraction to many of the tenets of social Darwinism.

The first of these books based on Roosevelt's western days, *Hunting*

Trips of a Ranchman, was in the main an account of stalking the buffalo, the black-tailed deer, and the giant grizzly, and in his story of the hunt lies the great charm of the narrative.[28] Yet there is more here than storytelling. For example, in the fate of the plains buffalo is a wider lesson, heavy with Darwinist accents:

> The rapid and complete extermination of the buffalo afforded an excellent instance of how a race that has thriven and multiplied for ages under conditions of life to which it has always fitted itself, by a process of natural selection continued for countless generations, may succumb at once when these surrounding conditions are varied by the introduction of one or more new elements, immediately becoming the chief forces with which it has to contend in the struggle for life.[29]

Indeed, the history of the West was a history of the change of nature by technology—largely for the good, as Roosevelt judged it. It was the long-range rifle, along with the advance of the cattle industry, that denied the Great Plains to the buffalo and enabled settlers to develop a frontier civilization.

Incidental to all this but especially fascinating to Roosevelt, was the evolution of the wood or mountain buffalo, which acquired habits widely different from those of the plains animal. His observations led him to note that the mountain buffalo had developed a keener sense of smell but had less sharp eyesight, and that the mountain variety grew longer and denser hair on a body that was more thickset. "As a result, a new race has been built up; and we have an animal far better fitted to 'harmonize with the environment.' " Roosevelt concluded that "the formation of the race is due solely to the extremely severe process of natural selection that has been going on among the buffalo herds for the last sixty or seventy years."[30] This kind of personal observation of evolution made a lasting impression.

Roosevelt afforded evolution a wide application that encompassed race relations between the white man and the red man. He believed that a good deal of "sentimental nonsense" had been written about the white man's taking of land from the Indians. Admitting that gross wrongs had been committed due to the brutality of the frontier and not infrequently deception by government agents, he denied that the plains had belonged to the Indians in the first place. "The simple truth is that the Indian never had any real ownership of it at all." Just as no one thought of the white hunters who roamed the wilderness as owning any part of it, so neither should the Indians be deemed proprietors of the lands they moved across. The wars against the Indians had been merciless, but also "just and rational." "It does no good to be merciful to the few at the cost of the many," was the way Roosevelt summed up his attitude regarding the sufferings of the Indians.[31]

In *Ranch Life and the Hunting Trail*[32] the basic evolutionary thesis had a different appeal. Roosevelt treated the frontier as a version or portion of the great American melting pot. Concerning the cowboys he wrote: "It would be impossible to imagine a more typically American assemblage, for although there are always a certain number of foreigners, usually English, Irish or German, yet they have become completely Americanized.[33] These cowboys were the vanguard of a permanent civilization on the plains, inasmuch as their employers, the stockmen, were "the pioneers of civilization and their daring made the after-settlement of the region possible." Both stockmen and cowboys alike were of the self-reliant breed who had proven their superiority over the Indians and the Mexicans. The Stockmen's Association was the seed from which a self-governing West would grow, a process uniting Darwinism and democracy and leading on to progress. Roosevelt found that "the frontiersmen show their natural aptitude for organization . . . lawlessness is put down pretty effectively."[34] For those who cared to read Roosevelt closely it was evident that his concern went beyond claw and fang, and that he discerned in the work of conquest and settlement the true measure of American history.

From a literary standpoint the best of the natural history trilogy is *The Wilderness Hunter.*[35] Roosevelt had greatly matured as a writer, avoiding annoying repetitions and extravagant generalizations from the limited samples of his own experience. He was intent on his storytelling and was ready to share his expanding knowledge of forest and game. But in the preface to *The Wilderness Hunter* he once again attempted to enlarge the meaning of the life of the wilderness hunter:

> In hunting, the finding and killing of the game is after all but part of the whole. The free self-reliant adventurous life, with its rugged and stalwart democracy, the wild surroundings, the grave beauty . . . all of these unite to give the career of the wilderness hunter its peculiar charm. The chase is among the best of all natural pastimes, it cultivates that vigorous manliness for the lack of which, in a nation, as in an individual, the possession of no other qualities can possibly atone.[36]

The hunter was the archetype of freedom and thus the best kind of citizen in Roosevelt's idealized democratic republic.

Francis Parkman, Theodore Roosevelt, and Frederick Jackson Turner—three American historians of the West—were three men tied together by circumstance and substance. It is not inappropriate to bracket Roosevelt with these renowned scholars whose work he much admired, for in *The Winning of the West* he, too, made a lasting contribution to the historical literature of the frontier.[37] Roosevelt's opus—not the magnum opus he dreamed of writing—was first published in four volumes: one and two in

1889, three in 1894, and the final volume in 1896. Altogether Roosevelt carried the story down through the purchase of the Louisiana Territory in 1803. In taking up *The Winning of the West* today, nearly one hundred years from the appearance of the first volume, certain allowances have to be made. There is much (too much for contemporary tastes) of spread-eagle triumphalism both in what Roosevelt wrote and in how he wrote it. Too often he chose to see his function as that of storyteller, neglecting institutions in favor of the lives of the men who conquered the land. The result is a series of vignettes that becomes locked in memory largely because the men described were cast in the mold of heroes. Then, too, Roosevelt's dislike and distrust of Jefferson is troubling, though it may be well to remember that Jefferson's stature has been greatly enhanced by historians and others writing long after Roosevelt registered his opinions. In his correspondence with Frederick Jackson Turner, in fact, he appeared prepared to soften his strictures. In a review of volume four Turner had scolded him for his harsh evaluation of Jefferson's conduct during the Citizen Genêt affair and pleaded for a more sober judgment. Roosevelt wrote in reply: "I am more and more inclined to think you are quite right as to the inadvisability of my taking the tone I did toward Jefferson. The trouble is," he explained, "that I meet so many understudies of Jefferson in politics and suffer so much from them that I am apt to let my feelings find vent in words."[38] Based on his own admission, the conclusion has to be offered that Roosevelt allowed subjective considerations to bias his historical writings. It was a fair admission, honestly made, but it indicates a serious shortcoming in his work.

The strengths of Roosevelt as historian of the West clearly outweigh the deficiencies. Not only did he make significant use of manuscripts and archival materials, but he did so under conditions not calculated to make his searches routine, as he explained in the preface to volume one of *The Winning of the West*. For the reader's information he listed the sources he had consulted, with a brief description of each. Apart from research in the archives in Washington, carried out between 1889 and 1895 when he was serving as a civil service commissioner—and an active one at that—Roosevelt made visits to Nashville, various locations in Kentucky, and New York to consult sources. Friends and contacts sent him material for use from Canada and from California. Compared with his research for *Thomas Hart Benton* and that done by other historians of the time, Roosevelt's research efforts were quite respectable.

A second aspect of *The Winning of the West,* which grows directly from the wide use of original sources, is the depth of the accounts Roosevelt offered. He brought his readers in close contact with many of the individuals who were in the vanguard of frontier conquest and who otherwise would have gone unnoticed. He was nothing if not thorough, exhausting what sources he had access to. The result is a spirited account, yet one in which the author is willing to linger over detail. Roosevelt demonstrated that he was something other than an amateur historian at a time when historians were just becoming conscious of themselves as professionals. The American Historical Association—Roosevelt would serve as its president in 1912—was organized in 1884, and the enduring work of Turner, Beard, and others lay ahead. Whether Theodore Roosevelt would ever have ranked with the great historians, had he decided to be a writer of history rather than primarily a maker, is debatable. He was not unaware of the deficiencies of *The Winning of the West,* as well as the superficiality of his studies of Benton and Morris. He agreed with Turner on the need to search the Spanish, English and French archives about the treaties of Jay and Pinckney, for example, and had he become a fully professional historian, no doubt he would have worked to overcome his faults.[39]

Beyond the historical apparatus expertly used, Roosevelt's standing as an historian derives from a willingness to offer a conception of history at once seminal and controversial. Let the very first paragraphs of *The Winning of the West* speak for him:

> During the past three centuries the spread of the English-speaking peoples over the world's waste spaces has been not only the most striking feature in the world's history, but also the event of all others most far-reaching in its effects and its importance.
>
> The tongue which Bacon feared to use in his writings, lest they should remain forever unknown to all but the inhabitants of a relatively unimportant insular kingdom, is now the speech of two continents. The Common Law which Coke jealously upheld in the southern half of a single European island, is now the law of the land throughout the vast regions of Australasia, and of America north of the Rio Grande. The names of the plays that Shakespeare wrote are household words in the mouths of mighty nations whose wide domains were to him more unreal than the realm of Prester John. Over half the descendents of their fellow countrymen of that day now dwell in lands which, when these three Englishmen were born, held not a single white inhabitant; the race which, when they were in their prime, was hemmed in between the North and the Irish seas, today holds sway over worlds whose endless coasts are washed by the waves of the three great oceans.[40]

In view of the foregoing passage there can be small doubt of Roosevelt's perspective, his prejudice, and his confidence respecting the English-speaking peoples and their place in modern times.

In *The Winning of the West* Roosevelt was striving for an acceptable historical framework into which he could fit the whole range of history since 1500, and with which the events of American history from the first settlements could be rightly understood. In this he was not following the lead of Turner, but was breaking new ground very much on his own initiative. He dedicated the four volumes to "Francis Parkman To Whom Americans Who Feel Pride In The Pioneer History Of Their Country Are So Greatly Indebted." Thus he stood between Parkman and Turner as historian of the pioneers and the frontier. Perhaps not nearly so good a historian as Parkman, and surely nowhere close to Turner in influence, Roosevelt nonetheless is justly associated with them. His analysis contained adumbrations of the democratic persuasions of the westward movement as it sought to justify the expansion of one people at the cruel cost to another. To Roosevelt the westward tide was irresistible by either Indian or Mexican. As he explained himself to Turner in discussing the Louisiana Purchase: ". . . the very point which Henry Adams failed to make [was] that the diplomatic discussions to which he devoted so much space, though extremely interesting, . . . did not at all determine the fact that the transfer had to be made. It was the growth of the western settlements that determined this fact."[41] What Roosevelt had done was to catch the cadence of western expansion, and he marched across four volumes of the American frontier experience in step with it.

Equally remarkable, Roosevelt's writing during the 1880s and 1890s was done while he continued to be directly or indirectly active in politics. He campaigned for Blaine for the presidency in 1884, stood for mayor of New York City in 1886, served on the Civil Service Commission from 1889 to 1895, and in the latter year began a stint as police commissioner of the City of New York. The quality of his writing may well have suffered by reason of his hectic public pace, but the quantity remains impressive. Though he wrote some quite ordinary books, as a consideration of *Thomas Hart Benton* and *Gouverneur Morris* will show, his need to relate contemporary politics to historical models through the device of books and essays affords compelling evidence of Roosevelt's instinctive reliance on learning.

During these years when Roosevelt was writing at such a furious rate, he was conscious of himself as a literary person. Less deliberately, at least in terms of an overarching philosophy, he was busy formulating a theory of history. The study of history became the intellectual bridge between Roosevelt's life of the mind and his active public career, and a necessary part of it was a study of the work of individuals who had helped create the present. Though attracted to the social Darwinist explanation of change and progress, TR was too much a traditionalist to ignore the feats of heroes. He therefore expected that contemporary public life could not be significantly improved without men of upright character and purpose. In writing *The Winning of the West,* he admitted that he had "always been more interested in the men themselves than in the institutions through and under which they worked."[42] For someone of this disposition, "the great man" theory of history was a sore temptation.

Roosevelt attempted three biographies, lives of Thomas Hart Benton, Gouverneur Morris, and Oliver Cromwell. He appeared convinced that history was more than forces or cycles, and that progress came about because men sought it. Roosevelt believed in man because he believed in men. Of the three biographies, that of Benton was the best.[43] It was, however, hastily written during the spring of 1886 while TR was on his Badlands ranch and deprived of even the most elementary library resources. At one point he wrote his friend, Henry Cabot Lodge, to ask assistance in getting some basic information about Benton's last years so that he might finish the manuscript and send it off to the publisher. What makes *Benton* noteworthy is its view of the senator as a westerner. Benton's efforts to make cheap land available to settlers, his appetite for as much North American territory as might be had to accommodate the expanding American race, and his advocacy of hard money in the style of another westerner, Andrew Jackson, gave Roosevelt ample reason to describe his subject in favorable terms. Furthermore, Benton was a nationalist at a time when nullifiers and secessionists plied their views. Roosevelt thought such attitudes totally abhorrent and judged Benton to be a better American for having used his position and influence to thwart them.

Despite a prolific pen, writing was not an easy matter for Theodore Roosevelt. "Writing is horribly hard work to me; and I make slow progress," he confessed at the time he was at work on *Benton*. "I have got some good ideas . . . but I am not sure they are worked up rightly; my style is very rough and I do not like a certain lack of sequitur that I do not seem able to get rid of."[44] Evelyn Waugh once described writing as putting words down on the page and pushing them one after the other, and Roosevelt's technique shared something of this mode. What carried him forward, what gave him the push, was his sheer enthusiasm, a habit that made him want to explain and to justify, in the case of a biography, the accomplishments of a historical figure with whom he was in sympathy. Thomas Hart Benton easily qualified in this respect, but Gouverneur Morris was less likable.

Gouverneur Morris was in the nature of an assignment by the editor of the American Statesman series, John T. Morse, Jr.[45] Roosevelt would have preferred to write about Hamilton or, better still, Lincoln, but once he was into Morris he found him a more apt subject for his pen than, for example, John Jay. Roosevelt had something less than total enthusiasm for Morris, a man thoroughly elitist in temperament. One who could refer to the people as "poor reptiles who bask in the sun," and who could predict that "they will bite 'ere noon, depend on it," was out of touch with TR's democratic spirit, however conservative Roosevelt has been judged. Consequently the Morris book was marked by frequent digressions, some of them quite gratuitous. At the start of chapter six, "The Formation of the National Constitution," Roosevelt chided Morris for not foreseeing that even with the loss of the colonies Britain would remain a great power, "that from their loins other nations, broad as continents, were to spring, so that the South Seas should become an English ocean and that over a fourth of the world's surface there should be spoken the tongue of Pitt and Washington.[46] Such commentary might be dismissed as silly except when taken as part of a continued awareness and support of the world movement of the English-speaking peoples, which, to Roosevelt's consternation, was about to be challenged by the Boers in South Africa. Neither the subject nor the author's literary reputation was well served by *Gouverneur Morris*.

The last of the biographical trilogy was *Oliver Cromwell*.[47] It appeared in serial form in *Scribner's* magazine from January to June, 1900, and was published as a book by Scribner's that same year. *Cromwell* was described only half-facetiously by Arthur Hamilton Lee as "a fine, imaginative study of Cromwell's qualifications for the governorship of New York."[48] TR was, of course, serving in that office when the biography came into print. *Oliver Cromwell* is best termed a character study rather than a formal biography. It is not clear why Roosevelt took up Cromwell, of all possible subjects open to him. If he had discovered many of Cromwell's traits, both his strengths and weaknesses, in himself and felt compelled to write about them through a thinly disguised literary device, the process would be consistent with his preoccupation with history as a way of explaining the contemporary, whether a scene or person. His admiration for the Lord Protector was genuine. He once wrote approvingly of the embattled Boer farmers as "belated Cromwellians," going on to say, however, that it was absolutely essential to the world movement that English be spoken south of the Zambesi.[49]

As for Cromwell, Roosevelt determined that his real historical importance lay in his establishment of political liberty. It was a half-wrought kind of liberty, because in victory Cromwell tied its enjoyment directly to religious tests. But once religious animosity had moderated sufficiently, freedom of conscience was allowed to develop under the law. In the course of his analysis Roosevelt displayed a good comprehension of the Whig version of English history and generally endorsed it, but he was acute enough to reject misinterpretations from the past. A perceptive distinction between Spanish and French Catholicism in the first part of the seventeenth century was one example of his rejection of stereotyping.[50] More than anything else, *Oliver Cromwell* revealed the Roosevelt passion to publish, stemming from his belief that thought must result in action. He viewed scholarship in somewhat the same fashion. Writing in *The Outlook* in 1912 he contended that "scholarship that consists in mere learning but finds no expression in production, may be of interest and value to the individual himself . . . but unless it finds expression in achievement" is sterile. ". . . Scholarship is of worth chiefly when it is productive, when the scholar not merely receives or acquires, but gives."[51] For Roosevelt, thoughts were not fulfilled unless they resulted in a tangible product. Having studied Cromwell he was intent on sharing his knowledge with others.

From 1923 to 1926 the Memorial edition of *The Works of Theodore Roosevelt,* edited by Hermann Hagedorn, was published in twenty-four volumes. Each set in the limited edition was numbered and signed by Edith Kermit Roosevelt. In his preface Hagedorn explained the organization of the numerous writings and observed that his aim had been "to arrange the material in a way that would make it as easy as possible for the reader to find out what Mr. Roosevelt's convictions were on any subjects; or haply just to browse in the green fields of his stimulating discourse."[52] The learned Roosevelt is present in each of these volumes, but perhaps nowhere does he show to better advantage than in volume fourteen, *Literary Essays.* In the preface to that volume Brander Matthews included a short essay, "Theodore Roosevelt as a Man of Letters," replete with comments on the literary Roosevelt. Comparing Roosevelt and Benjamin Franklin, he found they differed in "that Roosevelt was an author by profession and Franklin an author by accident." Matthews held further that Roosevelt "wrote well because he had read widely and deeply— because he had absorbed good literature for the sheer delight he took in it." He called TR "A normal human being" and candidly pointed out that Roosevelt "liked to celebrate himself and to be his own Boswell." But Matthews also noted that to TR, "life was more important than literature, and what he was forever seeking to put into literature was life itself."[53] *Literary Essays* brings to life an extraordinary mixture in Roosevelt— "distinctly a man of letters as a man of action."

"Social Evolution," an essay suggested by Benjamin Kidd's book of the same title,[54] exhibited an important moderation in Roosevelt's endorsement of evolutionary ideas as applied to society. He objected to any account of society that rested on the single postulate of natural selection because he was bound to reject the materialistic implications deriving from such a position. He also faulted Kidd because nowhere in his work was character granted a function in human affairs. Roosevelt espoused character as essential for the achievement of social progress. Character was "the mother who watches over the sick child; the soldier who dies at his post."[55] Both these models portrayed actions informed by convictions. "We need intellect," Roosevelt wrote, "and there is no reason why we should not have it together with character, but if we must choose between the two, we choose character without a moment's hesitation."[56] As for social evolution, the hypothesis that progress was greatest where competition was keenest was not substantiated by cultural realities. Were this so, he contended, "the European peoples standing highest in the scale would be the south Italians, the Polish Jews, the people who live in the congested districts of Ireland. As a matter of fact, however, these were the people who made the least progress. . . ."[57] The conclusion Roosevelt reached, one he continued to advance in essays and speeches throughout his lifetime, was that man's spirit, and in a sense, therefore, man's moral self, was the central consideration in accounting for social improvement.

Theodore Roosevelt's appreciation of literature of the more conventional sort is illustrated in three selected essays, "The Children of the Night," "The Ancient Irish Sagas," and "Dante and the Bowery." It is well known that when Theodore Roosevelt, Jr., on a White House visit from Harvard in 1905, showed his father Edwin Arlington Robinson's verse, the president was captivated. He asked his son to find out what he could about Robinson. Eventually the poet was invited to the White House for dinner, a sure sign of presidential approval. Roosevelt procured a sinecure for Robinson at the New York Customs House, since Robinson was virtually destitute when "discovered" by the Roosevelts. Feeling strongly that Robinson's work "should have attracted more attention," TR wrote to that effect in his essay that reviewed *The Children of the Night,* appearing in the *Outlook* in 1905.[58] He found in the poems "an undoubted touch of genius . . . a curious simplicity and good faith. There is in them just a little of the light that never was on land or sea . . . it is not always necessary in order to enjoy a poem that one should be able to translate it into terms of mathematical accuracy. Those who admire the coloring of Turner . . . do not wish always to have ideas presented to them with cold, hard, definite outlines. . . ." Roosevelt said of the poem, "Luke Havergal," for example, that "I am not sure I understand the poem; but I am entirely sure that I like it." And what of "Richard Cory," which has found its way unerringly into so many school anthologies? For Roosevelt the poem spoke "a very ancient but very profound philosophy of life with a curiously local touch which points its keen insight." Roosevelt, the optimist, seems to have understood the man who went and put a bullet in his head. Commenting on another poem, "The Tavern," the president as critic again revealed his poetic inner self. In "The Tavern," he noted, Robinson "writes of what most of us feel we have seen; and then again of what we have only seen with the soul's eyes." No doubt Roosevelt felt a special kinship with the man who could write "The Wilderness," which told of nature as TR knew and loved it. The author of *The Wilderness Hunter* identified with the poet's words: "And the lonely trees around us creak the warning of the night wind . . . / The winds that blow the message they have blown ten thousand years." The President's terse, last comment, "this little volume, not verse but poetry," summed up his admiration for Robinson.[59]

†"The Ancient Irish Sagas" showed Roosevelt's fascination with the old Celtic text whose stories were just then being paraphrased in popular form by Lady Gregory and others.[60] Just as he was later to praise the Abbey Theatre as "an extraordinary contribution to the sum of Irish literary and artistic achievement," he praised the sagas as the corresponding Celtic contribution to the corpus of ancient literature that the Germans, the French, and the English had helped to develop long ago. The contemporary Irish revival, in other words, owed a great deal to the new emphasis on the Cuchulain cycle and the Ossianic cycle. Such tales have much to tell the historian, thought Roosevelt, since they tend to portray life as it was lived in Erin in far-distant times. The greatness of these epics fell short of those of other peoples only because of the calamities and tragedies that befell Ireland. Roosevelt believed the Irish sagas truly remarkable in their treatment of women. Whereas women played no part at all in the "Song of Roland," and they were "alternately splendid and terrible" in the Norse and German stories, "it would be hard indeed to find among them a heroine who would appeal to our modern ideas as does Emer, the beloved of Cuchulain, or Deirdre, the sweetheart of the fated son of Usnach."[61] In his rendering of the story line of the Cuchulain cycle Roosevelt consistently demonstrated his poetic sense, striving to catch in plain prose the spirit of the epic itself. For him the sagas possessed "extraordinary variety and beauty, in their exaltation of the glorious courage of men and of the charm and devotion of women, they contained a curious attraction of their own."[62] Like the Irish players of the Abbey Theatre who sprang from the soil and dealt with things Irish, so the ancient sagas spoke of an authentic if irrecoverable Erin that was a meaningful but unappreciated part of Western civilization.

No less typical of Roosevelt, the man of letters, was his concern for poetry that made honest and imaginative use of the language of the marketplace, "today's market place—the Fulton Market" of New York, for example, and not the marketplace of Florence in the thirteenth century. This was the theme of "Dante and the Bowery."[63] "What infinite use Dante would have made of the Bowery!" he enthused. As he went on to explain, the nineteenth century was more apt than the thirteenth to boast of itself as being "the greatest of centuries," but except for its technology "it did not wholly believe in its boasting."[64] Thus a nineteenth-century poet, striving to make a point, was likely to draw material from ancient or medieval times rather than his own. In America, only Walt Whitman dared to use anything like the Bowery, that is, "what was striking and vividly typical of the humanity around him."[65] And even he, Roosevelt remarked, "was not quite natural in doing so, for he always felt he was defying the conventions and prejudices of his neighbors." The difference between Dante and Whitman was not so much between the artists themselves as their respective times. The conventions of Dante's century did not forbid him to use human nature just as he encountered it. Why not explore human nature by examples drawn from the Brooklyn Navy Yard as well as Piraeus, from Tammany no less than the Roman mob? TR urged. Dante had unhesitatingly used his contemporaries, or his immediate predecessors, alongside the great names passed on to him from antiquity, because the passions of men are the same in all ages, godlike or demoniac. Dante was "quite simply a realist," displaying the sort of realism that Roosevelt judged to be missing in all too much of the poetry of his day. "We do not express ourselves nowadays in epics at all," he lamented; "we keep the emotions aroused in us by what is good or evil in the men of the present in a totally different compartment from that which holds our emotions concerning what was good or evil in the men of the past."[66] The ex-president was not so sure that given the peculiar character of his times it could have been otherwise. "One age expresses itself naturally in a form that would be unnatural and therefore undesirable, in another age," he admitted. Nevertheless, he wanted the contemporary artist to see, as had Dante, the "eternal qualities" in the people around us, remarking that Dante himself would have preferred it so.[67]

Another of Roosevelt's literary essays was in the form of a review of *The Law of Civilization and Decay* by his good friend, Brooks Adams.[68] Of the Adams thesis it may be enough to say that it held out the prospects of the decline of Western civilization because the imaginative, artistic, and warrior classes were being preempted by the economic man—of industry, capital, and trade. TR wanted instinctively to reject the thesis outright since it ran counter to his belief in progress. In fact, he granted Adams some occasional points but found the tone of the argument in favor of decay intolerable. A more telling indicator of Roosevelt's erudition may be the numerous historical and literary references that he made good use of in developing his position vis-à-vis Adams. These included the Crusades, the British conquest of India, the house of Rothschild, the Knights Templar, the fall of Constantinople, the blind Doge Dandolo, Macaulay, Thucydides, Alexander the Great, Henry VIII, the historians Froude and Henry C. Lea, the "pope Hildebrand," Emperor Henry IV, Philip Augustus, Philip the Fair, Froissart, Malthus, Erasmus, jacqueries, Timothy Pickering, Henry Adams, Louis XV, Louis Philippe, Marlborough, Wellington, Nelson, Grant, Lee, Henry George, and Edward Bellamy. It must be added quickly that this was not unusual. Roosevelt moved as easily from one century to another as from one culture to another; he approached millennia as readily as epochs. He wrote in such fashion not for the sake of display but because his wide reading encouraged him to express himself in such terms.[69]

In Roosevelt the learned man overmastered the man of action frequently and with lasting effect. His presidency offered substantial evidence of this; learning was an operative factor once TR assumed office in September 1901. Viewed from this novel perspective an understanding of the Roosevelt presidency will not be altered in its broader outline. What is likely, however, is an enhanced appreciation of that presidency made possible by a fresh awareness of certain of his policies insofar as they were affected by his learning. With Roosevelt there was no touch of self-consciousness in mixing love of literature with love of political power. He was convinced that his understanding of society was enhanced by an understanding of the literature that society produced, that he was a better leader because he was better read.

Books aside, Theodore Roosevelt was well qualified for the presidency when he succeeded McKinley. In and out of politics for twenty years, he had been a state legislator, civil service and police commissioner, sub-cabinet officer, and one-term governor of what was the largest state in the nation, New York. "The Albany Apprenticeship," as it has been termed, was the most valuable part of his political education. Since it had come just before his election to the vice-presidency, he retained a feel for high-level administration. Roosevelt's military service in the Spanish-American War—he resigned as assistant naval secretary almost as soon as war was declared—earned him experience of a different kind that no doubt influenced his decisions as commander in chief. Characteristically, he wrote a book about his adventures, *The Rough Riders* (1899), another witness to his need to explain himself in a literary fashion. Roosevelt was at least as much a soldier as Andrew Jackson, but fell below the standards of Washington, Taylor, Grant, and, at a later time, Eisenhower. At heart TR was an amateur soldier; once the fighting was finished he was eager to return to politics, his natural milieu. Wooed in New York by reformers and the Republican machine alike to run for the governorship, he decided on machine support, convinced that he could be effective as a chief executive only with machine cooperation in the promotion of reform. Roosevelt and Thomas Collier Platt, the "easy boss" of the New York Republican organization, were almost completely opposite political types, yet there came to be an unlikely cordiality between the moral governor and the machine politico. Roosevelt was sufficiently successful as a reformer for Platt to want to move him out of Albany after a single term. Kicked upstairs to the vice-presidency in 1900, he turned out to be a darling of destiny. Assassination was a monstrous thing to Roosevelt, who once declared that the assassin stood on the pinnacle of evil fame, but he refused to be morbid about the circumstances of his elevation to the ultimate office. "Here is the task, and I have got to do it to the best of my ability; that is all there is about it," he confided to Henry Cabot Lodge within a week of his swearing-in.[70] Despite his age, and possibly because of it, Roosevelt was confident of himself in body, mind, and spirit.

Progressivism at home and imperialism abroad made up the twin theme of American politics during Theodore Roosevelt's presidency. In his approach to and handling of specifics relating to these large matters, the impact of learning was discernible, but in different ways. In domestic affairs the influence was exerted more subtly, more as a presupposition of many of his undertakings. In foreign affairs, by contrast, the authority of learning was at once apparent. Reasons for this distinction are embedded in the intellectual tendencies of the late nineteenth century. Evolution and social Darwinism were very much in vogue, and for America the application of their principles to imperialist expansion was so pervasive it was almost involuntary. Yet on the political home front the philosophy of laissez-faire, reinforced by the same cult of competition, was being challenged outright by new attitudes looking toward reform and derived from a combination of traditional human values and practical measures. Many such measures could be tentatively identified with pragmatism. While it might be premature to describe any but a very few of Roosevelt's policies as consciously pragmatic before 1910, it remains useful to think of his practical measures as a reformer as influenced by a sense of pragmatism.

The best place to look for the force of learning in Roosevelt's domestic policies is in his assessment of character in the individual and thus in the race, a position easily discernible in his writings. In terms of American politics Roosevelt viewed character as the central element in reforming society. "No man can lead a public career really worth leading," he was to write later in his *Autobiography,* "no man can act with rugged independence in a serious crisis, nor strike out at great abuses, nor afford to make powerful foes, if he himself is vulnerable in his private character."[71] This avowal of character meant that he was as sensitive as any behaviorist to the ills of American society and, as a result, was caught up in the Progressive movement. Though he might differ with many Progressives as to ultimate causes, one and all were disturbed by the same evils and frequently sought to overcome them by common methods, so that a distinction between them and the president (or ex-president) is not always understood. Indeed, it appears likely that, lacking Progressive support, Roosevelt could not have accomplished very much as a reform president. He managed at the same time to impart a strong, and popular, flavor of traditional morality to the general conception of what Progressivism stood for. The Progressive movement, despite its more radical possibilities, was to many very much in keeping with the old ways of thought in which nothing was more elemental than individual honesty and initiative. Roosevelt's understanding of the importance of the individual was a recurring aspect of his histories and his biographies, and received added emphasis in his biographical sketches of those he called "Men of Action."[72]

The president put the case squarely in an article in the *Outlook,* written as he was about to leave the White House in 1909. "A nation must be judged in part by the character of its public men, not merely by their ability but by their ideals. . . ." In the series of character profiles, written over a period of years, he singled out Washington and Lincoln as the great American public men; he described them as "of the type of Timoleon and Hampden."[73] Dealing with men of yesterday such as John Marshall and Andrew Jackson, he stressed qualities that he deemed made them great. Marshall "was in the best sense . . . a self-made man," "a hardworking Virginian who relied on his own reasoning," "entirely democratic . . . simple, straight forward and unaffected."[74] Not all historians might agree with Roosevelt's evaluation of Marshall, but none would deny him the strong and determined nationalistic spirit that TR thought so praiseworthy. Jackson, in turn, "belonged to a stern and virile race, the Presbyterian Irish." He combined "physical prowess" with "the resolute determination to uphold the cause of order." Roosevelt judged that Jackson, as president, had done "much good and much evil." He strongly censured the introduction of the spoils system and believed Jackson's bank policy replaced a less-than-perfect system with an infinitely worse one, the wildcat state banks. What redeemed Jackson was that he "was emphatically a true American."[75] In these accounts Roosevelt allowed himself heroes, but he was not uncritical of those he admired.

Lincoln was the great figure from the American past, Lincoln "the practical idealist." While in the midst of his presidency, Roosevelt wrote the preface to the Connoisseur's Federal edition of the writings of Lincoln, dated "Sagamore Hill, Sept. 22, 1905." In it he quoted from Lecky's fifth volume of *History of England.* Lecky contended that successful statesmen need not have the moral qualities of a hero or a saint; more wordly virtues would do: tact, knowledge of men, resolution, and the ability to meet emergencies. Lincoln, in Roosevelt's reading of history, exhibited the two sets of virtues that Lecky had represented as antithetical. For him Lincoln was "the wise and cautious radical," with TR again reflecting his own aspirations as a public figure through literary expression.[76]

Roosevelt wrote of his admiration for a great many among his contemporaries, including John Hay, Leonard Wood, Booker T. Washington, Augustus Saint-Gaudens, John Muir, and Frederick Courtney Selous. What he observed of these men provides a deeper awareness of traits he admired that, in general, were needed for a healthy society, or as Roosevelt would have insisted, "a strong nation." John Hay's blend of a "marked literary ability" with public service delighted him.[77] He identified Leonard

Wood with "boundless energy and endurance," while his conduct of colonial governance was untainted by "selfish interests, whether political or commercial."[78] Roosevelt quoted Scripture in a tribute to Booker T. Washington: "What more doth the Lord require of these than to do justice and love mercy and walk humbly with thy God? He did justice to every man. He did justice to those to whom it was a hard thing to do justice," according to Roosevelt, who valued Washington's "friendship and respect . . . a patriot and an American."[79] Admiration was not confined to public men of action, however. Praising the sculptor, Augustus Saint-Gaudens, he lauded his design of United States coins as both artistic and historically meaningful. The "pure imagination" of the piece of sculpture, "Silence," done for the Adams gravesite, greatly moved the President.[80] Linked with Saint-Gaudens was John Muir, the naturalist, whom TR credited with preserving beauty of a different kind, "those great natural phenomena: wonderful canyons, giant trees, slopes of flower-spangled hillsides."[81] And he saluted the big-game hunter, Frederick Courtney Selous, "a highly intelligent, civilized man," but "hard-bit who pushed ever northward the frontier of civilization" in Africa.[82] The character of people with whom he found himself involved in his conduct of affairs while president had a considerable effect on Roosevelt. He was comfortable and cooperated with the honorable man, but was easily put off by one whose behavior he thought was wrong, as his handling of the anthracite coal strike of 1902 bears out.

The anthracite strike, a major test of the new president's leadership, was governed in its outcome by three personalities: Roosevelt himself, who acted as a facilitator pushing hard for a peaceful resolution of the impasse between the miners and the coal operators; John Mitchell, the chief of the coal miners' union; and George F. Baer, president of the Philadelphia and Reading Coal and Iron Company, the spokesman for the owners. Roosevelt's observation of the two antagonists in the fight helped to persuade him of the path he ought to take, that of neutrality but with his sympathies for the workers only thinly disguised, as well as the path he ought to avoid, that taken by President Cleveland in the Pullman strike of 1894 in using federal troops to break the strike. TR gained a healthy respect for Mitchell because of his dignified manner and never forgot the arrogance of Baer as an example of the worst of laissez-faire capitalism.

The issues in the strike centered around a worker demand for a 10 percent wage raise, improved working conditions, including reduced hours per shift, and recognition of the United Mine Workers as a bargaining agent for the workers. Some one hundred and forty thousand hard-coal miners were off the job from May until October, a time of year when consumption of coal was off peak. In the absence of public inconvenience, much less suffering, the strikers won considerable public support. In essence, what the workers wanted was to sit down and talk with the operators and thereby come to an agreement. In such a process there could be give and take, and recognition of the union would come about. The owners showed themselves intransigently opposed to discussion, with Baer uttering some of the most extreme statements ever made publicly in labor-management confrontation. He announced when talks were first proposed that anthracite mining was a business, not a religious, sentimental, or academic proposition. Some weeks later he was prompted to deliver his now infamous confession of faith: "The rights and interests of the laboring man will be protected and cared for—not by labor agitators, but by the Christian men to whom God in his infinite wisdom has given the control of the property interests of this country." Baer's attitude was to take its toll on events. Mitchell, in contrast, was totally reasonable. He long had taken the position that the strike could have been avoided if a conference of the two sides had been convened, and it could be ended if such a conference were held at once. Baer's towering self-righteousness was set off sharply by Mitchell's moderation.

Over the summer months of 1902, though the president kept an eye on the situation, there was little sense of urgency. This mood was certain to change as coal inventories fell and cold weather loomed just ahead. Ordinarily priced at $2.40 a ton, coal had gone to $6.00 a ton and predictions were that it might reach $30.00 with little to be had unless the miners were soon digging coal. Roosevelt saw the unhappy prospects for what they were. The difficulty was that under the Constitution he was powerless to act to benefit the community at large. At one point he complained of being at his wit's end over how to proceed. Undeterred by constitutional incapacity to act, he continued to explore possible options and to worry about the outcome. Most importantly, he never stopped discussing the crisis with those he trusted: Elihu Root, Murray Crane, Philander Knox, and Cabot Lodge. With his persistent sense of history he informed Crane, the governor of Massachusetts, "I felt that the crisis was not one in which I could act on the Buchanan principle of striving to find some Constitutional means for inaction. . . ."[83] Roosevelt, being Roosevelt, wanted to do something.

In early October the president played his trump card, calling a conference of representatives of the operators and the miners to meet with him and his attorney-general, Knox, in Washington. Both Baer and Mitchell attended. Though the meeting failed to resolve the crisis, it succeeded in convincing Roosevelt that George F. Baer was a reprobate and John Mitchell an honorable man. In the course of the October conference Mitchell once more iterated the position of the workers: a series of talks between miners and owners whereby a compromise might be secured. Failing that, the union was willing to accept a presidentially appointed arbitration commission and to abide by its decision. Baer would have no part of such an arrangement. He accused Mitchell of fomenting anarchy and violence and defiance of the law, and went to the length of berating Roosevelt for the very idea of having Mitchell in the same room as the president and himself. Roosevelt's sympathies were readily enlisted on the side of Mitchell and thus on that of the workers, though he was quick to assure J. P. Morgan that he would not allow himself to be swayed by such considerations. Of course Roosevelt was swayed by the behavior he had witnessed. Mitchell was a gentleman, Baer was not. These things mattered to TR, however much he might disavow their influence.

Meanwhile, the war of nerves continued. Roosevelt dispatched Elihu Root to New York for talks with Morgan about a renewed proposal for a presidential conference. He named General Schofield as the army officer who would be in charge of maintaining law and order in the coal fields, should the government have to seize the mines. He welcomed the offer of ex-President Grover Cleveland to have a part in any scheme of arbitration. All this amounted to the kind of pressure Baer could not resist indefinitely. Finally, on 11 October, agreement was reached on arbitration. The following March the commission voted a 10 percent wage raise for the miners along with some reduction in hours. While the union did not win formal recognition as a bargaining agent, the newly formed National Board of Conciliation was to have union representation. An important corner had been turned in the union's fight for legitimacy.

Historians have agreed that Roosevelt acted out of mixed motives in his handling of the anthracite strike: fear of social upheaval, Republican party political advantage, and a desire to be in the eye of the storm. But in no small measure the type of men who were party to the dispute helped to shape his judgments and, accordingly, to direct his actions. It seems altogether unlikely that, if Mitchell had been as arrogant and un-cooperative as Baer, the president would have wanted to facilitate the kind of settlement that was reached. Mitchell's character made it easy for Roosevelt to blend the public welfare with the good of the workers to the advantage of his reputation as a "square deal" president. Roosevelt's long-harbored suspicions of the economic man were confirmed by the callous disregard for humanity that Baer personified. It was difficult for the president, or for any third party, not to side against a man who, when reminded of the sufferings of the miners, retorted that the miners were not suffering, adding, "why, they don't even speak English."

Few remarks could have more offended Roosevelt's belief in the melting-pot thesis. In dealing with Baer, therefore, TR discovered not only an enemy of the miners, but an enemy of his vision of an America that took the various peoples who came to its shores and molded them into a single race. Once when writing about "true Americanism," he reviewed the history of immigration and settlement in America, a study that showed that to the successive waves of immigrant groups, America was "a matter of spirit, conviction, and purpose, not of creed or birthplace or language." The history of "the ancient republics of Greece, the medieval republics of Italy, and the petty German states of the last century" showed what particularism could do. The contrast between these historical examples and events in the United States meant that America would not be allowed to succumb to this local or regional sentiment that centered in race or language. The ghetto mentality had no place in America as the strange peoples were gradually assimilated.[84]

The *Northern Securities* case (1904), which was another presidential triumph in the name of progressivism, involved a play of personalities as had the coal strike, but with a difference. In the coal dispute Roosevelt was a third party, whereas in the litigation involving the giant railroad combination engineered by Morgan, E. H. Harriman, and James J. Hill, the president was an antagonist. In the eyes of the business world TR was both antagonist and troublemaker. Business had long enjoyed virtual freedom from governmental regulation. As competition gave way to consolidation, monopoly conditions were achieved by the giant trusts. As early as 1902 Roosevelt had ordered his attorney general to institute proceedings against the Northern Securities Company, which had managed to clamp a stranglehold on all freight traffic out of Chicago to the upper West. Such a railroad combination was an ideal target for Roosevelt's ambition to show himself an enemy of the malefactors of great wealth and a friend of the people. After all, the combination included some of the biggest names in the corporate and financial world: Morgan, Harriman, Hill with Kuhn, and Loeb and Company thrown in for added measure. No sooner had Philander Knox instituted the legal proceedings than Morgan paid a visit to Roosevelt in Washington and made his bid to put TR in his pocket. "If we had done anything wrong," he advised the president, "send your man to my man and they can fix it up." To Morgan, life was that simple.

Roosevelt was not about a little "fixing" of his own and in a way that was to bear on the *Northern Securities* case. In 1902 with the death of Justice Horace Gray, the president named Oliver Wendell Holmes, Jr., to the United States Supreme Court. TR sized up Holmes as a good Republican, the son of a worthy father with a gallant Civil War record, and a man with twenty years of valuable experience on the Supreme Judicial Court of Massachusetts, where he had established his reputation as a liberal and reform-minded judge. Looking ahead to the time when reform laws would be put to the judicial test at the national level, Roosevelt was convinced Holmes was the right man for the job. The Holmes appointment revealed both the president's belief in the centrality of individuals in the working out of complex problems and a great faith in the power of men to control events. To him, the issue in the *Northern Securities* case was clear-cut: business had to be made responsible to the will of the people through the agency of government. From what he knew of the man, he thought Holmes would see the matter as he did.

The decision was handed down in 1904. The effort to apply the Sherman Anti-Trust Act to the railroad combination was upheld by a five to four vote. To Roosevelt's surprise and annoyance, Holmes had voted against the regulation of railroads and for big business. More importantly, the rather unpromising Sherman act had been used to curb railroad monopoly in the public interest. The decision marked a notable advance in the war on the trusts, and other successful suits followed soon thereafter. Looking back on the outcome, Roosevelt chose to remember the case in terms of the men who had been involved. He complained that he could have carved from a banana a judge with more backbone than Holmes had displayed. Writing to Owen Wister, he put his finger on the main issue, singling out James J. Hill, probably because of the latter's outspoken criticism of the decision: "Mr. Hill was doing what I thought wrong in the Northern Securities case," he told his friend.[85] Roosevelt had met numerous wrong-headed men in life and in literature. Hill was a familiar type. TR also believed firmly that he knew what was right and what was wrong, and that there could be no difference between private and public ethical standards in the conduct of business. The railroad trust had been judged in technical violation of a law, but in Roosevelt's interior judgment the crux of the matter was that the railroad men had done wrong.

"Of all Roosevelt's constructive endeavors, the movement for conservation was most marked by sustained intellectual effort and administrative force." This is the estimate of William H. Harbaugh, who has written further that in no other public enterprise "did the President blend science and morality quite so effectively."[86] The tribute, which sums up the thinking of contemporaries and historians alike, is well deserved. Had TR been born a century or more earlier, he might well have had an important place in the conquest of great continent. As it was, it fell to him to describe that conquest as a historian, and, as a public official, to preserve as much of the continent and its resources as possible "for generations yet unborn." The historical, the literary, and the public Roosevelt were again forged as one.

The fight for conservation turned out to be a difficult one, in the process of which TR learned anew the meaning of "special interest" and congressional stonewalling, as well as the high price often extracted of a man of principle. In the effort to make conservation an enduring national commitment and not simply a passing policy of his administration, Roosevelt put the issue above partisanship; as a good Republican, he did not find that easy. No doubt the final outcome was favorably influenced by the man

Roosevelt worked with in the conservation fight, Gifford Pinchot, a man with the qualities he admired in his father and in his historical heroes. Pinchot was the knight-errant in Roosevelt's quest for the holy grail of conservation. Wealthy, well connected, and well educated at Yale and at the School of Forestry in Nantes, France, he was a man of action who himself guided his official behavior by the learning he had acquired through study and experience.

Pinchot was an easterner, as was Roosevelt, of course, determined to save the westerners from the effects of their continued reckless use of natural resources. Ironically, the Roosevelt-Pinchot conservation program alienated westerners, including many of the plain folk as well as the giant timber and mineral tycoons. To westerners of all ranks, government regulation was seen as interference with economic freedom. The president understood this attitude perfectly, while not agreeing with it. As he told one meeting of the Forest Congress in Washington in 1905: "In the old pioneer days the American had but one thought about a tree and that was to cut it down; and the mental attitude of the nation toward forests was largely conditioned on that."[87] But as a learned Roosevelt had discerned long ago, the freewheeling West was a phase in the evolutionary process. As the West matured and grew more complex it had to be regulated for the welfare of the people there and for the nation of which the West was an organic part. Roosevelt was prepared to follow the lead of forest technology, which was learning of a specialized kind. The scientists had the practical knowledge and the president sought to work through them to save the natural resources of America. At the same time he insisted that his own insights about the West, his careful study of its ways, and his experience as a ranchman gave him a special warrant to speak out.

Throughout his presidency Theodore Roosevelt pushed hard for conservation reforms by means of laws, executive decrees, and state cooperation. He supported the Newlands bill aimed at the construction of irrigation and reclamation projects as early as December 1901. His attitude was distinctly nonpartisan. Roosevelt set aside national forest reserves, on one memorable occasion just a step ahead of a congressional effort to tie his hands, adding millions of acres to this natural treasure. He supported tree-planting experiments on federal lands, became an advocate of selective cutting, acted to support flood-control works, and called for and got legislation that reorganized the federal bureaucracy responsible for supervising the conservation program. This latter reform was one Roosevelt identifed with especially. He spoke of the need for a corps of professional foresters—"a new profession, a profession of the highest usefulness; a profession as high as the profession of law, as the profession of medicine, as any other profession most ultimately connected with the highest and finest development of a nation"[88]—to the Society of American

Foresters in 1903. Whatever the reform, it devolved upon individuals of character, of knowledge, and of energy to frame the laws and make them effective. Under Pinchot's firm guidance the forestry service became an outstanding component of the civil service. What the president had expressed as hopes for the conservation of American natural resources were well on the way to fulfillment by the time he left office.

Looking back over the various administration-led attempts to regulate private economic interests for the social good, Roosevelt is often heard invoking what he called "the Puritan spirit."[89] He recalled on one occasion that the Puritans were people who possessed a to remarkable degree the power of individual initiative and self-help. Combined with these traits was practical common sense that taught them the wisdom of joining with others when it was necessary to get a job done. "The spirit of the Puritan . . . never shrank from the regulation of conduct if such regulation was necessary to the public weal."[90] Roosevelt urged this spirit on the nation in his day. "The American people became firmly convinced of the need of control of the great aggregations of capital," he said, "especially when they had monopolistic tendencies."[91] Using the Puritan past as a touchstone, the president argued that as the Puritans had found a certain degree of regulation appropriate to the requirements of the seventeenth century, so regulation, different but generically the same, was essential to effective government in the twentieth century. Roosevelt claimed that in this spirit of just regulation "we have shown there is no individual and no corporation so powerful that he or it stands above the possibility of punishment under the law."[92] Underlying the justice of regulation was the Puritan spirit of order and discipline. This use of the Puritan experience looks like a straining on Roosevelt's part to thread the historical needle, a demonstration that he could stray beyond limitations imposed by lessons drawn from the past.

"I am, as I expected I would be, a pretty good imperialist."[93] Roosevelt pronounced this verdict on himself to his English friend from Spanish-American War days, Arthur Hamilton Lee, while touring Africa in 1910. What were the sources of that imperialism of which he spoke so confidently? They ranged from some primordial urge to conquer coming from deep within him, through a belief in the superiority of America as the highest expression of contemporary Western civilization, to a commitment to improve the lot of mankind generally by playing both master and servant to "the lesser breeds without the law." It was strongly Kiplingesque: brutal, self-serving, self-sacrificing, uplifting, and romantic. That it was also intellectual was made evident through two distinct but intersecting principles. The more basic one was evolution; its derivative, the authority of Anglo-Americans as the most advanced race, was evidenced by their achievements. From time to time Roosevelt called upon these principles to explain and justify the sweep of modern history and to account for particular actions taken during his presidency, actions for which he was ultimately responsible and that identify him with imperialism.

Greatly taken with the leading scientific proposition of his era, the process of natural selection, or what he once called "the line of descent from protozoan to Plato," Roosevelt made a careful study of both evolution and its outgrowth, social Darwinism.[94] Darwin and Huxley had "succeeded in effecting a complete revolution in the thought of an age," so that "the acceptance of the fundamental truth of evolution is quite as necessary to sound thinking as the acceptance of the fundamental truths of the solar system."[95] Yet he inclined to set Darwin and his work in perspective. Writing to Oliver Wendell Holmes, Jr., in 1904, he allowed that Darwin was "the chief factor in working a tremendous revolution," going on to express the opinion that in the future Darwin would be read "just as we read Lucretius now; that is, because of the interest attaching to his position in history."[96] Early results of his study of evolution, as already shown by his opinion of Kidd's *Social Evolution*, strictly qualified the function of natural selection by insisting on the function of character. He later expressed mature judgments along these lines in "Biological Analogies in History." Accordingly, Roosevelt put great reliance on the achievements of the Anglo-Americans that exemplified the place of character. Of these none stood higher than the establishment of self-governing communities at home and the lessons of self-rule that they offered to colonial peoples. Successful self-government by a community was the equivalent of character in the individual. It required the adapting of a political system to changing circumstances while keeping intact the eternal principles of justice and truth. Imperialism called not for the exportation of the American system of government, but the American spirit of government. Just as "it was Roman influence on language, law, literature, the governmental system, the whole way of looking at life" that had given Rome its historical significance, so the contributions of the American people would be judged.[97] The frontiersmen had swept across a vast continent, carrying their ideals and building up a superior nation. The superiority thereby demonstrated justified a continuing westward movement across the Pacific as well as American domination of the Caribbean. Weaker peoples, the Filipinos in particular, were to be servant and served alike. Destiny and responsibility met in imperialism no less in the twentieth century than two thousand years before.

Roosevelt inherited an imperialistic state of affairs when he took office in 1901. His mind-set was one that approved, in general terms at least, the policies that had brought about American presence in the Pacific and ascendancy in the Caribbean. The particulars of the situation, and therefore what he was bound to deal with once he was president, were, however, the result of the McKinley way of doing things. In the Philippines the nationalist insurrection under Aguinaldo had been put down by early 1901, so that as a new president, Roosevelt was not beset by the problems arising from a vicious guerilla war. He had enthusiastically approved the use of force against the native nationalists, likening Aguinaldo to Sitting Bull, but he sincerely rejoiced that such difficult times had passed. As he had looked forward to the end of the conflict as vice-president, he had told William Howard Taft, who was serving as governor general of the Philippines, that "the military arm should literally be an arm directed by a civil head."[98] Believing fully in civilian control of the military establishment, he was from the start of his time in office prepared to give to Taft, and to William H. Hunt in Puerto Rico, "the largest liberty of action possible and the heartiest support," knowing that Taft and Hunt were themselves committed to civilian supremacy in the Anglo-American tradition.[99]

The attainment by the Filipino people of self-rule was one of the objectives of Roosevelt's policy toward the Islands. But he was equally convinced that it had to be a gradual process if it were to be a permanent achievement. "It is not a light task for a nation to achieve the temperamental qualities without which the institutions of free government are but an empty mockery. . . ." "Our people," he went on to underscore in his first annual message to Congress, "are now governing themselves because for more than a thousand years they have been slowly fitting themselves, sometimes consciously, sometimes unconsciously. What has taken thirty generations to achieve we can not expect to see another race accomplish out of hand." Having urged caution both on Congress and the Filipino people, the president nonetheless declared: "We hope to do for them what has never been done for any people of the tropics—to make them fit for self-government after the fashion of the really free nations." Meanwhile American occupation of the Islands was imperative, an occupation depending directly on the American army, the same force that had denied the Filipinos their independence.[100]

Buried in the rhetoric and the reality of American control was the inherent contradiction in the proposal of any imperialistic power to make the conquered fit for self-rule. The more pronounced the success of preparation for independence, the less justification there was for continued occupation by the colonial power. Irrespective of how cordial relations between colonial power and colonial people might have been, the contradiction became the controlling factor. It was a contradiction that Roosevelt could not escape and was prepared to face.

The president insisted that his administration was encouraging in every way the growth of those conditions that made for self-government, but the Congress appeared to want to move faster in the matter than Roosevelt. The Cooper Act, which the President signed into law in July 1902, made the Islands an unincorporated territory and declared that all citizens of the Philippines should enjoy the protection of the United States. The law also provided for the safeguarding of individual rights and specified a census, to be taken in preparation for the election of a lower house of a Philippine legislature. The Cooper Act further called for a strong, independent judiciary with the right of appeal to the United States Supreme Court when the Constitution or any treaty was involved in a dispute. The census was completed in 1905, the elections took place in July 1907, and in October of that year the first Filipino Assembly came together.

With his pronounced Anglo-American affinity, Roosevelt was inclined to compare American imperialism with its British counterpart, judging the former to be superior. "We have done more for the Philippines than the English have done in Egypt," he wrote Lodge in April 1906, and "our problems . . . were infinitely more complex." He noted further that while the British appeared to be exploiting the Malay Settlements, the cardinal doctrine of American rule in the Philippines was to avoid all forms of such behavior. As far as Roosevelt was concerned, Leonard Wood in Moro country had a more difficult job than his counterparts in Malaya and he had done his job better. In the same vein he told Lodge that the "performance of Taft, like the aggregate performances of Wood, surpasses the performance of Lord Cromer" in Egypt. Whether boasting or representing the facts, such estimates sharpened the contradictions in benign imperialism. Roosevelt accordingly garnished his optimism with a touch of restraint, saying that it would be unwise to "turn the attention of the Filipinos away from the problem of achieving the moral and material responsibility requisite . . . and toward dangerous intrigues for complete independence."[101] At the end of his presidency TR continued to insist that the Filipinos had made great progress but that national independence was unthinkable, not only because of his judgment about the political maturity of the people of the Islands, but also because of what Captain Mahan had called "the problem of Asia."

Fascination with China and the lure of the China trade continued to work their magic on American foreign policy once Roosevelt became president. Mahan's book, *The Problem of Asia* (1901), marked his full emergence as a geopolitical thinker and, with other of TR's friends, including Brooks Adams and the English diplomat, Sir Cecil Spring Rice, he anticipated that China would be the great imperialist prize of the new country. All these observers tended to agree that Russia was the lurking menace. "I think the Russians have got the Chinese now whenever they like," Spring Rice wrote Roosevelt as early as 1896; "when they command and drill the Northern Chinese they will be a pretty big power-such a power as the world has never seen."[102] Only later did the president become fully convinced of the potential danger of the Russians to the

American position in the Far East. The Boxer Rebellion in 1900 occa-sioned Roosevelt to write Arthur Lee: "The stupendous revolution now going on in China is an additional reason why we [America and England] should work together."[103] Later the president would orchestrate the peace negotiations bringing an end to the Russo-Japanese War because he said he thought the war a senseless slaughter of gallant men (a lesson learned well in Cuba) and because a continuation of the conflict would derange the balance of Far Eastern power. The Philippine Islands had to figure in the construction of an American strategy for the area, so that the United States could hardly forego possession of this stepping stone to the Asiatic mainland.

Before Roosevelt was long in office he came to realize the impossibility of America's doing more than maintaining the status quo in the Orient. Balance of power became the watchword. In such a policy British cooper-ation was vital. The English-speaking peoples would have to act together. The Taft-Katsura Agreement of 1905, wherein Japanese hegemony in Korea was acknowledged by Washington and American preeminence in the Philippines was recognized by Tokyo, and the Root-Takahira Agree-ment of 1908, which saw each nation accept the status quo, were com-pletely consistent with the Anglo-Japanese Naval Treaty of 1902, signaling the friendship of these two countries. The aggressive American attitude of 1898–1901 was distinctly moderated by Roosevelt, who admitted, toward the close of his presidency, that the Philippine Islands, from a military standpoint, might be "our heel of Achilles."[104]

During Roosevelt's ascendancy the United States became an active policeman in the Caribbean and the watchdog of much of the western hemisphere. Cuba, Venezuela, Santo Domingo, Colombia, as well as Can-ada, in the dispute over the location of the Alaskan boundary, were all made to feel the power of the United States at one time or another. This was a posture based on strength and it immediately suggests the evolution-ary ethic of survival of the fittest, giving a scientific justification for the dictum that might makes right. Roosevelt's disdain for Latin Americans generally went undisguised. "The bandits of Bogota," "banana re-publics," and "nests of a wicked and inefficient type" were all phrases of his manufacture. The sense of superiority they spoke was towering. As Roosevelt once remarked to the German ambassador, von Sternburg, "if any South American State misbehaves toward any European country, let the European country spank it."[105] These states were like children, to be disciplined by adult nations as required by circumstances. They had not evolved to a sufficient degree of political maturity to enable them to manage their own affairs, necessitating American supervision.

Given the American sense of mission to uplift the peoples of the Philippines, it is appropriate to inquire whether the supervision in the

Caribbean was in any way benign, in intention if not in effect, and whence the intended good derived. When there was a softening of the evolutionary thesis in Roosevelt's thinking about South America, it was due more to a general sense of justice and fair play and had limited relationship to Roosevelt's intellectual commitments. But the impression persists that the Latin American aspects of Rooseveltian foreign policy retained a distinct emphasis on power that was, in considerable part, traceable to Roosevelt's evolutionary outlook. His apologists have contended that TR did not believe that "might makes right" but that "might makes right possible to achieve." This is an intriguing distinction that, while possibly exonerating the president from extreme charges against him as a blatant imperialist, still does not deny the resort to force that was characteristic of the ethics growing out of the evolutionary dispensation. Yet force was a fact of life long before evolutionist teaching in the nineteenth century. Roosevelt had recognized this fact of life in building his body as a youngster, in his adventures as a Dakota ranchman, and in his military experiences during the Spanish-American War. Meanwhile, evolution as a cosmic explanation of things became part of his intellectual makeup. His learned mind gave no resistance to it. As for the tenets of social Darwinism, as opposed to evolution, he found he could not always morally or intellectually accept them. If Colombia was manhandled during negotiations over the building of a canal at Panama, force was utilized as a means to an end, but not as an end in itself. The application of force would eventuate in a result useful to mankind. As the president confided to his son, Kermit, the interests of civilization must take precedence over those of a wildcat republic like Colombia.[106] There were times to draw on a knowledge of history for guidance and, again, there were times when it was plainly better to make history.

Much the same argument can be offered in evaluating Roosevelt's uses of the Monroe Doctrine, though the president appears far more imaginative, or creative, in his reliance on that historic pronouncement. Before he became president, TR spoke often and with passion about maintaining the Monroe Doctrine intact and applauded the efforts of others, not excluding the Democrat, Grover Cleveland, to see that it was honored. Yet Roosevelt was practical enough (and just possibly incipiently pragmatic enough, in the strict use of that word) to grasp the idea that the Monroe Doctrine had to be a tool of American power rather than a mere frame of reference. To be limited in its utilization by inherited versions of what the doctrine meant, inhibited meeting the fresh kinds of problems arising from an alarming dependence by many South American states on large European loans. The Roosevelt Corollary to the Monroe Doctrine, which he enunciated in his annual message to Congress in 1904, was an extension of the meaning of the doctrine necessitated by new conditions. If pragmatic truth comes about by the wedding of old ideas with new ideas to produce new truth, then Roosevelt may well have been acting in a clearly pragmatic way. And if the test of the new truth was to be its workability, his policy in Santo Domingo, where the corollary was first applied, proved that it was eminently true. European creditors were satisfied and the western hemisphere continued inviolate. As for Santo Domingo, it had surely received a moral insult to its sovereign status, but, practically speaking, it was better off with Americans collecting customs than when Dominican officials undertook the task. An immature nation, it had to rely on a more advanced nation for its immediate welfare. Roosevelt's incipient pragmatism had closed the intellectual circle, which helps to explain Roosevelt's confidence in his Santo Domingo policy despite heavy criticism in the Congress and the press.[107]

The demands of the presidency on Theodore Roosevelt were heavy. The nature of the office and the changes that were part of the era combined with TR's own passion for action, resulting in what was a hectic pace. He retained his fondness and friendship with learning, nonetheless. Occasionally he dipped his pen into the literary well, though mostly he was preoccupied with matters and papers of state. He wrote several review-essays, including "The Mongols," a critique of *The Mongols: A History* by Jeremiah Curtin, and "The Children of the Night." He kindly wrote prefaces to *The Master of Game* by Edward, Duke of York and *Hunting the Elephant* by C. H. Stigand. "The Ancient Irish Sagas" appeared in the *Century Magazine* for January 1907.

During TRs days in the White House the doors were always open and through them came many distinguished men of learning and intellectual accomplishment. The president delighted in such visits and was as prepared to listen as he was eager to speak his own viewpoints on law, poetry, history, science, or whatever else his guests might like to discuss. Most of all he loved people who loved books. He had abiding personal friendships with James Bryce, Henry Fairfield Osborn, Owen Wister, Cecil Spring Rice, the brothers Adams, John Hay, Cabot Lodge, and G. O. Trevelyan, several of whom exchanged long and serious letters with him. A forty-thousand-word account of his Afro-European tour of 1909–10 in letter form to Trevelyan is an example of his rare gift as a raconteur.[108] "Literary salon" would be too tame a description of the White House during Theodore Roosevelt's occupancy. It was more like a literary merry-go-round. And when there was a break in the action the president turned to books, classics and contemporary works alike, which, after his wife and family, were his dearest companions.

For all of that Roosevelt often has been dismissed as anti-intellectual. Henry F. Pringle in his Putlizer Prize–winning biography of Roosevelt, a book that is distinguished by a lively but serious prejudice against its subject, has advanced the argument that Roosevelt was "far from an objective critic," judging literature "in the light of his own stern moral code."[109] He certainly distrusted Zola and Tolstoy; and he rejected naturalism in literature as in bad taste at the very least. But he was ready to read these novelists, and if he dismissed them on moral grounds he did not proceed blindly or without what he considered substantial reason. As a critic of the *Kreutzer Sonata,* for example, all he really said was that Tolstoy had written a bad book.[110].

Roosevelt was not reluctant to moralize about literature or history. In his 1912 address as president of the American Historical Association[111] he insisted that "the greatest historian should also be a great moralist. It is no proof of impartiality to treat wickedness and goodness on the same level. . . . Carlyle offers an instance in point. Very few men have ever been a greater source of inspiration than Carlyle when he confined himself to preaching morality in the abstract." But the ex-president believed that Carlyle "was utterly unable to distinguish either great virtues or great vices when he applied his own principles concretely to history. His 'Frederick the Great' is literature of a high order. . . . But 'morality' therein jubilantly upheld is shocking to any man who takes seriously Carlyle's other writings in which he lays down different principles of conduct." Put very simply, the "morality he praised had no connection with the morality as understood in the New Testament."[112]

Theodore Roosevelt left the high office of president on an upbeat note. He was determined to keep his 1904 decision not to seek a second successive elected term, and to this effect he openly favored Taft's nomination by the Republican party, thus heading off a possible stampede for Teddy. His plan was to retire gracefully to private life and to his house at Oyster Bay, Sagamore Hill, much as Jefferson had sought out Monticello a century before, confident that Taft would be elected and would continue to follow the basic policy line he had laid out. "There is something rather attactive, something in a way living up to the proper democratic ideal, in having the president go out and become absolutely without reservation a private man," was the way he summed it up for St. Loe Strachey, the editor of the *Spectator.* As he was only fifty-one at the time, in good health and with a zest for life, there was, however, the real problem of a suitable occupation. He believed it would be an "unpleasant thing to be pensioned and given some honorary position," but at the same time he rejected one or two lucrative offers because of his suspiciousness of the marketplace.[113] Apart from his not being a wealthy man, the very thought of idleness was so repugnant that Roosevelt was keen on both counts to do some worthwhile work. His earlier experience as an author naturally pointed him in a literary direction. He contracted with Scribner's to do a book on his pending hunting trip to Africa, and on his return from the

Afro-European tour of 1909–10 he accepted an offer from Lyman Abbott to be a contributing editor of the *Outlook*. In 1909 it appeared that Roosevelt's career in the overall might go from books to books with high offices sandwiched in between.

The final decade of Roosevelt's life was far from totally bookish. The impression is that he went about like a roaring lion, such as he had missed killing while on safari, and that books and what they suggested had been put aside altogether. His need to be at the center of public life drew Roosevelt inexorably to active politics as early as 1910, and to political disaster in 1912 when the Bull Moose cause, for all its nobility and glamor, foundered on the reality of the two-party system. Any chance for a nomination in 1916, when he would have been fifty-eight and electable, was squandered in 1912. Meanwhile, another chasm opened, threatening both career and reputation—the 1914 war. Roosevelt believed almost from the start that America should join Britain and France in the fight. By 1915 he had gone fully public in his shrill demands for American entry on the Allied side and in his overbearing assaults on President Wilson's policy of neutrality. Frustrated by his lack of power, Roosevelt at this stage appeared to reverse the dictum of Lord Acton. It was a want of power that corrupted the ex-president, to the point that he resorted to name-calling to vent his spleen: "the trouble with Wilson is that he is plain yellow." This was not the learned Roosevelt speaking.

Prescinding from the misfortunes of his public life, Roosevelt had a great deal to say in his postpresidential years. It is altogether remarkable that he was able to combine public outcry with literary productivity, and political action with reflective writing. His previously cited "History as Literature" comes to mind at once. Consider the date of this address to the American Historical Association: 27 December 1912. TR had finished the arduous Bull Moose campaign six weeks before, a campaign in which he had blanketed the country, survived gunshot wounds to the chest, and roared his defiance at the old guard of his beloved Republican party in a cause he knew was lost. He took his defeat in stride but it cut him to the quick. Then in late December in Boston he gave his address to the AHA, an address that, although generally neglected over the years, contained some stunning observations. For all his insistence that the great historian must be moral, he believed strongly in science as a healthy influence on historical writing. Morality in historical writing "does not mean that good history can be unscientific; the great historian can do nothing unless he is steeped in science," he told his fellow historians. "He must accept what we know of man's place in nature. He must realize that men have been on this earth for a period of incalculable length." He saw no conflict between morality and science, in other words. Roosevelt's own scientific bent and training go a long way toward explaining the ease with which he made this accommodation. Much more memorable were the two additional notes he sounded that have a striking contemporary ring to them. "The great historian of the future will have easy access to innumerable facts [computer assisted?] and can not be excused if he fails to draw on the vast storehouses of knowledge [data banks?]." Furthermore, Roosevelt contended, the historian of the future must be able to distinguish between the usual and the unusual in this world of innumerable facts.[114]

A second novel way in which the ex-president called for a new version of history had to do with the commonplaces of the past. The great historian "must be able to paint for us the life of the plain people, the ordinary men and women of the time of which he writes." "Nothing that tells of their life will be amiss to him: implements of labor, weapons of warfare, wills written, bargains made, songs that they sang as they feasted and made love." Nor were these observations simply to be made in passing. Roosevelt labored his injunction that "the historians deal with common things" and deal with them "so that they shall interest us in reading of them as our common things interest us as we live among them."[115]

"History as Literature" was also remarkable for its final thoughts. After speculating on how the historian of the future would write about the nineteenth and early twentieth centuries in America, Roosevelt was prompted to make a prediction. The historian would tell "of the frontier, of course, but also of the portentous growth of the cities," "the far-reaching consequences of industrialization," and of the new race arising from the melting pot. And "The hard materialism of our age will appear, and also the strange capacity for lofty idealism which must be reckoned with by all who would understand the American character."[116] Roosevelt's final paragraph is worth quoting as well:

> Those who tell the Americans of the future what the Americans of today and of yesterday have done will perforce tell much that is unpleasant. This is but saying they will describe the arch-typical civilization of this age. Nevertheless, when the tale is finally told, I believe that it will show that the forces working for good in our national life outweigh the forces working for evil, that with many blunders and shortcomings, with much halting and turning aside from the path, we shall yet in the end prove our faith by our works, and show in our lives our belief that righteousness exalteth a nation.[117]

In uttering these thoughts, the obvious fruit of reflection on the ultimate meaning and nature of the American experience, Roosevelt might well have been speaking to the audience of a much later time. For all its preachy overtones it constitutes an extraordinary commentary on American life and character. Composed and delivered in the aftermath of the

1912 election, it serves as a reminder that the learned Roosevelt was never that distant from the man of action.

TR's life during the whole of the 1909–19 decade may be characterized in the same way. While a contributing editor for the *Outlook* and in a private capacity as well, Roosevelt turned out journalistic and political pieces with no lasting value on a variety of subjects, but he also did some impressive work of a substantial nature. He brought out two books on travel, *African Game Trails* and *Through the Brazilian Wilderness,* his *Autobiography,* a collection of essays under the title, *A Book-Lover's Holiday in the Open,* and several deserving essays that contained reviews of important books of the day, including Arthur E. P. B. Weigall's *The Treasury of Ancient Egypt* (1911), Octavius Charles Beale's *Racial Decay* (1911), H. J. Mozans's *Woman in Science* (1914), and Henry Fairfield Osborn's *The Origin and Evolution of Life* (1918), the latter appearing just a year before his death.

Of all his contributions to the *Outlook* none stirred more controversy and none has been so widely used to misrepresent his attitude toward the arts than "A Layman's View of an Art Exhibition," his critique of the famous New York Armory Art Show of 1913.[118] It has been described as the towering protest of an influential philistine against modern art. And it is true that Roosevelt was unsparing in his hostility to cubism and other futuristic art forms. "Probably we err in treating most of these pictures seriously," he wrote. "It is likely that many of them represent in the painters the astute appreciation of the power to make folly lucrative which the late P. T. Barnum showed with his fake mermaid." To him "the lunatic fringe was fully in evidence." Roosevelt observed that he was struck by the "resemblance of some of the art to the work of the palaeolithic artists of the French and Spanish caves." The palaeolithics were "interesting samples of the strivings for a human form . . . stumbling effort [that] represented progress. . . . Forty thousand years later, when entered into artificially and deliberately, it represents only a smirking pose of retrogression, and is not worthy of praise."[119] These and like comments on some of the modernist entries have marked Roosevelt as an enemy of art. Too little notice has been taken of what he found in the Armory show that moved him. "In some ways," he wrote,

> it is the work of the American painters and sculptors which is the most interesting in this collection, and a glance at this work must convince any of the real good that is coming out of the new movement, fantastic though many of the developments of these new movements are. There was one note entirely absent from the exhibition and that was the note of the commonplace. There was not a touch of simpering, self-satisfied conventionality anywhere in the exhibition [of the Americans]. Any painter or sculptor who had in him something to express and the power

of expressing it found the field open to him. He did not have to be afraid because his work was not along ordinary lines. There was no stunting or dwarfing, no requirement that a man whose gift lay in new directions should measure up or down to stereotyped or fossilized standards.[120]

Specifically, he singled out " 'Arizona Desert,' 'Canadian Night,' the group of girls on the roof of a New York tenement-house, the studies in the Bronx Zoo, the 'Heracles,' the studies of the Utah monument, the little group called 'Gossip' which has something of the quality of the famous fifteenth idyl of Theocritus, the 'Pelf' with its grim suggestiveness"—these and many more he found worthy of notice and respect.[121] Without denying the virulence of the ex-president's dislike for much in modern art, it is wrong to remember him as an enemy of art or of all new directions in the art world.

Roosevelt's decision to write an autobiography, at least in its timing, resulted in a book satisfying neither for him nor for posterity. "I am having my hands full writing certain chapters of my past experience," he admitted frankly to his sister-in-law, Emily Carow.[122] The whole project, in fact, started tentatively. When installments began appearing in the *Outlook* in February 1913, they were entitled "Chapters of a Possible Biography." The completed account was published in book form by the end of that year, Roosevelt having decided after all that it might be useful to have his version of events on the record. He faced two problems in recounting his life and public career. First, aware that he was writing what would be an important historical document, he wanted to be candid; conscious that such candor would offend any number of people still alive and active in politics, he was persuaded that he must be balanced and dispassionate in what he set down. The result is a story of a tepid kind in view of Roosevelt's personality, yet it also sounded more self-serving than it would have if it had provided a full, unrestricted version of things. The second was a more complicated problem. TR decided to end his biography as his presidency came to a close, not unlike General Grant, whose *Memoirs* went no further than Appomattox. The note of triumph was intended to produce a lingering effect in both accounts. For Roosevelt this meant that the whole new nationalism phase of his career, climaxing in the Bull Moose campaign, went unregarded. Still nurturing political hopes, Roosevelt decided it was best to say nothing of 1912, but the *Autobiography* is a poorer historical source as a result.

This truncated life suffered further, of course, from the fact that it was not to include the controversial role the ex-president took in the battle over American neutrality after 1914. Those were dark days, and even Roosevelt's more friendly biographers have been somewhat wary in their treatment. For all its extremism, Roosevelt's position was not totally indefensible, and it would have benefited him a great deal had he taken the opportunity to make some measured and formal statements in his own behalf, as distinct from the fulminations he uttered that have so warped his wartime image. As it turned out he was not vouchsafed the time required for this much-needed apologia.

Still, the *Autobiography* captured some of the variety and vitality of the man. It was a big book, as it had to be to accommodate the many-sided individual it described. It was a confident book, though there are hints of self-doubt from time to time. For all its deficiencies it added an important account to the historical record, which all too few presidents, either before or after TR, have attempted to do, except with the aid of ghost writers and rewriters and other adjuncts. At the very least it is certain that TR himself put pen to paper. Therefore, both contemporaries and historians have a better knowledge of the inner workings of a man whom Henry Adams once described as "pure act." The *Autobiography* also provides another major piece of evidence of Roosevelt's compulsion to resort to a standard literary form.

African Game Trails was a worthwhile book.[123] Subtitled "An account of the African wanderings of an American hunter-naturalist," it was the product of knowledge, enthusiasm, courage, and a devotion to the written word. It is a big book, occupying nearly five hundred pages in volume 24 of the Memorial edition of Roosevelt's *Works*. With a sense of the romantic, TR signed the preface "Khartoum, March 15, 1910." One of the book's winning features is that one may open it at almost any page and enter into the adventure: stalking the rhino or the elephant, making the dangerous trek into the high grass country, or viewing the awesome natural settings. Roosevelt is so very much alive on the trail of game in Africa. But he is also the naturalist and the literate man. He is writing about hunting the giraffe, when he pauses to explain:

> The country in which we were hunting marks the southern limit of the "reticulated" giraffe, a form or species entirely distinct from the giraffe we had already obtained in the country south of Kenia. The southern giraffe has blotches with dark on a light ground, whereas this northern or northeastern form is of a uniform dark color on the back and sides, with a network or reticulation of white lines placed in a large pattern on this dark background. The naturalists were very anxious to obtain a specimen of this form from its southern limit of distribution, to see if there was any intergradation with the southern form, of which we had already shot specimens near its northern, or at least northeastern, limit. The distinction proved sharp.[124]

A page or two later, Roosevelt describes the sighting of a rhino amid a great herd of zebra. As the purpose of the day was not to hunt, he did not want to kill the rhino, which remained in a position obscuring the party's view of the zebra. TR wrote: "I did not wish to kill it, and I was beginning to feel about the rhino the way Alice did in the Looking Glass country, when the elephants 'did bother so.' "[125]

Roosevelt believed that apart from great sport "with the noblest game in the world," he was making some contribution to scientific knowledge. He had offered the Smithsonian Institution specimens of what he proposed to shoot and several field naturalists and taxidermists were members of the party. What makes *African Game Trails* all the more extraordinary as an account of the expedition is that it was written during the trekking itself. For that reason the adventures recounted have an immediacy and a freshness that produce a winning effect. During one six-week stretch, Roosevelt managed to put down forty-five thousand words, often writing by camp fire and under adverse conditions of weather and fatigue. The contributions the expedition made to scientific knowledge, while not great, were valiantly done, and the literary Roosevelt, put to the severest of tests, passed with high marks.

The literary Roosevelt was revealed further in the "pigskin library." In planning the African trip, Roosevelt proposed to take a number of books with him for solace by night after having hunted the big cats by day. His sister Corinne Douglas collected copies of the books he wanted, and had them cut to pocket size and bound in pigskin as a protection against jungle rot. It is necessary to cite only a few of the items he took. The Bible and Shakespeare, of course, along with Homer's *Iliad* and *Odyssey,* headed the list. also included were Bacon's *Essays,* Lowell's *Biglow Papers,* Emerson's *Poems,* Milton's *Paradise Lost,* Dante's *Inferno,* Mark Twain's *Tom Sawyer* and *Huckleberry Finn,* as well as *Vanity Fair* by Thackeray and *Pickwick Papers* by Dickens. The pigskin library was never intended to be a listing of the world's great books. As Roosevelt wrote, there was no trace of dogmatism in preferring this book to that. It was a matter of personal choice: classics to reread as well as more contemporary novels, and poems to roll off the tongue. He conceded that he did not take scientific books "simply because as yet scientific books do not have literary value." Throughout his life Roosevelt had counted books among his friends, and some of those that were his best friends he wanted as companions.[126]

Through the Brazilian Wilderness was Roosevelt's personal account of what was officially the "Expedicao Scientifica Roosevelt-Rondon."[127] Invitations from the governments of Argentina, Brazil, and Chile to visit those countries brought Roosevelt to South America in 1913. Once there, he was encouraged both by his fellow explorer, Father John Zahm, and the Brazilian government to undertake an exploration of the interior of Brazil. It was to be a scientific expedition to gather information about plant and animal life as well as to learn more about the geography and geology of the area. During the course of the exploration, Roosevelt, accompanied by his son Kermit, Colonel Rondon of the Brazilian army, and a small number of others from the general party, undertook to descend the River of Doubt to determine its location and how it flowed into the Amazon. This latter phase of the trip proved to be extremely dangerous. At one point the ex-president nearly died of infection and the accompanying high fever. That he persevered as an explorer is no more surprising than that he persevered as a writer. Under conditions far more severe than those encountered in Africa—for days the party was totally out of contact with the rest of the world and disasters lurked at every step—TR wrote his daily notes as the basis for his book, attired in head net and heavy gloves as protection against the insect stings that were a relentless fact of life. Two things were notable about the expedition. It led to a first-rate account of the adventure in which Roosevelt's modesty, courage, vulnerability, curiosity, and physical stamina were all visible; it was perhaps the most honest book in terms of himself that TR was to write. Second, the expedition was responsible for important scientific finds, geographic, geologic, and zoologic. In recognition of his work the ex-president was awarded the David Livingstone Centenary gold medal by the American Geographical Society. No less than a dozen separate bulletins and papers were issued by the Brazilian government on the basis of the findings of the expedition. In addition, specimens of birds and mammals, almost two thousand in all, were collected for the American Museum of Natural Science.

Roosevelt had clearly risked his life in this further try at "a great adventure." Very probably his health was undermined, as he suffered ailments off and on for the remainder of his life. He had taken the trip out of a sense of adventure, and equally out of a desire to advance scientific knowledge. What had happened in the course of his explorations had more than fulfilled his expectations on both counts. The Brazilian government named the great interior river that he had helped to locate "Rio Teodora," as a tribute to this North American friend and compatriot. Later Roosevelt delivered various lectures founded on his experiences to the National Geographic Society, the Royal Geographic Society, and the American Museum in New York. The Brazilian wilderness was a long way from the Adirondacks where in 1874 TR had made his first extensive scientific listing of summer birds. Yet there was a unity in his endeavors that combined these two treasure troves of nature. It was the unity of nature itself. Not surprisingly, he continued to probe nature and its ultimate secrets in his last intellectual efforts, offered in several essays and book reviews.

When "Biological Analogies in History" and "History as Literature" are added to the essays and several other pieces that Roosevelt wrote in the years 1909–19, it is an easy matter to appreciate the ongoing literary man in the sometime president. For all the allure and command of science he remained a humanist at heart, protesting not long before he died that the study of science must not be carried out at the expense of the study of man. But who was man, what was his purpose in the final accounting? In "Racial Decadence," Roosevelt addressed the then delicate subject of "deliberate sterility in marriage."[128] It takes a preacher of great compassion and a writer of taste to delineate views on such a subject without giving offense. The critique of Octavius Charles Beale's book was somewhat lacking in subtlety, advocating without qualification an anti-materialistic version of human life. In his analysis, Roosevelt came to the causes of a declining birth rate directly and forcefully. It was due, in his judgment, to "coldness, to selfishness, to love of ease, to shrinking from risk, to an utter and pitiful failure in sense of perspective and in power of weighing what really makes the highest joy and to a rooting out of a sense of duty, in a twisting of that sense into improper channels." To a large extent he equated the salvation of society with the fulfillment of duty by the individual. Flowing from duty were warm generosity, a willingness to take risks in a good cause, a healthy perspective on pleasure, and procreation.[129]

In "Woman in Science" the ex-president raised his voice in praise of women and of women in history and deplored the deprivations they had endured for whatever reason.[130] Yet he did so largely on empirical and rational grounds, rarely evoking God or sentiment. Though he respected women in a chivalrous fashion, he developed his celebration of womanhood from sterner stuff. After viewing what he termed "the so-called arguments" used to keep women down, he recognized that in the first flush of emancipation women might exult in their newly won freedom. But he was confident that women would not "shirk their duties" "any more than the average man in a democracy would be less dutiful than the average man in a despotism." Nor did Roosevelt believe he was being especially avant-garde in taking this position, describing it, rather, as part of "the right thinking of the day." He agreed with the contemporary French writer Jean Finot that humanity would be happier when women enjoyed equality with men. No less for women than for men, duty was the paramount consideration.[131] No doubt Roosevelt's wife, Edith, to him a model woman, was not far from his thoughts as he wrote "Woman in Science." The mother of five of his children, she was endowed with a fine mind, a resolute will, and a sense of femininity, a combination that made her both companion and confidante.

Modern man, moral and scientific, was the inheritor of an anthropological and a historical past. Roosevelt entitled his review of E. P. B. Weigall's book on pre-Christian Egypt, "Our Neighbors, The Ancients."[132] He discovered ready similarities between ancient and twentieth-century people. Using Ikhnaton to make the point that ideals and realities often clash, he flayed the doctrinaire reformers of his day for their insistence on immediate and total change. In effect, the human race was a constant in the ever-changing circumstances of time and place. Virtue and vice remained the same, though epochs might be separated by thousands of years. The unity of the human experience meant much to the philosopher in Theodore Roosevelt.

The ex-president's last significant book review appeared in the *Outlook* just a year before he died. It was a critique of Henry Fairfield Osborn's *The Origin and Evolution of Life,* a book he pondered.[133] Osborn stressed that the beginnings of life to a physicist like himself lay not in form but in energy. But he offered his views without any dogmatic inflections. Roosevelt appreciated this because, as he had to admit, he himself was without the requisite physicochemical knowledge to dispute the scientists. As he had done numerous times before, he endorsed the evolutionary thesis as readily as the principle of a heliocentric solar system or the Newtonian postulates about gravity. But in pondering Osborn's treatment of the beginnings of life Roosevelt was moved to state his qualification of human evolution in a singularly trenchant fashion:

> The tracing of an unbroken line of descent from the protozoan to Plato does not in any way really explain Plato's consciousness, of which there is not a vestige in the protozoan. There has been a non-measurable quality of actual creation. There is something new which did not exist in the protozoan. It has been produced in the course of evolution. But it is a play on words to say that such evolution is not creation.[134]

In the contention between science and humanism that was perhaps the leading intellectual battle of his day, Theodore Roosevelt came down on the side of the traditional estimate of man, of woman, and of humankind.

No one is likely to deny to Roosevelt that whatever he did he did with flair. His writings were no exception, nor was the range of his pursuits or the confidence of his expression. Many times he wrote books or articles that appear to have no direct or immediately useful purpose. As has been suggested from time to time, he often wrote such literary pieces to organize his thinking in a general way rather than to advocate or justify a specific proposal or policy. Writing was part of his thought process to an unusual degree, but his flair too often worked to obscure this fact.

Roosevelt's style should not be taken as a model for other learned presidents, and specifically not for Taft or Wilson. Taft's writings were much less general, less wide of focus, and less interesting in consequence; much the same must be said of his mind. Wilson, on the other hand, possessed the professional qualities of Taft, but he wrote for more general audiences, conscious of his intention to instruct the reader. Taft, as a professor of law, brought something of that to his writings. Each of these presidents was unique, but TR had one special characteristic. He was the first in line. Being first in this remarkable series of learned individuals did not mean that it was easier for Taft and Wilson to follow in the presidency, but that it was more congruous that as learned men they should occupy the office. Roosevelt alone could not have revived the tradition of a learned presidency; Taft and Wilson, coming after, were no less essential. The three men, taken together, responded to the intellectual impulses of their age, imparting a fresh vigor to the presidency as it entered the twentieth century.

2
WILLIAM HOWARD TAFT
Legal Mind

William Howard Taft—the one man to be both president and chief justice—has a secure place in American history. Only occasionally, and
perhaps unfortunately, have ex-presidents remained politically active to
the point of holding important public office: John Quincy Adams represented his district of Massachusetts in the lower house of the Congress
after being president; Andrew Johnson was reelected to the Senate, though
he did not live long enough to take his seat; and Herbert Hoover made a
singular contribution at the head of the commission that bore his name
and that helped to reorganize the federal government. Taft did much more.
After four years in the White House he was appointed to the Supreme
Court of the United States as chief justice in 1921 and presided over the
Court for a decade. Some might contend that in passing to the Court he
had taken a higher place. More than one respected voice—Justice Oliver
Wendell Holmes, Jr., among them—has been raised to argue that service
on the Supreme Court is the supreme public achievement. Certainly Taft
expressed himself in such terms from time to time, which is not to suggest
that he contemned the presidency. He thought of himself, rather, as better
suited to be a jurist than an executive. Such judgments, after all, are a
matter of individual temperament, taste, and training, which in Taft's case
combine to explain his preference for the judiciary. His heritage, education, and early experiences were of the law, his inclinations and ambitions
were judicial, and his learning was the offspring of these kindred elements.[1]

Insofar as his writings are evidence of Taft's learning, they fall into three
categories. His judicial philosophy is readily identified from his decisions
both as a state judge and a federal jurist and from his Supreme Court
opinions written during the 1920s.[2] His several books and other extended
observations on government and especially on the presidency show Taft to

good advantage as both an erudite and thoughtful student of American government.[3] Finally, his writings on international peace and arbitration extend the range of his mind, demonstrating qualities of both judge and statesman.[4] There is, furthermore, a basic intellectual consistency threading itself through these sets of writings, along with a number of clues that point to the role that learning played in Taft's presidency. What he had gleaned from study was reinforced by his experience in the ways of men. Tolerance for opinions with which he did not agree, a caution against precipitous conclusions, recognition that there was a meaningful difference between moral right and moral wrong, the need to be of service to others, and a consciousness of the frailties of humankind were all attitudes Taft exhibited. His dependence on learning in all this was much like his respect for it; it was assumed, internalized, practical, and quite without the self-advertising enthusiasms of a Theodore Roosevelt.

Though born and raised in Ohio, William Howard Taft belongs more to New England than the Middle West, in the view of his principal biographer, Henry F. Pringle.[5] A New England mentality was in many ways distinctively his, and perhaps this is illustrated best by the heritage of learning that passed to him from his mother no less than his father. Both parents were bred in a tradition of intellectual commitment amid the practical affairs of everyday living, classic New Englanders torn between a passion for righteousness and a desire to get on in the world.

The Tafts came from England in the mid-1670s, the first of them a Robert Taft, "a plain unlettered man" and a carpenter by trade. He lived for a time in Braintree, and it is not unlikely that he knew the family of John Adams, which by then had attained some prominence in the town. By 1679 Robert Taft had settled permanently at nearby Mendon. Over one hundred years later President George Washington, while on a tour of New England, made a brief stop at Samuel Taft's farm and tavern, located on the turnpike connecting Boston and Hartford. The future president's father, Alphonso, was the first of the family to gain national prominence, as an Ohio judge and as secretary of war and attorney general in the dying days of the Grant administration. In the 1880s he was United States minister to Vienna and St. Petersburg. Alphonso Taft was a remarkable man in many ways. He worked his way through Yale, graduating with honors in 1833. At the time Yale was fast in the grip of a Calvinistic revival, but Alphonso was cold to the evangelistic temper he encountered in New Haven, a harbinger of his later Unitarianism. After Yale he read law, migrated west, chose Cincinnati as his new home, and prospered as a lawyer almost at once. In the process, two traits became identifiable in the senior Taft. By the later 1840s he had largely forsaken conventional Protestantism, following the lead and lectures of Ralph Waldo Emerson. Only somewhat less significantly, his legal experience suggested to him that people, and especially children, who were lawbreakers were often in that position not by choice but because of circumstances and environment. Such conclusions were hardly unique to Alphonso Taft, but he appears to have arrived at them largely on his own. Each of these positions, one theological and philosophical and the other legal and philosophical, associates the elder Taft with some of the new directions evident in mid-ninteenth-century American thought.

Taft's second wife, and the mother of William Howard Taft, was Louisa Maria Torrey, also derived from old Dissenter stock in Massachusetts. She spent a year at Mount Holyoke Academy, studied in New Haven with Miss Dulton, and attended public lectures given by the Yale faculty, after which she taught at Monson Academy in Maine. She was very much the enlightened female, and though many years junior to her husband, they were ideally suited, not least in their intellectual disposition. On one occasion Alphonso scolded his wife because he believed she was allowing her children and her household to distract her from reading and an interest in public affairs. Their home on Mt. Auburn was a meeting place for notables, from William Holmes McGuffey to the Reverend Lyman Beecher. The Tafts attended lectures by visiting celebrities, including Frederick Douglass and Emerson, and delighted in performances of the opera. Taft, along with Rutherford B. Hayes, was a charter member of the Cincinnati Literary Club. The atmosphere in which young William grew up was distinctly cultured; learning was prized both for its own sake and for the practical uses to which it might be put for individual and social betterment.[6]

William Howard Taft, lacking a brilliant mind, was to master learning by diligent application to the task at hand, whether at school, college or the bar. If the word brilliant is reserved for the very few, as it should be, it would be accurate to characterize Taft as able; it was a combination of talent and hard work that led him to excel. His formal education began in earnest when he entered Woodward High School in Cincinnati in the fall of 1870. Woodward was one public high school that prepared students for college. Taft's courses included Greek, Latin, history, literature, and mathematics in large doses. He did well in his subjects, but after the manner that all was grist for his mill. Judging from the grades he earned over the course of four years, he was very much the ideal student. At Woodward he came to understand that he must work hard to do the best with his talent. It also seems likely that high school failed to excite young Taft's curiosity, so that what he took to Yale as a freshman in 1874 was a mastery of fact and a commitment to disciplined study, rather than a sense of an intellectual adventure on which he was about to embark.

Alphonso Taft had graduated from Yale and there was no doubt that his son William would go east, as was expected of all his boys, to get his college education, just as there was no doubt in Alphonso Taft's mind that such an education was requisite preparation for success in the modern world. With the onset of the 1870s, Yale had undergone a series of changes that brought it from what many called a poor place to learn to a university in the making. Many of these changes were due to a movement called "Young Yale," which began to gather momentum shortly after the close of the Civil War. In keeping with the times, and the times were largely scientific and practical in tone, many young Yale alumni believed that Yale had to change to meet the challenges and opportunities of a changing world. Complaints were common that too little attention was given to the sciences, political philosophy, and economics in the university curriculum. Furthermore, the alumni felt that Yale should be a national institution and not simply regional in influence. It should attract students from Cincinnati, whether or not their fathers were Yale graduates. Alumni chapters were organized and by 1869 William M. Evarts, the noted barrister and public man, was calling for alumni participation in the affairs of the university. The alumni recognized that they might well hold the key to Yale's future. If it was to enjoy enlarged libraries and be equipped with modern laboratories, such improvements would cost money. Where was the money to come from? Leading members of Young Yale had a simple answer. Involve the alumni in the business of the university, and the alumni would proceed to provide the financial support. "Young Yale" was turning out to be "revolutionary Yale."

Eighteen seventy-two was *annus mirabilis.* The quest for a broad-gauged curriculum and a more liberal spirit to animate it had borne first fruit. Yale had a new president, Noah Porter, not the most avant-garde of intellectuals but a marked improvement over the aged Woolsey. Money was beginning to flow in, new professorships were endowed, and elected alumni members joined the governing board of the Yale Corporation. No single individual better exemplified the new atmosphere than the man who shook Yale to its intellectual foundations and who became, by Taft's own admission, the greatest single influence on him while at college. His name was William Graham Sumner. The new Yale and the future president were to owe much to Sumner, who was appointed professor of political economy in 1872.[7]

By the time of his death in 1910 Sumner had achieved considerable fame for himself and for Yale by espousing the rights of capital in a laissez-faire economy; his rationale included a naked emphasis on force. All of this added up to Sumnerology, concerning which the equally celebrated William Lyon Phelps was to write a memorable reminiscence, "When Yale Was Given over to Sumnerology." But in Taft's years at Yale, 1874–78, Sumner was still in the process of developing his theories, particularly his arguments in favor of a monometallic money standard, free trade, and the rights of private property. His theories reflected his unflinching admiration for the sociology of Herbert Spencer and Spencer's "great services to true science and to the welfare of mankind," as Sumner phrased it in one of his many essays about "the forgotten man." No doubt Sumner was a professor of pronounced opinions vigorously stated. Fifty years later Taft was to recall that "he had more to do with stimulating my mental activities than any one under whom I studied during my entire course."[8]

While Taft was not to accept Sumner's free-trade thesis, he found Sumner's position on the centrality of private property in a free society altogether congenial. In this respect, Sumner was preaching to the already saved because all of Taft's background and prejudice favored that order. What Sumner had done was to go beyond prejudice to supply a philosophy whose ethical postulates were derived ultimately from power: "I regard economic forces as simply parallel to physical forces, arising just as spontaneously and naturally, following a sequence of cause and effect just as inevitably as physical forces—neither more or less." These and similar dogmatic assertions were consistent with the vogue of social Darwinism current in the 1870s, which added to the weight of Sumner's argument. Taft and his fellow students were stamped by Sumner's manner as well as his message. As Sumner was wont to say, "I plant myself squarely upon the fundamental principles of the science of which I am a student." There is not much evidence that Taft, sitting at Sumner's feet, saw fit to question the master or to think critically in such matters.

One lesson that Sumner was fond of repeating to his students was that "the human race has made no step whatever in civilization which has not been won by pain and distress. It wins no steps now without paying for them in sacrifices." What the professor was espousing was a version of a world of superiors and inferiors, of the strong and the weak, of survival of the fittest, of root, hog or die. Indeed, he argued that equality was nowhere found in nature, that survival of the weakest was the law of anticivilization. Sumner was an expert phrasemaker, a sure way to capture undergraduate fancy without necessarily conquering the mind. His "forgotton man"— "the simple, honest laborer, ready to earn his living by productive work" in a world filled with parasites and weaklings—was just such a piece of memorable and quotable Sumnerian rhetoric, combining as it did the work ethic, the frontier spirit, and the scientific doctrines of the time. It is small wonder that President Taft, surveying Yale undergraduate education from the perspective of fifty years, remembered Sumner with particular vividness. Most Yale men did.[9]

William Howard Taft became only a partially wrought social Darwinist, after all. There were competing elements in his heritage, and other professors at Yale, for that matter, who helped to shape his total outlook. Among the college teachers who influenced him were Cyrus Northrup, Thomas T. Thacher, and, more importantly, Henry A. Beers, the authority on romantic literature. It was Beers who stimulated Taft's lifelong fondness for the novels of George Eliot. Beers was a young assistant professor during Taft's course at Yale but he was even then in the process of becoming a legend. He had studied at Heidelberg and came to know both Lowell and Emerson while a student at Bronson Alcott's Summer School of Philosophy. This friendship with Emerson no doubt made him attractive to Taft, whose father greatly admired the Sage of Concord. Beers was a sensitive man, in many ways the antithesis of Sumner. He wrote poetry, refined his interest in the English romantics, and appealed to the humane and kindly in Taft, of which there was a generous share, much as Sumner spoke to his prosaic side.

At Yale Taft had a traditional and a worthwhile educational experience. The college year was divided into three terms in those days, which probably gave the student a somewhat more diverse exposure to learning than the two-semester year. While a freshman he read the *Odyssey* in Greek, Roman history, and parts of Herodotus, Livy and Horace; studied Euclid, algebra, and Chauvenet's *Geometry* and *Trigonometry;* attended lectures in botany and did work in rhetoric, composition, and declamation. Much of the same regimen was followed in his sophomore year. In Greek he studied Demosthenes, Aeschylus's *Prometheus,* Xenophon's *Memorbilia,* and Sophocles' *Antigone.* In Latin there was more of Horace (*Satires* and *Epistles*), Juvenal *(Satires)*; Cicero *(De Senectuti),* and Plautus *(Captivi).* French was a second-year subject with stress on inflection and syntax and readings in Fénelon's *Télamaque.* Peck's *Mechanics,* rhetoric, composition, and declamation rounded out the year. As a junior Taft read more Greek and Latin authors, moved into physics and mechanics more fully, and added some work in German and astronomy. Instruction in rhetoric required a knowledge of Morris and Skeat's *Specimens of Early English* and Craik's *History of English Literature.* The logic text was Jevon's *Logic,* and in natural philosophy, Ganot's *Physics.* Only in his last three terms did Taft have lectures in political and social science. Apart from Sumner's early writings he also read Fawcett's *Political Economy.* Other required books were Lieber's *Civil Liberty,* Schwegler's *History of Political and Social Science,* Woolsey's *International Law,* and Tocqueville's *American Democracy.* In his final terms he also studied both British and American constitutional law, and mental philosophy (based on Noah Porter's *Human Intellect*), geology, anatomy, and physiology.[10] It would appear that at Yale, students touched most of the established academic disciplines, getting a good overall view of the world of learning. Furthermore, Taft excelled in many of his courses. He was third in his class as a freshman and won two sophomore composition prizes, an award for mathematics as a junior, and another for his essay, "Availability as a Ruling

Consideration in the Choice of Presidential Candidates." His brother Horace, recalled that William Howard had displayed a "clear, strong mind" as a student. In addition to his excellence in studies, Taft emerged as a social and moral leader among his fellow students.[11] Combined with a clear, strong mind was a clear, strong character, and he was greatly admired and widely remembered by his classmates on both counts.

Taft delivered the traditional senior oration, "The Professional and Political Prospects of the College Graduates," as the salutatorian of the class of '78. He dealt with political corruption, the abuses of governmental authority by the Republican party, and the centralization of power brought on by the Civil War. "The Republican Party has lost its grip on the affections of the people," he lamented. When times had been good the people winked at Republican wickedness, but now that times were bad the party was judged and found wanting. Taft was especially hard on the Republican-controlled Congress, which seemed to pass laws in every direction. "We became the worst governed people because we were the most governed people" aptly summed up his position. Voicing opposition to soft money and other proposals from the "insane West," he was hopeful that an educated and informed electorate would be able to turn the tide. People of higher education had particular responsibilities in this regard. At bottom Taft expressed great faith in the Constitution and the Republic: "Discontent in France makes a riot, in America a political party. In France the commune sought their ends by violence, in America a safety-valve is found for dangerous mutterings in the ballot box." He discovered other safety valves in emigration, opportunity, and wealth; he called the latter "the great civilizer and source of a nation's happiness." All in all, Taft's address was a standard oration. It expressed deep concern about the present but confidence in the future because of a national inheritance from the past. While Taft's address exhibited much that was declamatory, it also offered a reasoned assessment of the nation's woes, if not a way to overcome them.[12]

Taft's university education was not remarkable. What had happened was that Yale had substantiated a number of his socioeconomic presuppositions and reinforced his adherence to them. His understanding and appreciation of the variety of human aspiration had been broadened and deepened through readings in literature. But in each instance these were attitudes that he was more or less inclined to accept because they had been presented to him by convinced and effective teachers. It would be some years before he tested such theories critically. As in his political career, where Taft was not to show himself aggressive, so at Yale he was not intellectually enterprising. Although he was an outstanding student, he did not stand out by reason of intellectual acumen. Yet as Will Taft departed New Haven for Cincinnati, for further study in the law, his academic preparation, whether for a private career or public service, was much superior to that of most men he would meet.

The one special habit of learning that Yale instilled in him was a sense of discipline. This was no small thing given Taft's temperament, which tended toward procrastination. He was to profit from the Yale regimen for the rest of his life. His education remained incomplete, nonetheless. The elements of righteousness had been confirmed, but the means of getting on in the world were still indistinct. A study of law was to supply this last ingredient, providing him the practical learning that was essential for his future. Yet the law did more. It pointed him toward a judicial career, a direction to which, in his heart of hearts, he steadfastly adhered, though he would have to put it aside for many years while serving in the executive branch of the national government.

The Cincinnati Law School, which William Howard Taft entered in the fall of 1878, had been founded in 1833 and had the distinction of being one of the three or four such schools in the country at the time. Over the years it had built up a reputation for sound legal training. Rufus King was the dean when Taft matriculated, and he had assembled an able, if small, faculty of experienced men in the law. Instruction was still through lectures on law rather than the case method, which C. C. Langdell had introduced at Harvard in 1870. Cincinnati was slow to change. The professors lectured to explicate legal principles already established and paid slight attention to law in the making, one of the great merits of dealing with cases. Various readings were assigned, from Coke and Blackstone to more recent commentaries on the law, such as Austin's *Principles of Jurisprudence*. Standard treatises on evidence, contracts, and the like were also studied. This approach gave the student a sense of the large outlines of the law, a feel for the history of its development, which the case method by itself did not always convey.

At the Cincinnati school, formal instruction was only part of the legal training. The practical side, somewhat more than the equivalent of the case method, was learned by entering a law office to work as a kind of apprentice. But Taft's experience was different. He took employment as a court reporter on Murat Halstead's *Cincinnati Commercial*. It was from this vantage point that he observed the law and came to understand better the reality of its influence on the everyday lives of the people. He once told friends, when Halstead was urging him to abandon law for journalism, that his work as a court reporter was entirely motivated by his desire to know more about the workings of the law.

His law school lectures had made Taft more fully aware of certain changes in American jurisprudence that influenced the understanding and practice of law in the latter decades of the nineteenth century. As it had grown out of the English common law, American law in the aftermath of the Revolution had progressively accommodated itself to the New World and its environment. Law changed due to the vast differences in conditions between England and the expanding American nation. It became a social and an economic instrument, responding to young America. By the mid nineteenth century these new modes of law had, themselves, hardened into a set of formal legal rules, which became more and more rigid as property and property rights were more and more the preoccupation of the American ruling classes. Many such laws reached the plateau of immutability. Law was expected to defend property rights and did so with considerable success both in the pre—and post—Civil War years. Perhaps too little emphasis was placed by the Cincinnati Law faculty on the challenges to this legal formalism being prepared in the 1870s. Oliver Wendell Holmes, Jr., Melville Bigelow, James Bradley Thayer, and others were working to produce certain fundamental alterations in the prevailing legal framework. From the time of Jeremy Bentham, political commentators in England had been calling for a reworking of the legal system in order to make it more intelligible and more practical. German scholars had been delving deeply into legal history, and their views of law were based on new findings respecting ancient legal forms. An interest in Roman law, wherein the sovereign authority seemed clearly to promulgate the rules according to which society was regulated, dovetailed nicely with fresh developments in German philosophy. The result of all this was to introduce metaphysical concepts of absolute right and absolute prohibition, growing chiefly from Kant's principal contention that man is an end in himself and that his rights and duties can not be reduced to mere social convenience. This absolutist view of the law was consistent with what had occurred in American legal development, especially regarding the absolute rights of property.

No American was more determined to undermine such legal formalism than the young rising legal scholar, Oliver Wendell Holmes, Jr. Years later Holmes and Taft would sit together on the High Court, and while there were not many times when they agreed on critical issues before the Taft Court, they consistently maintained a cordial friendship based in part on a mutual respect for legal learning. But in the 1870s Holmes was making his reputation as a legal scholar by advocating a version of legal realism. He was a Malthusian and a social Darwinist who saw fundamental reality in the cruelty of the struggle for existence. If law was to be evaluated properly, it must be done according to empirical standards, however much this might offend morality and sentiment. Holmes's efforts as a legal authority would come under the influence of these hard certainties. He put it provocatively in his great book, *The Common Law,* published in 1881, when he argued that "the ultimate *ratio,* not only *regnum,* but of private persons is force, and . . . at the bottom of all private relations however tempered by sympathy and all social feelings, is justified self-preference." Morality in life as well as in the law was based on power.[13]

The importance of property and the successive alterations in society growing out of a Darwinian struggle for survival were familiar enough to William Howard Taft as a result of his encounters with William Graham Sumner. How far he might be willing to apply the whole of the Darwinian ethic of might makes right was another matter. While there was much about Darwin's philosophy that encouraged Taft to embrace notions of extreme property rights, there was equal reason for him to reject a system based on force. The passion for righteousness was no small consideration in his total outlook. In any event, Taft was not properly a legal scholar at this juncture in his intellectual fleshing out. He was still an avid learner of the detailed functioning of the law. Very much occupied with the trees, he had not had many occasions to survey the forest. His decision in 1881 to accept an appointment as assistant prosecutor for Hamilton County (Cincinnati) was prompted in the main by the further opportunities it afforded for learning law. At the same time it made his family wonder about what appeared to be an unconscious effort on his part to avoid the practice of law. No doubt he had already begun to think of the fulfillment of his legal career as a judgeship and proposed to shape his experience with that in mind.

If Taft was not more cognizant than the average lawyer of the pending changes in American legal philosophy that would one day blossom into sociological jurisprudence, he was a man who thought earnestly about a judicial career and was by no means indifferent to the changing patterns of Supreme Court decisions in the 1870s and 1880s, especially as these affected private property. The Court, after some initial hesitation in the years immediately following the passage of the Fourteenth Amendment, swung around decisively in favor of economic liberty, that is, the use of property free of regulation by the national or state governments. In due course the Court became both the promoter of liberty, now understood to have an economic dimension foremost, and a bastion against government efforts to curb property rights in the public interest. The possibilities for action through judicial review increased and multiplied and filled the docket of the Supreme Court with numerous progeny. *Munn* v. *Illinois* (1877), the case in which the Court upheld a state law regulating private property that was "clothed with a public interest," did not mark the beginning of a trend but, rather, punctuated the end of an era. By the time Taft had assumed his position as assistant prosecutor, the legal world confidently anticipated a reversal of the *Munn* ruling. Justice Stephen Field's dissenting opinion in the case was an augury. To Field, property rights were the very cornerstone of public morality and as such could not be infringed. William Howard Taft was appointed judge of the Superior Court of Ohio—he later was elected to a full term—the year after the United States Supreme Court in 1886 handed down the *Wabash, St. Louis and Pacific Railroad Company* v. *Illinois* decision. It reversed the *Munn* ruling and riveted sanctity of property onto American constitutional law for the next two decades. The Progressive movement, in fact, had only limited success in altering the conservative posture of the judiciary, and conservatism remained a fact of American constitutional practice down to the days of the New Deal. That Taft was in general and in a good many particulars sympathetic to the Stephen Field brand of judicial interpretation is hardly disputable. However, though much of his learning was conventional in character, he did not meekly follow where ethos might lead. From his work as an Ohio judge, his tenure as solicitor general of the United States from 1890 to 1892, and his eight years as a judge on the United States Court of Appeals for the Sixth Circuit he was to acquire an increasingly critical sense of the law. His accumulation of legal learning, which was not that of a scholar but of an active judicial official, was evident in several important decisions he handed down, all of which involved his interpretation of property rights under the Constitution.

The final decade of the nineteenth century was replete with industrial disputes as labor, in the process of organizing to protect its interests against already well entrenched capital, resorted to formidable weapons, including the strike and the boycott. Cincinnati was to have its share of industrial conflict. Taft's most important decision while serving as an Ohio superior court judge grew out of one such confrontation. The case was *Moores and Company* v. *Bricklayers Union No. 1, W. H. Stephenson, P. H. McElroy et al.* (1890). The bricklayers were involved in a dispute with Parker Brothers, a local builder. Unable to obtain satisfaction of their grievances, the workers attempted to prevent materials from being shipped to Parker Brothers by threatening to refuse to use materials other suppliers brought to Parker Brothers job sites. Moores and Company, suppliers of limestone, was boycotted as a consequence. After a court of first instance awarded Moores and Company damages, the case came to the superior court on a motion for a new trial.

Taft's opinion, upholding the lower court, was both erudite and in favor of property rights. He appealed to English law, noting that "every man, be he capitalist, merchant, employer, laborer, or professional man is entitled to invest his capital, to carry on his business, to bestow his labor, or to exercise his calling, if within the law, according to his pleasure," In the case at hand, however, Taft contended that under the common law "there are losses willfully caused to one by another in the exercise of what otherwise would be a lawful right, from simple motives of malice." He found that malice was the intention of the bricklayers in their threats against Moores and Company. To support his judgment he cited precedents from English law remote in time and circumstances from the matter before the court. While labor might combine as suitably as capital for reasons of self-interest, labor could not on that account act when the result was to interfere with property rights.[14]

Taft embraced a double standard of social morality to the detriment of labor by discovering "intent" and "malice" in the behavior of the bricklayers. Such a position ran counter to the assertions of legal realism, which was just then making its principles heard in the courts. The realists were interested not in intentions but in the empirical results of the actions in question. Taft had gone fishing in the distant waters of history long past, an affront to the new jurisprudence, which preferred to take each case as it came and to judge it by an external standard rather than by intent, real or supposed. His ruling, nonetheless, placed Taft with the overwhelming majority of his judicial brethren. He had not ruled from whim or fancy or malice; neither was he altogether indifferent to personal rights when they conflicted with those of property, as some of his later decisions would demonstrate.

Other opinions of William Howard Taft written while he was a superior court judge enrich the image of a learned man. In *Societé Anonyme de la Distillerie de la Benedictine* v. *Micalovich, Fletcher & Company,*[15] he did research in the history of the French liquor industry, discussed the meaning of certain obscure French words, and enjoyed—to all appearances—the opportunity to spice usually turgid court opinion with some erudition, all in the name of justice. The impression persists, nevertheless, of a rather matter-of-fact judicial mind, traditional in its orientation, conservative in its reasoning, and determined to preserve the socioeconomic status quo. Not totally deaf to pleas of justice based on "fair play," Judge Taft responded only occasionally to appeals made on that basis.

For just over two years, from 1890 to 1892, William Howard Taft served as a solicitor general of the United States. The young Ohio judge possessed all the political requirements for the position. He was a midwestern Republican of known party loyalty, the son of a well-placed and equally Republican father. In another sense his appointment was in the public interest because of his valuable experience as a sitting judge. Since a solicitor general functions as a legal and expert advisor to the attorney general, the position required that Taft renew and deepen his study of the history and the mystery of the law, a task to which he gladly lent himself. This was an important phase in his ongoing legal education. The most notable sucess he achieved in office had to do with the *Bering Sea* case.[16] He offered the opinion that inasmuch as the United States and Great Britain were at the time engaged in negotiations over a fishing rights treaty for the Bering Sea, a foreign power (Great Britain) could not pursue litigation aimed at making the Court censure the conduct of another branch of the national government. The Supreme Court concurred in Taft's argument. Such bright spots were not common in the work of the solicitor general. Taft took some satisfaction that his efforts were still with the law and not politics, that he did have an indirect influence on some decisions of the Supreme Court, and that, were the gods to respond to his fondest hopes, he, too, would one day attain a seat on the High Court.

His resignation as solicitor general, which Taft was not reluctant to offer, was occasioned by President Harrison's nomination of him as a judge for the United States Court of Appeals for the Sixth Circuit. He remained a federal judge from 1893 to 1900, when he was called to Washington by President McKinley and offered the post of governor general of the Philippine Islands. This position, while far removed from the court he had grown to love, required his kind of judicial temper and wisdom. Not only was he a successful civil governor, but his work caught the eye of Theodore Roosevelt, who had known Taft from the early 1890s in Washington when TR was on the Civil Service Commission. He was so impressed with Taft's handling of delicate matters in the Philippines and his administrative skill that he named him secretary of war, a post he held from 1904 to 1908 when he was elected to the presidency.

Meanwhile, serving on the sixth circuit court, this rising Republican man of the law was to add to his reputation as a judge of learning and of increasing awareness that the rights of property might well be balanced by the rights of the laborer. One important case in which Judge Taft had a hand was *Toledo, Ann Arbor and Northern Michigan Railway Company* v. *Brotherhood of Locomotive Engineers* (1893). The railway had brought a suit in equity, asking an injunction in federal district court against the striking locomotive engineers. To isolate the railroad the workers threatened not to handle any freight on lines connecting with those of the Toledo, Ann Arbor and Northern Michigan Railway Company. On appeal, Taft upheld the injunction of the lower court on the grounds that interstate commerce had been unlawfully disturbed. He took his reasoned argument from the opinion in the *Moores and Company* case. A man had "an inalienable right to bestow his labor where he will, and to withhold his labor where he will." But, Taft went on, "generally speaking this is true, not absolutely." Exceptions arose when workers resorted to a boycott, thereby interfering with the property of other parties not involved in the original dispute.[17] Taft also found elements of intended malice in the actions of the engineers. His conservative jurisprudence prompted him to read intent into the actions of the defendants while his determination to protect property rights had a definite Sumnerian ring to it. During his tenure as an appeals court judge Taft was to issue a number of injunctions restricting the practices of labor unions in industrial disputes, and he soon had the reputation of being an antiunion judge. Years later when contending for the presidency, this side of Judge Taft's public philosophy would haunt him.

In 1894 Taft sentenced Frank Phelan, an aide to Eugene V. Debs, president of the American Railway Union, to six months in jail for contempt of court. The action grew out of the Pullman strike of that year in which Debs had come to the assistance of strikers at the Pullman Palace Car Company by ordering his union, the American Railway Union, to refuse to handle trains of which Pullman cars were a part. Phelan had been assigned to Cincinnati to organize a tie-up of rail traffic there, and was arrested for obstructing the business of the New Orleans & Texas Pacific Railway, a company that was in federal receivership. Taft cited Phelan for contempt when informed that he had refused to obey an injunction against union action. On the face of it, *In Re: Phelan* appeared to be a renewed effort by Taft to defend property rights, whatever the cost. What makes the case remarkable is that in the course of his opinion he articulated the first clear judicial definition and defense of the right to strike. In part he wrote:

now it may be conceded at the outset that the employees of the receiver had the right to organize into or join a labor union which should take joint action as to their terms of employment. It is of benefit to them and to the public that laborers should unite in their common interest and for lawful purposes. They have labor to sell. If they stand together, they are often able, all of them, to command better prices for their labor than when dealing singly with rich employers, because the necessities of the single employee may compel him to accept any term offered him. The accumulation of a fund for the support of those who feel that wages offered are below market prices is one of the legitimate objects of such an organization. They have the right to appoint officers who shall advise them as to the course to be taken by them in their relations with their employer. They may unite with other unions. The officers they appoint, or any other person to whom they choose to listen, may advise them as to the proper course to be taken by them in regard to their employment, or, if they choose to repose such authority in any one, may order them, on pain of expulsion from their union, peaceably to leave the employ of their employer because any of the terms of their employment are unsatisfactory. It follows, therefore (to give an illustration which will be understood), that if Phelan had come to this city when the receiver of the Cincinnati Southern reduced the wages of his employees by 10 per cent, and had urged a peaceable strike, and had succeeded in maintaining one, the loss to the business of the receiver would not be ground for recovering damages, and Phelan would not have been liable to contempt even if the strike much impeded the operation of the road under order of the court. His action in giving the advice, or issuing an order based on unsatisfactory terms of employment, would have been entirely lawful.[18]

In so many words Judge Taft had brought organized labor, at least in his court, out of the legal shadows and into the sunlight of legitimacy. While he continued to differentiate between strike and boycott—upholding labor's right to use the former and rejecting its recourse to the latter—he had laid down a strongly reasoned justification for the existence and for the rights of organized labor. In so doing he had exhibited a sense of intellectual independence. By 1894 Taft had seen enough both of life and the law to cause him to attenuate, perhaps essentially, the dogmatic assertions of Professor Sumner.

The year 1894 was a bad one for organized labor. Following the unsuccessful Homestead strike of 1892, the Pullman strike was broken and Debs was sent to jail. Labor appeared to be in full retreat, overmastered by the power of the corporations and disdained by the Congress and the courts alike. Taft's position respecting the rights of organized workers was all the more noteworthy in consequence. It had elements of a Progressive public philosophy, the first clear indication that William Howard Taft was to make a significant contribution to the development of American law.

Two further cases demonstrated Taft's sense of fair play regarding laborers, if not the labor movement. In the *Voight* case (1896)[19] he ruled that an employer, in this instance a railway company, was liable for injuries suffered by a worker while he was on the job, thereby rejecting the old common law principle of assumed risk by the worker. At the same time he somewhat weakened the sanctity of contract rule inasmuch as the employee had signed a work agreement relieving the company of liability for injuries that might be incurred on the job. The Supreme Court was to reverse Taft's ruling; but vindication was to be his with the passage of a federal Employers' Liability Act and its eventual acceptance by the Court. In the *Narramore* case (1899), the Cleveland, Cincinnati, Chicago and St. Louis Railway Company was likewise held liable for a brakeman's injury due to a safety violation by the company of which the worker was aware. A portion of Taft's opinion in this case read:

> Will the courts enforce or recognize against a workman an agreement, expressed or implied on his part, to waive the performance of a statutory duty of the master, imposed for the protection of the servant, and in the interest of the public? We do not think they will. . . . The manifest legislative purpose was to protect the servant by positive law because he had not previously shown himself capable of protecting himself by contract, and it would entirely defeat this purpose thus to permit the servant "to contract himself out of the statute." . . . .
> The sole question in this case whether the statute requiring the railroad company in penalty of a fine to block its guard rails and frogs, changes the rule of liability of the company and relieves the injured man

from the effect of the assumption of risk which would otherwise be implied against him.

To confine the remedy to a criminal proceeding in which the fine to be imposed on a conviction was not even payable to the injured employee or to anyone complaining, would be to make the law not much more than a dead letter.

The intention of the legislature of Ohio was to protect the employees of railway from injury from a very frequent source of danger by compelling the railway companies to adopt a well known safety device. And although the employee impliedly waives a compliance with the statute and agrees to assume the risk from unblocked frogs and switches by continuing in the service without complaint this court will not recognize or enforce such an agreement. . . . The imposition of a penalty for the violation of a statute does not exclude other means of enforcement and to permit the company to avail itself of such an assumption of risk by its employees is in effect to enable it to nullify a penal statute and is against public policy.[20]

In each of these judgments Taft was striking out on his own while winning considerable notice in legal circles will beyond the jurisdiction of the sixth circuit.

In defending the rights of workers, especially if they were vulnerable to the might of large corporations, Taft was also prepared to act, on occasion, against a corporation itself. At least one important case, that involving the *Addyston Pipe and Steel Company* (1898),[21] moved him to invoke the Sherman Anti-Trust Act, holding that the company had conspired with other manufacturers of cast-iron pipe to fix prices and thus to eliminate competition. The facts of this case were surprisingly similar to those in the much publicized *E. C. Knight* case (1895) in which the Supreme Court had resoundingly rejected the application of the Sherman act to alleged price fixing in sugar. But Taft dared to take a different line, insisting that in the case before him the sales contracts that actually fixed prices constituted a restraint of trade between the states, something the Sherman act expressly forbade. More surprising still, the Supreme Court affirmed this decision. This ruling may have dismayed corporation counsel but it generally failed to soften the image of William Howard Taft as an antilabor, big-business judge of the law. For Taft himself these were good and satisfactory years on the bench. He had always felt that he could learn as much by doing as by study alone; sitting on the circuit court enable him to combine these two approaches to the law.

Much of Taft's later career was prefigured in the six years during which he sat as a federal appeals judge. The future president became more fully aware of the problems of labor and management in conflict and of the place of corporations in a free capitalistic society. His response to these and related matters was spelled out in a practical fashion. He laid down some of the broad principles of the law that he would articulate more fully in his opinions while chief justice. Finally, beginning in 1896, his service as dean of the Cincinnati Law School, where he also lectured regularly on the law of property, provided experience on which he was to draw while teaching law at Yale. The circuit judgeship had worked to deepen Taft's comprehension of the complexities of the law and to sharpen his understanding of its application to changing conditions. Always conservative in matters of legal change, he was convinced from the cases that came before him that law must be rescued from the historical graveyard to do service in shaping the future along basically conservative lines. He was never to take the path of legal realism, but he was equally dubious about the determination of twentieth-century cases by nineteenth-century rules of law. As events were to show, his legal learning, compounded of study and experience, stood him in good stead in the variety of public employment he was to have over the course of the next thirty years.

Invited to Yale in 1906 to give a series of lectures on the Dodge Foundation, Secretary of War Taft delivered four addresses at the university. He had retained a great fondness for Yale and its traditions of learning. In the late 1890s there had been talk that he might be offered the presidency of the university on the basis of a distinguished public career and his well-known love for his alma mater. Taft moved quickly to quash the idea of the Yale presidency, however. He judged his Unitarian religion as both a proper and an insurmountable obstacle to the appointment, and expressed grave doubts as well about his qualifications as an educator. But to serve Yale in other ways, to return to give formal lectures to "the President and the Gentlemen of Yale," for example, was another matter and altogether attractive. Taft being Taft, he did not push himself forward, but he was always ready to serve. As chance would have it, he met Arthur Twinning Hadley, the Yale president, in St. Louis several weeks before the lectures were to be given, and Hadley suggested that Taft take up some matters of great public importance that might be discussed from different points of view. The secretary of war agreed and the result was four distinct but interrelated lectures under the general title, "The Duties of Citizenship." In succession, the lectures examined the viewpoint of a recent graduate of a university, a judge on the bench, the colonial administrator and the national executive. The next year Scribner's published the lectures in book form under the title *Four Aspects of Civic Duty*.[22] As it turned out, it was an excellent time for the future president to have the outline of his political faith in print.

In 1906 Taft's federal judicial post was six years in the past and his tenure as civil governor of the Philippine Islands had ended three years previously, time sufficient to have lent useful perspectives on both these important positions. He was also three years from the presidency and had been close enough to the incumbent to have watched with instructive effect the discharging of presidential responsibilities. The Dodge lectures were an occasion for Taft to reassess the past under the mantle of calm provided by a university lecture platform and to discuss the role of government as Americans tended, even then, to focus on it. The lectures were not learned in the sense of being heavily laden with documentary evidence for this or that observation. They were learned in the style of a philosopher-king, discoursing on the challenge and opportunity of free men governing themselves. Not in-depth reading in political theory, but wide experience in political reality had operated on Taft's educated sense to provide him the raw material on which to base his judgments and his advice.

In the introductory lecture, "The Duties of Citizenship Viewed From The Standpoint Of A Recent Graduate Of A University," quite apart from the conventional appeal to Yale men to be good and active citizens once they had gone from the university and entered the real world, Taft cleared the ground for his later lectures by enunciating a number of fundamental views on man and government. He began by expressing his concern over the place and function of wealth in American society, revealing thereby an abiding debt to his Puritan forebears.[23] Wealth that was earned was far preferable to inheritance because "under the spur of necessity" character is formed. As for those born to wealth, "in no one respect can it be made more useful than in support of young men willing to devote their attention to politics and public affairs."[24] Taft held up the English example of men of means who performed well in public service as worthy of American emulation. Of course he wanted the wealthy to remain wealthy. After all, he said, "The motive for gain and accumulation of money is the main-spring of nearly all the material improvement which has been so marked in America."[25] No populist, William Howard Taft continued to express his belief in rule by the wise, the well born, and the well to do. The university graduate, he thought, would quickly learn, once he had passed into the world beyond the university, to moderate the strict rules of political economy and sociology that he had learned at college. At first the recent graduate would be impatient because theory and reality did not come together as one, that there was no perfect matching. Soon, the secretary of war contended, the young man would become more moderate and the "certainty and severity of views found in the lecture room and in the abstract study of political science" would give way to the hard facts of life.[26] But he was quick to add that professors knew all this, and it was the tendency of students to remember the principles and to neglect the nuances that were also part of instruction. Recalling that his own genera-tion at Yale had been taught the sacred principles of laissez-faire, Taft added in a light vein that "when I graduated we looked upon the Post-

Office Department with great suspicion." But theory must give way to practice.[27] "Experience will show that there are fields of business action which the Government can better cover than private enterprize; and there are also fields over which, because of the probability of abuse by private enterprize, the Government should assume control . . . by way of effective regulation." Given this moderate Progressive stance Taft could only condemn "a few graduates of universities who concentrated on the persistent abuses in society without counting the progress that had been achieved" and who, in consequence, "yearn for an entirely different system and radical change, in which men are to be governed by love and not by any motive of gain."[28] He was prepared to understand although never to condone agitators for extreme change who had been victims of capitalistic exploitation, but he had no tolerance for the university men who were agitators, dismissing them as "parlor socialists."[29]

Taft expressed a belief in a divine plan for the universe, saying that progress had been achieved in human history because of the impulses of men toward personal freedom and the right to possess property. He thought of the two rights as coequal, arguing that their parallel growth made it "hard to separate them in historical discussion." What followed from this assertion was a version of a free society directly attributable to John Locke and very much an extension of the Whig view of progress through history.[30] Taft's conclusions were thus highly predictable. "The institution of private property with all its incidents is what has led to the accumulation of capital in the world." Capital represented and measured the difference between civilization and barbarism in Taft, linking material comfort with human happiness and "the greater opportunity for the cultivation of the higher instincts of the human mind and soul."[31]

The size and complexity of the modern nation, and he had the United States explicitly in mind, made it necessary in Taft's view to use government to regulate capital to some degree, at least in light of the rights of the public. This regulation was rendered more difficult—and, paradoxically, more safe—when it was in the hands of political parties than when controlled by a single ruler or by an oligarchy. As Taft was eager to encourage his young listeners to be active in politics, he took up the role of political parties in the American system of government. "The existence of parties, their maintenance, and their discipline are essential to the carrying on of our popular government."[32] He refused to label the major American political parties conservative or liberal as could be done in a country such as France, which he cited as his example. Instead he spoke of American parties as positive or negative, depending on whether a party was in power or in opposition. Without stating it explicitly Taft hinted that this was almost the only real distinction between Republicans and the Democrats.[33] He also expressed doubts about the value of the independent, or nonparty, voter, inasmuch as independents voted but did not govern. In America only parties governed, and it was only through party government that social progress could come about. Party loyalty was therefore an estimable thing in Taft's political creed, though such loyalty did not justify the sacrifice of high principle. Whereupon the secretary added, "but this life is all a series of compromises."[34] Principles, seemingly, might be bent but not broken. Finally, Taft warned his audience that once active in a political party the men of Yale would have to learn to work with the whole of the American electorate, fourteen million male voters strong. "This will bring him, doubtless, in contact with some people whom he would not wish to have as permanent associates or companions," and, not surprisingly, the saloon keepers were singled out as examples of Taft's unsavory average politico. For all of his priggishness he was ready to advocate that Yale men rub shoulders with the people. The Yale man "must stand in an exact equality with men of less education and less advantages." The university graduate had much to teach and much to learn from fellow Americans of ordinary background. Theory must be put aside in the rough and tumble of politics, American style.[35]

Taft's address had touched on any number of scattered points, yet it was predicated on a philosophical unity: the exercise of the right of private property in a free society led to the accumulation of wealth that was as fundamental to civilization as to individual human experience. The orchestration of freedom and property in a complex society needed the direction of positive government in many particulars, and the safest way, both for freedom and for property, to achieve a resolution of conflict was through party government in the hands of an educated and experienced citizenry. All of Taft's thinking was derivative, and it appears especially so when reduced to the elemental level. But it was a philosophy of government well enough, if briefly, stated, and it must have left Taft's Yale audience more than a little curious about the remaining lectures.

In "The Duties of Citizenship Viewed From The Standpoint Of A Judge On The Bench," Taft was on familiar and much-loved ground. Once again he appeared to scatter a good many observations about the judicial aspects of the law, but a basic unity and a historical awareness were readily discernible. He began in a bantering and somewhat self-deprecatory vein by telling his audience that he had gone on the bench at the age of twenty-nine, that he perhaps knew too little law at the time, and that the bench was one of the best law schools even though the judge got his training at the expense of the public.[36] He was decidedly in earnest once he turned to his first concern, the jury system. In response to a rising demand that juries be placed above and independent of the judge, a movement he associated with southern and western states, Taft pointed out that the English common law contemplated the court and the jury as one, "that the ultimate decisions rested not on the verdict of the jury alone, but on the verdict as approved by the judge holding the court." It was the jury and judge together that made "an admirable tribunal."[37] This, he insisted, was what was intended by the American Constitution when it spoke of trial by jury. Juries unguided by judges tended to abuse power and to mishandle the law. For example, in suits against corporations the jury was too often "an almoner of its charity" by mulcting the corporation of large sums of money through fines and damage awards.[38] In effect, Taft was entering a plea for greater authority for judges, especially in various southern and western states, observing that "the common law is preserved in its entirety in the Federal courts."[39]

Taft was far from advocating the abolition of the jury system. He was emphatically in favor of juries when their responsibilities were rightly interpreted, saying that "the great advantage of a jury trial in a popular government is that it gives the public confidence 'that justice will be done.'" The jury concept, the future chief justice, argued, had worked better in Anglo-Saxon than Latin nations, not because of any innate difference between races but because of the long training in the use of juries common to the Anglo-Saxon peoples. Taft did not explore what ultimately led to the preference for juries by these peoples. Similarly, a jury composed of educated individuals was bound to be superior to one composed of uneducated people. Finally, the judge, like Caesar's wife, must not only be above suspicion but must maintain the appearance of rectitude.[40]

As is typical of men of the law, Taft came out forcefully for upholding its supremacy. He saw a number of contemporary challenges to that idea and sought to spike them *seriatim*. Laws not capable of enforcement should not be passed for it was at variance with sound policy to enact a law which by reason of the conditions surrounding the community in which it is declared to be the law, is incapable of enforcement.[41] Prohibition of the sale of intoxicating liquors by a state legislature for local communities where public sentiment was against such a prohibition was a case in point, leading Taft to come out strongly in favor of local option. Second, Taft took special pains to denounce lynch law, which was the very antithesis of a government of law. Law must not come from human emotions but from sober methods of justice.[42] On the other hand, he also took aim at those in society who advocated that "it is better that 99 guilty men should escape than one innocent man should be punished." Such a dictum "has done much to make our criminal trials a farce," he concluded. Also threatening the supremacy of the law was the power of wealth and the pernicious idea that the wealthy were exempt from obeying the law.[43] Taft considered this an inversion of the law, since men of property should be more concerned with having the law enforced than those lacking a stake in society. If the law was not guaranteed, property could not be protected. A law like the Sherman Anti-Trust Act must be enforced, therefore, as part of the supreme law of the land whenever contracts or conspiracies in restraint of trade between the states were proven. Taft believed the muckrakers were in part responsible for the growing disrespect for law. In his view the muckrakers "have overdone the picture."[44] Granting corruption, chicanery, and abuse of privilege, he believed that much wrong could be eliminated by sound law, soundly enforced and adjudicated. There was really no other way. In the process the role of the courts was critical because adjudication was the final step in the logic of the process. "The Courts are the background of our civilization. The Supreme Court of the United States is the whole background of the Government." Its power rested, quite simply, in "the supremacy of the fundamental law."[45]

William Howard Taft's well-known predilection for the law as faithfully administered by the courts had been given a fresh and vigorous statement in this second lecture. If property was the basis of American civilization, as had been asserted in the opening address, law was the instrument to keep property inviolate, and the courts were designed to wield that instrument as provided in the Constitution. Yet Taft had recognized, by indirection, that law was a living phenomenon and not something inert, held fast by history. Conservative as he was, he had an awareness of the needs of the people in the throes of living and the abuses that were perpetrated by the wealthy classes. Avoidance or at least control of the inherent conflict between the haves and the have-nots demanded the supremacy of the law.

William Howard Taft was the most experienced and the most successful of American colonial administrators. He had a right to a respectful hearing from an audience well beyond the boundaries of Yale. His lecture on "The Duties of Citizenship Viewed from the Standpoint of the Colonial Administrator" was, surprisingly, the least effective of the four talks.[46] After a brief review of the history of the American presence in the Philippines, he went on to criticize many of the actions of his countrymen who were sympathetic to United States occupation, no less than those of advocates of independence for the Islands. He was against exploitation and independence in equal measure. The only possible justification for a continuation of the American presence there was that it afforded the United States the opportunity to prepare the Filipinos for self-government at some time in the future. In this process the former governor general urged Americans to cultivate the friendship of the Islanders and encouraged the Islanders to maintain their allegiance to the insular government. Taft's basic proposition was that time and experience would prepare the people for self-government while the presence of the United States served to allow the Filipinos to learn the difficult art of self-government without fear of foreign interference (Taft singled out Japan in this respect). In such passages the secretary of war was advocating his version of the white man's burden, sincerely and without a trace of self-consciousness. He was frankly proud of what the Filipinos had accomplished under American tutelage and made favorable comparisons with British rule in the Far East and in Egypt. Taft sounded remarkably like Theodore Roosevelt when he contended that Lord Cromer had done a good deal less for the Egyptian people while he was agent general in Cairo than Americn administrators had done for the Filipinos.[47]

Taft was conscious of the paradox implanted in the American efforts to cultivate self-governing qualities in the Islanders: the greater the success, the less justification for continued American supervision of the Philippines. The upshot would be withdrawal of the United States from the archipelago and, with it, serious ramifications for American Far Eastern diplomacy. In such matters Taft found himself straying into policy areas.[48] It was policy in which he had had a hand, but that he was ill at ease in discussing. He was more comfortable commenting on law than defending policy. This third lecture tended to have less of learning and more of polemic. After all, Taft felt himself called to explain and justify his belief in his work in the Islands.

The final lecture took up the national executive; it was more abstract than might have been anticipated in light of Taft's remarks on colonial administration. He first concerned himself with the criticism by a free press of public officials and their actions. The influence of the muckrakers was evidently still on his mind. "The press is essential to our civilization and plays an unofficial but vital role in the affairs of government" inasmuch as "the exercise of power without danger of criticism produces an irresponsibility in a public officer."[50] Nonetheless, the tendency "to criticize public servants unjustly" had to be curbed because this was "frequently a serious hindrance to the accomplishment of valuable results from a patriotic and governmental standpoint."[51] While restraint of criticism was always appropriate, the future president believed that in foreign policy matters extreme partisanship was a misdirection of effort. "My country is right" was his consistent position, and he cited the American policy toward the Philippines as an example.[52] Taft believed that unwarranted partisan criticism had extended the war against the insurrectos and made it more costly. A self-serving judgment, no doubt, looking at all the facts, but one consistent with Taft's conservatism.[53]

Examination of the lecture makes it clear that Taft had thought seriously about the presidency. He urged his listeners to recognize that even the most powerful of rulers was always subject to the limitations of circumstances, and therefore the strongest of presidents suffered from inherent limitations, apart from the authority delegated by the Constitution. A president should try to surmount obstacles to the legitimate use of power. He should be an active agent of new legislation and not a passive creature subject to the will of Congress. A president who failed to lead disappointed his party as well as the electorate. Such leadership depended much on the ability to compromise; Taft was a foe of the doctrinaire conservative as well as the doctrinaire liberal. In fact, Taft worried aloud about the encroachments of Congress on executive privilege. He thought the history of American politics from the days of Andrew Johnson was sufficient evidence for concern. Rather typically, however, he sought to strike a balance, holding that investigations and criticisms of executive actions by Congress were "important influences toward a better government."[54]

In carrying out his work the president should be able to rely on a sound civil service. For an administrator who preferred to delegate authority, capable subordinates were essential.[55] Taft told his audience that despite some false starts the American civil service system, as represented in the federal government, at least, had come into its own. He lauded the passage of the Pendleton Act some twenty-five years before and expressed the hope that future chief executives would add to the number of positions based on merit. Ultimately, Taft concluded, the people would have to decide on matters of executive leadership and on the wisdom of legislative actions as well. Describing the American people as "intelligent and keen," he was prepared to repose his trust in them.[56]

Taking these lectures all together, it is possible to identify many of Taft's points with the principles of Adams, Jefferson, and Madison and to conclude that in much of what he held regarding man and government he had been guided by the philosophy of the founding fathers. The estimate of the place of wealth in the ways of men is a reminder of the thesis John Adams advanced in *Discourses on Davila,* in which he described the poor man as downcast and envious and the rich man as a model for emulation. It is less easy to identify Taft with Jefferson, for they were a world as well as a century apart. Each of them was an admirer of John Locke, though one may have spelled out Locke's meaning in a fashion different from the other. The respect for party government that the secretary of war advanced on several occasions, finding parties both a neutralizing factor in the conflict between interest groups and a positive element in promoting necessary political compromises, could have been proposed by any faithful Madisonian. If few of Taft's observations exhibited much originality at their core, they imparted a contemporary inflection, especially apropos the early years of Progressive reform. Taft reflected on the American system of government as it operated rather than as an abstraction. Furthermore, he was willing to work out his ideas in a semipublic forum so that both he and others might better understand and appreciate the place of free government in the everyday lives of men. Even so, the cloistral hush of Yale tended to make his commentary remote from the actuality of governing.

As a well-known and popular figure in the Roosevelt cabinet, Secretary of War Taft was called upon to give any number of public addresses that as with political speeches in all ages, had a full share of rhetoric. These speeches might be given in Shanghai, China, or Kansas City, Missouri; they might deal with the Panama Canal or the panic of 1907; or they might propose to define Japanese-American relations or invoke the memory of General Grant. Such occasions, subjects, and audiences were not generally calculated to promote a high level of discourse. Nevertheless, Taft's learning often protruded, revealing a mind well stocked with ideas. He showed a realistic awareness of China's condition and history; spoke of being engaged in a study of Lincoln in his address dedicating Grant's Tomb in New York; called upon a considerable knowledge of the development of capitalism from the time of the Middle Ages to explain the philosophy of the Republican party to an audience in Boise, Idaho; and with understandable zeal expounded to the 1905 graduating class of the Yale Law School the history of the writ of habeas corpus across the centuries. On these and other occasions Taft showed that he was at ease in his use of learned evidence to make a point more forcefully. This was one of the many reasons that Theodore Roosevelt liked Taft, trusted his judgments, and was confident he would make an exemplary president.[57]

In contrast with Theodore Roosevelt and Woodrow Wilson, for each of whom the presidency was the centerpiece of a distinguished career, William Howard Taft had the office made available to him—another example, as he himself remarked, of a capacity for having his "plate the right side up when offices were falling." That Taft did not like politics and especially the campaign trail he often said; that he did not seek the presidency is the received wisdom; but that his presidency was inevitably a failure is a matter of dispute. When Taft did not choose to identify with the Progressive wing of the Republican party, many members of which he did not like personally and on principle, his actions as chief executive often belied his conservatism. Viewed from another angle, Taft, on balance, did not fail the conservatives within the party, which was one important reason why he won renomination in 1912. Sufficiently flexible to move in opposite political directions, he somehow failed to promote himself as a leader who could bridge party differences. The result was a "troubled Taft" in the White House. The explanation of this is not hard to determine. The president's lack of political shrewdness, which manifested itself as an inability to appear to be different things to different men by adroit political maneuver, stemmed from his dislike of politicking. After

1910, when Roosevelt had thrown down a challenge for control of the party, Taft displayed less a lately developed political skill than an instinct for survival.

Whether judged in the main a success or a failure, the presidency of William Howard Taft bespoke his intellectual training as much as any one attribute. His choice of cabinet officers was one of the earliest indications that a respect for law and its institutions would carry over into his work as an executive. In 1909 there was no serious doubt on the part of the new president that he would be able to lead the legislature to enact more laws based on the reform beliefs that Theodore Roosevelt had lately preached. This was the reason TR had forced Taft on the Republican party, and why Taft had been willing to agree to take up residence in the alien abode of politics. But the Ohioan was to have his own presidential style, different from that of his patron and predecessor. He believed that if he was to be an effective president he must have capable cabinet subordinates. Men trained in the law, by that fact alone, had special appeal. Given the likelihood of an ongoing clash between capital and labor, Taft preferred corporation lawyers because they seemed best fitted to carry out reform laws without doing harm to business interests. As he wrote one Ohio friend, he must "get the best men" for the cabinet. "I mean by that I must get the men with the best qualifications."[58] Not surprisingly, there were five lawyers in Taft's cabinet. These appointments revealed a touching faith in the capacity of the legal mind and too little stress on the political savvy required of high-ranking subordinates in an effective administration.

In his final Yale lecture of 1906, which dealt with the national executive, Taft had recognized the responsibility of the president to promote legislation and to remove whatever obstacles might stand in the way. The Speaker of the House of Representatives, Joseph Cannon—unaffectionately called Uncle Joe—was just an obstacle. Cannon possessed the oldest of the old guard mentality within the Republican party and was able to be a legislative dictator in view of his power to appoint committees in the House and to dominate the powerful Rules Committee. Cannon, furthermore, was no friend of reform. At first the president appeared to lead Progressive forces against the Speaker, but he was too firmly entrenched to be dislodged by a presidential wish, and a passing wish at that. Taft was politically incapable of following through on actions he was intellectually convinced were necessary. "Cannonism" was to die out before Taft left office, but the president was reduced to being an observer of its passing rather than an active, effective proponent of its demise. A pattern had begun to emerge. The man of thought was not readily capable of translating his ideas into the practical instrument of law, which, ironically, he was prepared to honor so much.

Taft's opposition to Cannonism, and his failure to do something about it, was bound up with the issue of tariff reform. Cannon and Senator Nelson Aldrich of Rhode Island, among others, made no secret of the determination to thwart any downward revision of tariff rates, an attitude long maintained by the hard core of the Republican party and not a few Democratic congressmen as well. In his campaign for the presidency, however, Taft had promised to work for a lower tariff; once he was in office his responsibility in the matter was as clear to him as his promises had been to the voters. Taft's resolve was reinforced by Cannon's dismissal of the president's pledge as so much campaign rhetoric. But for all of that, Taft had to acquiesce in Cannon's continued possession of the Speakership, extracting a less-than-convincing promise from Cannon that he would support the president's legislative program, which included tariff revision as one among several initiatives. In Taft's view of the Constitution, only through cooperation between the executive and the legislature could needed and promised legislation be secured.

Seeking to fulfill his tariff pledge the president called a special session of Congress in mid-March 1909. In so doing he found himself in his first political fight, and the experience must have been sobering if not disheartening for him. Cannon and Aldrich were consummate parliamentarians and tough political infighters, overmatching the president on all fronts. They were also die-hard protectionists. Not that Taft failed to fight valiantly; at one point over the summer he appeared able to insist that iron, ore, coal, hides, oil, and lumber be placed on the free list. In its final form the Payne-Aldrich law made provision for substantial reductions on these and similar items. In summary, the Payne-Aldrich Tariff Act turned out to be something less than half a loaf of what reformers had been calling for over the years and what the prepresidential Taft had insisted would satisfy him. The president was charged by the disappointed low-tariff factions with having caved in to special interests. Certainly he had cooperated with Cannon, whom he disliked personally, and Aldrich, of whom he grew fond, and these men were the embodiment of protectionism. The indictment of the president by the reformers appeared not unfounded. In evaluating Taft's conduct two considerations should be borne in mind, both having to do with his prepresidential conception of what a president was required to do by the Constitution and by history. Taft's commitment to cooperation between the executive and the legislature in order to produce results was virtually a truism for him. The structure of government under the Constitution required it. Furthermore, as he had stressed in the first of his Yale lectures in 1906, "the existence of parties, their maintenance and their discipline are essential to the carrying on of our popular government." Not having worked with party leadership in the Congress would have contradicted a maxim sanctioned by history. To have thrown in with the insurgents, who constituted only a small portion of total party members in the Congress, would have undermined the Republican party as an effective instrument of government. Heritage and instinct as well as thought and reflection prevented Taft from such a move. To him party loyalty was an essential. That same party loyalty caused him much political grief. Stung by the reformers' criticism he was moved to defend the Payne-Aldrich act as the best of tariffs—which it manifestly was not—and his political woes multiplied.

At a distance of three-quarters of a century the Ballinger-Pinchot controversy continues to loom large in any account of Taft as president. The rights and the wrongs of the affair apart, Gifford Pinchot played the same kind of political hardball that he ascribed to his opponents. The controversy is a ghost that still haunts. Too easily remembered in broad outline, too little comprehended in specific detail, it has unduly damaged Taft's reputation. The president's role in the episode may be somewhat better understood by reference to a philosophy of administration and the principles followed in its implementation. Charges made by Pinchot, chief of the forestry service, that Secretary of the Interior Richard Ballinger was in league with the Morgan-Guggenheim group for the purpose of exploiting federal coal fields in Alaska, posed a serious problem for Taft. The president was by his own word heir to Theodore Roosevelt's conservation policies; yet one of his cabinet officers was charged with violating what the Roosevelt-Pinchot mentality looked upon as a sacred trust. Taft insisted on viewing the matter as an administrative issue and not the political problem it was, much less the acid test of progressivism that it was to become. As he had consistently maintained since coming into office, the president had to rely on his executive team to carry out the law and could not, therefore, undercut the authority of the interior secretary for the sake of politics. Pinchot had breached one of the fundamental rules of good administration, direct-line authority, by persisting in conduct that finally forced Taft to dismiss him. As for the law involved, the president was convinced that Ballinger had done no wrong and was prepared to stand by him for that important reason as well.

There is a third factor to take into account respecting the president's position in the Ballinger-Pinchot controversy, a clue to which is contained in the last of Taft's Yale lectures. A president, he had observed, must be able to rely on a sound civil service, from the top down to the lowest level of responsibility. In his December 1911 message to Congress he was to recommend a massive extension of the merit principle, applying it to all fourth-class postmasters as well as to a general run of federal officials who served local communities. Meanwhile, by executive order he had added seventy thousand jobs to the civil service payroll. Friendly estimates of Taft's initiatives in this respect are undoubtedly true: no president before him had done as much to make a patronage-free civil service closer to reality. The Pendelton act had come of age. In light of this concern for an honest civil service the president's dismissal of Louis Glavis, the minor Interior Department official who had supplied the highly sensitive information about the Alaskan coal lands to Pinchot, was hardly unexpected. In his own way Glavis had mixed politics with the civil service. As much as Taft may have regretted the political harm his decisions produced, including the immense strain put on his friendship with Roosevelt, Taft was true to his abstract Yale formulation. In this instance, having thought through what a president in principle should do, he went ahead and did it. The price of principle was a deadly political fallout.[59]

Taft's indifference to politics was responsible for the failure of the public and the press and some historians of the period to appreciate the mildly Progressive reforms he favored and that, in some ways, he was effective in promoting into law. Use of the Sherman Anti-Trust Act against monopoly capitalism—eighty cases were initiated in four years—achieved some spectacular results in suits against American Tobacco and Standard Oil in 1911. Such prosecutions by the attorney general were always done with a careful regard for the law and the Constitution. New proposals for corporate regulation, such as the 1910 Mann-Elkins Act, aimed at increased control of railroads in the public interest, were also characterized by a respect for private property and a concern for the common good. Taft's touch was evident in the preparation of the Mann-Elkins Act, especially in the commerce court feature of the proposal. The court was to have broad powers of review of rates set by the Interstate Commerce Commission. The Mann-Elkins Act, once it became law, showed the scars of political infighting between the regular Republicans, the insurgents, and the Democrats, but the presidentially inspired commerce court survived the rigors of partisan strife. Taft's high hopes that the court would develop into a workable piece of moderate Progressive machinery went unfulfilled. It was shortly abolished by Congress, but not before it demonstrated once more the president's penchant for the judicial process, a further example of the guidance Taft's legal learning gave his practical steps.[60]

In his foreign policy William Howard Taft, while agreeing with Roosevelt's conviction that America stood at the head of a world movement of superior peoples, struck out in his own direction. Promotion of United States commerce abroad, never high on TR's list of priorities, involved Taft in attempting to enlarge trade with China and with South and Central America. The policy was touted as Dollar Diplomacy. In the total of his foreign policy moves Taft was subtly influenced by the social Darwinist teachings of Professor Sumner as these were modified by personal experience as civil governor in the Philippine Islands. The desire to benefit American business through commerce also showed Taft's strongly capitalistic preferences, which rested on the secure foundation of property rights under the law. But, mostly, President Taft reflected the spirit of the age in which he lived, whether he was promoting American trade or acting to ensure American leadership in international politics.[61]

Two considerations stand out in the conduct of Taft's foreign policy. First, the president proposed to lay down a broad course of action and leave the work of spelling out the details to Secretary Knox and the State Department. Conscious of the necessity for a trained civil service, as a new president Taft sought to upgrade both the diplomatic and the consular services. The Department of State was reorganized according to geopolitical divisions. As in other departments, delegation of authority presumed qualified personnel as well as a sound organiztion. To Taft this was the essence of efficiency in government. Second, Taft shifted his position with respect to the exercise of constitutional power. Limited power in domestic affairs was transformed to increased power when dealing with foreign policy. Whether this shift made him more of a Progressive is dubious since Progressives themselves tended to divide on the subject of executive discretion in diplomacy. This enlargement of presidential authority did show that Taft was not a hidebound constitutionalist after all. His attitude toward trouble brewing in Mexico said as much. He was willing to use his prerogatives to order mobilization of twenty thousand American soldiers, yet when badgered by members of his own party to resort to force to calm the Mexican border areas, he adroitly observed that he had an obligation to consult the full Congress, thereby evolving a policy of preparedness without intervention after the fashion of John Adams.

By far the feature of his foreign policy most characteristic of President Taft's learning and intellectual bent was the effort to arrange comprehensive arbitration treaties with Great Britain and France. Arbitration procedures based on solemn treaty commitments were to become working parts of a system of international law that would promote international peace. The advanced nation must take the lead in this high-minded experiment. Taft the jurist was speaking when he contended that "I don't see any more reason why matters of national honor should not be referred to a court of arbitration any more than matters of property or national proprietorship. . . . I don't see why questions of honor can not be submitted to a tribunal."[62] A tribunal, because it was a tribunal, could be trusted. There is no doubt that Taft believed that issues "justiciable in nature," should be arbitrated by applying the rules of law and equality. The arbitration treaties the president sent to the Senate in 1911 were intended to render international law something more than a collection of unenforceable customs. The Senate so emasculated these treaties with Britain and France that Taft was discouraged from submitting the amended versions to London and Paris. Looking back on the whole matter of arbitration treaties the president told Major Butt that had they been passed they would have been "the great jewel of my administration," a final testament to President Taft's reverence for the law and his expectations of it as well.[63]

The passage of William Howard Taft from the presidency was easily accomplished. Whatever the office had been or not been, he looked forward to postpresidential years that would take him back in the direction of the law. In December 1912 he accepted the Kent Professorship of Law at Yale, and the prospect of the law and Yale together brightened his outlook. On the other hand, the former first lady, Nellie Herron Taft, was not so sure. She took some solace in the 1912 defeat of Theodore Roosevelt who, in her judgment, was the main source of grief for Taft and for the Republican party. For her the time seemed ripe for memoirs. Nellie Herron Taft was a remarkable woman and, in the political sense at least, Taft's better half. She was the daughter of a prosperous Cincinnati attorney and was part of the society in which Taft moved. They married in 1886. Her keen intelligence was outstripped only by her ambition for her husband. Despite his fondness for the law Nellie Taft preferred the excitement of politics to the routine of the bench. She appeared to be the driving force behind Taft's presidential special, the engineer at the throttle as station after station flashed by on the way to 1600 Pennsylvania Avenue. The civil governorship of the Philippines was to her a necessary first step into the political arena, whereas to Will Taft the assignment was a matter of patriotic duty. As President Theodore Roosevelt came to rely increasingly on his secretary of war, Nellie Taft could think of little else except the White House. And so the presidency came to Taft and so it passed from him.[64]

If 1912–13 meant denouement for Nellie Taft it promised the beginnings of a happy interlude for her husband. After a brief Georgia vacation he reported to Yale the first day of April and immediately took up his duties. He remained officially at Yale until 30 June 1921, the date of his appointment as chief justice of the Supreme Court by President Harding. These were years of exceptional intellectual productivity for Taft. He wrote and lectured widely, published two solid books on government, and during World War I emerged as a leading spokesman for international peace and world order. Indeed, once at Yale he was eager to get back to work. As a professor of law he was expected to teach a senior course on the Constitution and to make himself available to the law school for such assignments as the dean might choose to give him. As it was too late in the term to teach conventional courses, he delivered a series of eight formal lectures on the Constitution, using the preamble as his text. These lectures, together with two addresses given on other occasions to the American Bar Association, were incorporated in book form and published by Yale University Press in 1913 under the title *Popular Government*.[65]

Popular Government was a timely book. Progressivism was about to climax and among the dreams and demands of the reformers were such innovations as initiative, referendum, recall, and the direct primary. The Progressives appeared bent on building a better mousetrap. Taft was dubious about the entire trend toward more popular government. He called upon history and experience in nearly equal measure to challenge the pretensions of what he called political novelties. He dismissed Charles Beard's economic interpretations of the Constitution, for example.[66] Taft blamed current political failures not on the system but on the failure of the people to use the system properly. New systems would not change human nature, which is what he thought was the purpose of the reformers, and it was folly to think so. The system in place was sound, which he proposed to show by emphasizing the historic differences between Jefferson and Marshall on the nature of the Constitution.[67] Taft agreed with Marshall's construction and spoke approvingly of the relative remoteness of government from the people, as required by the document, and of the authority of the Supreme Court free from the influences of popular passions. This was preliminary to his key assertion: "popular government is not an end in itself" but a means "to secure to each individual and to each class of individuals the greatest measure of happiness."[68] Whatever the collectivist requirements of the times might be, Taft gave individual rights first priority. Mere majority rule would not do; tyranny of the many could be as dangerous as that of an unrestrained monarch. "Such was the fate of Greece, of Rome, and of France," But the ex-president was more comfortable when drawing on the history of his own country.[69] He pointed out that of the four million Americans in 1787 only about one hundred and fifty thousand men—one person in twenty-five—actually voted on ratification of the Constitution. He quoted Blackstone and James Wilson to the effect that under given circumstances "a certain number of men might assume to act in the name of the community."[70] In contrast, Taft opposed Rousseau's original contract theory as "not a true statement of what had happened in history."[71] Wedding theory to experience he argued that any form of government that made continuous and heavy demands on the mass of people to participate was likely to fail. Fully popular government could not sustain itself. Taft's views had an echo and perhaps more than an echo of conservatism as he discussed the beginning of the constitutional period. New England Federalists such as Jeremy Belknap argued that the people should be taught that government comes from the people, but that they must also be taught they are incapable of governing themselves directly. Experience had demonstrated, however, that a majority of the people would participate in elections for their representatives and they in turn would do the work of government.

Taft was a strong advocate of the representative system of government. He looked on the worship of democracy, as the term was being loosely used, as a fetish. He traced the roots of representation back to the Saxon witenagemot, bringing its development forward in brief compass from pre-Norman England to the twentieth century.[72] In so doing Taft noted that as times had changed, the responsibilities and expectations of government had grown more numerous and complex. The task of organizing popular government was dramatized in the modern world by the increasing need for experts and specialists whose technical knowledge was beyond the average citizen; he cited the intricacies of currency and banking as examples.

The ex-president agreed with Edmund Burke that representatives should first seek the good of the whole nation in the measures they supported and only then the interests of their constituents.[73] Political parties became essential to representation because the individual lawmaker was able to identify with his party's program, which could be cast in large terms. Taft admitted that parties could abuse prerogatives of government. Corruption defiled them and unworthy leaders became party bosses against whom such devices as the initiative, referendum, and recall were aimed.[74] Conditions of party waywardness were all too real and had to be reformed. The new school of radical political progressivism was an inevitable outgrowth of abuses, and Professor Taft agreed with its impulses. He dissented from its methods, and the speed of change with which reform was urged. "Great reform should not be brought about overnight." It was at this point that Taft launched his attack on "the new devices."[75]

Professor Taft expressed any number of worries respecting the use of the initiative, referendum, and recall. These devices were used on issues that rarely were clear-cut; a majority pro or con was not necessarily a majority of the electorate; delegation of legislative authority was involved, which might be unconstitutional; the effect of the use of these devices could be harmful on the ordinary procedure of government; and manipulation and corruption were possible inasmuch as human nature was a constant. Yet Taft's strongest objection to the use of such instruments of direct rule was that they "eliminate all distinction between a constitution as fundamental law and statutes enacted for the disposition of current matters. When exactly the same sanction . . . is given to a statute as to a constitution, to an appropriation bill and a bill of rights, so that one may be repealed as easily as the other, the peculiar office of the constitution ceases to be."[76] In citing Justice Miller in *Loan Association* v. *Topeka* and Lord Acton on the American Constitution, Taft's defense of the Constitution was unyielding.[77] In refuting the arguments of the proponents of what he persisted in terming "the new devices," the former chief executive showed himself acquainted with a considerable range of historical fact and political theory and possessed of a thorough understanding of the development of the law.[78] The entire set of lectures sustained the impression of a learned man, as he cited the work of Max Farrand on the records of the Constitutional Convention, rehearsed the history of the Republic in its many phases in simple but spirited terms, called on the work of Marshall and Taney to emphasize a contention, and quoted knowingly from *The Federalist* and from his own veto message respecting the initial petition of Arizona to enter the Union.[79] As a cohesive commentary on American political institutions, Taft's *Popular Government* was marked by four characteristics. In addition to erudition it contained a lofty patriotism, a high regard for the Constitution and the law, and a plea for public morality based on a personalist ethic of the strictest sort. By no means a great book or even one of permanent value, it did find Taft at home with ideas and with history.

In the year following the appearance of *Popular Government,* Taft published *The Anti-Trust Act and the Supreme Court.*[80] It was the most scholarly of his books. Earlier in his career, when he was a circuit judge, he had written the occasional piece for law journals. "The Right of Private Property" appeared in the *Michigan Law Journal* in 1884 and the next year "Criticism of the Federal Judiciary" came out in the *American Law Review,* but these were rare accommodations to journal literature. With more time to devote to an investigation of the history and operation of antitrust legislation, Taft set about the task of explaining antitrust laws.[81] He was moved to write by the agitation then current in the country concerning a revision of the Sherman Anti-Trust Act of 1890. Taft believed there was a good deal of misunderstanding concerning the Sherman Act and proposed to "make clear the Law against trusts and monopolies as it grew up under the common law, as it was changed by statute, as it had been enforced by the courts, and as it is today."[82]

Convinced that the Sherman act had become a political football he first of all wanted to depoliticize it by a consideration of the long history of such legislation. Taft delved into English common law at the time of Henry V, when freedom from restraint of trade was pronounced law. This freedom was maintained for over two hundred years. Some effort was made to permit restraint in the days of James I, and Taft noted exceptions that were made. But in general, monopolies, especially those in the trade of foodstuffs, were condemned by statute.[83] From this historical base the future chief justice reviewed the various practices that grew up in light of the general prohibition, showing how and why certain exceptions to the prohibition were allowed. He discerned from history, in other words, that there might be reasonable restraint of trade, if conditions called for it. Taft borrowed his idea of "reasonable restraint" from the English practice, termed "judicial guidance."[84]

From England Taft moved to New England, quoting various cases wherein fear of monopoly was registered. As colonial law was strongly influenced by English law, an influence that continued to some degree after independence, Taft felt justified in intermixing English and American precedents to demonstrate the further history of laws against restraint of trade.[85] He quoted from the English case, *Mogul Steamship Company* v. *McGregor,* to the effect that a "combination of workers to seek higher wages was 'lawful at common law.' " Taft proceeded to modify this rule by arguing that while a combination of workers was not actionable, efforts to compel third parties to join in to bring pressure on employers—the secondary boycott—were illegal. Showing that in his own way he was not completely out of tune with sociological jurisprudence, he claimed that secondary boycotts were reprehensible because in their effects the entire community could be made to suffer.[87]

Taft next took up the Sherman act itself. Quoting authorities that included Oliver Wendell Holmes, Jr., Sir Frederick E. Pollock, Roscoe Pound, Frederick Maitland, and James Barr Ames, he pointed out how all these commentators discerned the need for change in law—what Taft called moral progress in the law. Change put special pressure on judges. Judges were men subject to the prejudices and preferences of time and place. A great judge, according to Taft, was one who knew what must be retained in the law and, conversely, what might be usefully discarded. As the Civil War had brought many changes to America, including a reawakening of the electorate, Congress had been busy passing new kinds of laws. This situation placed a renewed emphasis on "judicial guidance," and led to Taft's reiteration in favor of an independent judiciary. The rapid alteration of the legal landscape in the Progressive era made an independent judiciary imperative. Not that Taft had a totally conservative legal outlook. He expressed the opinion, for example, that had the *Lochner* case come before the Supreme Court in 1913 it would have met "a different fate."[88]

Next Taft made a measured assessment of the famous *E. C. Knight* case of 1895. Reviewing the facts of the case, he quoted extensively from Chief Justice Fuller's majority opinion, which rejected the application of the Sherman Anti-Trust Act to the operations of the American Sugar Refining Company even though the company controlled 95 percent of the sugar refining capacity of the nation. He also referred at length to Justice Harlan's dissenting opinion. Part of the failure of the government to win the case was due, in Professor Taft's judgment, to the poor preparation of the briefs filed by the attorney general.[89] *E. C. Knight* and other cases were cited in order to provide Taft historical buildup to the two great 1911 Court decisions in the Standard Oil and American Tobacco Company cases. In each of these latter decisions the Court declared that the monopolies enjoyed by the companies constituted restraint of trade and the monopolies were therefore illegal. At the same time the Court insisted on the rule of reason, with the Court in the best position to determine when a trust was reasonable and when unreasonable. To Taft's mind this was nothing other than taking the concept of restraint of trade back to an earlier common law practice that had relied on "judicial guidance." He maintained that the scope of the Sherman act had been enlarged rather than narrowed. Taft took issue with the popular notion that the Court was using its position to enforce its own economic and political views. Instead, by appealing to history as his witness, he expressed the conclusion that the Court was "merely following a common law standard."[90]

There is no disguising Taft's view that further antitrust legislation (such as the proposed Clayton bill) was unnecessary. He was content with the "rule of reason." Additional laws, furthermore, might have a detrimental effect on corporate structures and corporate profits, major factors in the overall well-being of the nation. The Sherman act was sufficient in its wording to enable the Court to orchestrate an appropriate harmony between capital, labor, and the public in the free American system. All these considerations had prompted Taft to write *The Anti-Trust Act and the Supreme Court* in the first place.[91]

Meanwhile Professor Taft had settled in comfortably at Yale and felt very much at home in New Haven. He had returned to the New England of his heritage. The Tafts rented a large house near the university with room to accommodate the professor and his books. He soon became a familiar and welcome patron of the university libraries. The subjects of the books he borrowed ranged from history, philosophy, and ethics to religion, law, political science, and world organization. He also became an avid reader of serious periodicals, using articles from the *Review of Reviews, International Journal of Ethics, Proceedings of the American Philosophical Society, Spectator,* and *Political Science Quarterly,* among others, as material for lectures and papers. During these years at Yale Taft employed no research assistant, taking his own notes and composing his thoughts quickly and confidently.[92]

One of the most popular of Taft's lecture topics became the presidency. He gave a series of lectures on the subject, first at the University of Chicago, later at the University of Virginia and the University of Toronto, and finally at Columbia University in New York in the fall of 1915. Editions of this lecture series appeared under various titles, the most complete of which was *The President and His Powers,* given on the George Blumenthal Foundation and published by Columbia University Press in 1916.[93]

The President and His Powers is often cited for the strictures that Taft offered on Theodore Roosevelt's use of presidential power, and often dismissed because the ex-president appeared to have little of use to say otherwise. The book catches the eye of those who look for supporting evidence for their own castigation of TR and remains unappreciated as evidence of the scholarly Taft. Neither man is particularly well served in consequence. Taft intended to offer some understanding of the presidential office by appealing to history and his personal experience when in office. If in the process Theodore Roosevelt came in for some hard knocks, he was not the victim of malice. Taft was not a malicious man, but by the conclusion of his assessment of the presidency Taft had moved inexorably into the twentieth century and ended his commentary with an evaluation of the uses of presidential power by his immediate predecessor.

In his introduction to the 1925 Columbia edition of *The President and His Powers* Nicholas Murray Butler made the observation that these lectures on the presidency were both objective and philosophical and conveyed to the reader "a clear and exact comprehension of the functions and duties" of a modern president.[94] Taft chose to divide his discussion of the office into six major categories: the distribution of powers within the government, giving special attention to the presidential veto power; certain minor powers of the office that involved the relationships of the cabinet to the presidency and the cabinet officers to the president; the power of appointment, which involved considerations relative to the civil service; the execution of the laws, with emphasis on the president as commander in chief; the conduct of foreign affairs, to which was incongruously attached a treatment of the pardoning power; and, finally, the limitations of the president's power, which contained Taft's criticism of Roosevelt, although by no means did he confine his attention to TR in stressing the limitations of presidential power.

Over the course of his commentary Taft offered any number of informed and interesting observations on the presidency. He began by admitting that in its very nature, as distinct from congressional power, the executive authority was more difficult to interpret under the Constitution.[95] Considerable evidence was given from English constitutional history, and from the proceedings of the Continental Congress and the Constitutional Convention to show that the founding fathers discerned the problem of restricting executive power in relation to the other branches of government. In fact, Taft thought, a single term of six or seven years would have been preferable to the open-ended arrangement that the convention chose.[96] One effective way of delimiting presidential power would be a budget, coordinated and submitted by the president to Congress. Taft noted that Great Britain had such a system and that the state of New York was even then experimenting with the idea.[97] He hoped that success in New York would usher in a budget system for the United States. This first lecture was also an occasion for him to insist that American presidents were really not all that powerful, if compared with a German or Russian emperor; that a parliamentary form of government had many advantages over the presidential system; and that any major changes in the form of government should be undertaken slowly and with caution.[98]

As for the veto power, the ex-president called it "purely legislative," reminding his readers that the power was essentially passive in character, a response to initiatives taken by others.[99] A chief executive, he thought, would be unwise to depend very heavily on the device of the veto. Unacceptable laws were better headed off by executive pressure against them while they were being considered in the Congress.[100] Nonetheless, Taft believed that the president, when he did resort to the veto, often represented the popular will more surely than a majority vote in the two houses of Congress. A guideline he urged particularly on a president considering a veto was the constitutionality of the law in question. No amount of expediency could justify presidential acceptance of a law that he deemed to be against the Constitution.[101] This was not surprising from someone who had perennially held the Constitution to be sacred. In the course of making these and numerous other salient comments, Taft displayed a strong grasp of Anglo-American constitutional growth and of the history of the revolutionary and constitutional periods, and a thorough understanding of late-nineteenth-century American political history.[102]

Referring to his expressed admiration of the parliamentary form of government, he went on to express the hope that some start would soon be made in the direction of rendering the president's cabinet a more important part of the machinery of the national government.[103] Taft recalled that in his annual message to the Congress in 1912 he had urged an enhanced and, in fact, a somewhat altered role for cabinet officers. The cabinet principals, he said, should confine their attention to those duties "which require wise discretion and intellectual activity.[104] Housekeeping matters should be left to under secretaries in each department. Nor was such a proposal unheard of in the past, Taft pointed out. Justice Joseph Story in his *Commentaries on the Constitution* had urged the wisdom of such a change, and in 1881 a select committee of the Senate recommended the passage of a measure designed to bring cabinet officers into contact with the Congress, after the British model.[105] All in all, Taft's eye had a marvelous ability to note details. He deplored, for example, that presidential papers did not automatically become public property after a president left office. "Thus there is lost to public record some of the most interesting documents of governmental origin bearing on the history of an administration."[106] Taft's voice for a policy of open access to the full history of a presidency has not often been recognized. Other matters that he took up under "minor powers" were the decision of Woodrow Wilson to appear in person to address the Congress (a change Taft applauded), the wisdom of John Marshall in inaugurating judicial review in *Marbury* v. *Madison* (which was reviewed at scholarly length),[107] and the question of whether a sitting president might leave the country for some good and serious reason (with which Taft had no quarrel).[108] There is a remarkable mix of ideas, history, law, and good sense throughout the Taft lectures on the presidency, some of it surprisingly timely for the 1980s. Expectedly, he worried about machine politics and the spoils system. Unexpectedly, perhaps, he expressed concern over the formation of associations of civil servants into what he noted were "in effect, trade unions."[109] He perceived the likelihood that the interests of the workers in obtaining higher pay would clash with the interests of the public in receiving services, but he did not go so far as to predict strikes by public employees.[110]

In explaining the responsibility of presidents for a "faithful execution of the laws," Taft argued that, while presidential power was indeed limited, what power the chief executive had under the Constitution should be used to the extent required by any situation he might confront.[111] This was the very nature and necessity of the office. Taft had no difficulty in this respect in defending his actions while secretary of war when the United States went into Cuba at the direction of President Roosevelt, in order to prevent the slide of that country into anarchy.[112] This action was a reasonable interpretation of the authority of the president under the Teller Amendment. Similarly, in providing for the government of the Canal Zone, which Congress had neglected to do after 1904, President Roosevelt had proceeded constitutionally to correct a deficiency.[113] Taft also justified the American invasion of Nicaragua. Intervention had been requested by the president of that country, and the introduction of American marines preserved his administration from overthrow by insurrectionaries.[114] Taft saw little difference between what he had ordered done in Central America and what President Grover Cleveland had done at the time of the Pullman strike in 1894; that is, both had used the executive power to maintain law and order. In the area of foreign policy, it is evident that Taft preferred a broad interpretation of presidential power. He expressed doubts about the role of the Senate in the treaty-making process, a point made sore for him by the emasculation by the Senate of his arbitration treaties with Great Britain and France. "The treaty making power [of the president] is very broad," he observed, and he did not think that the Senate could sit in continual judgment on a body like a league of nations— were the United States a member—on the basis of its power to advise and consent.[115]

The ex-president's treatment of the conduct of foreign policy moved logically in the direction of limitations on the president's power. As he had noted at the start of his extended commentary, the Constitution had left the executive authority undefined when compared with that of the legislature.[116] Therefore, abuse had to be more of a concern for the Court and the public. For example, under the Constitution the president was charged with maintaining the peace of the United States, Taft observing that "I think he would have this power under the Constitution even if Congress had not given him express authority to that end."[117] Similarly, the president's determination of the movements of the army and the navy were beyond congressional control. Drawing on specific historical examples from Jefferson to Grant, Taft defended the independence of the presidential office, which drew its power from the Constitution, from law, and from custom. He noted that Roosevelt's action in withdrawing lands from development and exploitation, which had drawn the ire of Congress in 1908, had been sustained by the Supreme Court.

What then was William Howard Taft's quarrel with Roosevelt's use of presidential power? First, he stated that "the true view of the executive function is . . . that the president can exercise no power which can not be fairly and reasonably traced to some specific grant of power or justly implied and included within such express grants as proper and necessary to its exercise."[118] In this assertion he quoted President John Tyler's secretary of state, Abel Parker Upshur. Upshur had taken issue with the view that any power not legislative or judicial that government enjoys must be, by process of elimination, presidential.[119] To Upshur this was a monstrous doctrine, "utterly at war with the whole genius of our government."[120] Taft quoted him approvingly. He then referred to Roosevelt's "Chapters of a Possible Biography," in which his former chief put forth the view that it was not only right but the duty of a president to do anything that the needs of the nation might require unless such action was forbidden by the Constitution or the laws passed under it.[121] Taft called this the doctrine of undefined residuum of presidential power. He judged it dangerous. Though plainly irked by Roosevelt's dismissal of him as a Buchanan type of president when at the same stroke TR implied that he was a Lincoln type, Taft purged his argument of personal animosity by quoting extensively from the writings of Edward Livingston, the brother of Chancellor Livingston.[122] A man of superb education, Edward Livingston had become embroiled in a land dispute with the government of the United States. Jefferson was president at the time and at least in Livingston's judgment, had dangerously enlarged the powers of the executive office in order to obviate Livingston's claim.[123] The Yale library records show that Taft had made an exhaustive study of the life of Edward Livingston and had made use of his considerable knowledge of the subject to add to his criticism of Thomas Jefferson and Theodore Roosevelt when either assumed there was an undefined residuum of presidential power. Yet it is well to note that in the conclusion of his lecture on the limitations of the president's power, ex-president Taft stressed the "the Constitution does give the President wide discretion and great power and it ought to do so. . . . He is no figurehead."[124]

This brief review of Taft's lectures on the presidency shows several things. Again he displayed a keen sense of history and a good grasp of its details. Central to that history was the framework of the law that, organizing men's lives as they lived them, was a unique tool for understanding their history. He also revealed a deep knowledge and abiding love for his country, a nation to which the law had been essential in its growth to prosperity and greatness. As he described Jefferson, the strict constructionist who exercised wide power once in office, he implied that he was also susceptible to the charms of power. It was for that very reason— Taft's awareness of the weakness of human nature when presented with the temptation to abuse power—that he believed his thoughts on the powers of the president were worth sharing with his fellow citizens.

Another area to which William Howard Taft attached the greatest importance and in which he was active through lecturing and writing was the peace movement. In the various offices he had held, including that of secretary of war, he had gained a justifiable reputation as a man of peace. During his presidency he had worked for arbitration and experienced frustration when his efforts were negated. By the time he entered his Yale retirement, international peace appeared more fragile than ever. Though only a private citizen he continued his pleas for the cause of arbitration between nations lest civilization slip into the abyss of a great war. Once war was declared in 1914, Taft strode to the head of the peace movement in the United States and became a leading spokesman for the cause. His reputation had been firmly established by numerous speeches and papers delivered in behalf of world peace. In four lectures in particular, which he gave at the New York Peace Society over the winter of 1913–14, Taft brought his full learning and wisdom to bear on the subject. These lectures appeared in the *Independent* and were published in book form by Scribner's in 1914 under the title *The United States and Peace*.[125]

Taft's views were at once scholarly and humanitarian, American and internationalist, and hopeful and realistic. He defended with considerable vigor the operation of the Monroe Doctrine, but insisted that its motivation was less American aggrandizement than a desire for the well-being of the various peoples and nations of the Americas.[126] Admitting that the doctrine rested "ultimately on the strength of our army and our navy," a steady support of the doctrine by the United States had reduced the likelihood that force would be needed to defend the hemisphere from outside attack.[127] "The exercise of force on our part [if required] is certainly not a reason for the most sincere advocate of peace to insist on sacrificing its beneficent influence," Taft declared.[128] Until such time as all countries of the western hemisphere had organized into a single body for cooperative action, the Monroe Doctrine appeared to Taft a necessity for the good of all.

The ex-president expressed himself deeply concerned by the failure of the United States government to protect resident aliens in their treaty rights.[129] The American record in this respect he thought disgraceful, with Chinese, Mexicans, and Italians among the most frequent victims of mob violence and lynch law. This kind of xenophobia at home was the flammable material for wars abroad. He acknowledged the clumsiness of a federal system of government, noting that the police power of the states tended to inhibit the authority of the United States in fulfilling its treaty obligations. Nonetheless, legislative action had to be taken. As he said, "the treaty-making power of the United States is the widest power that is has," so that laws enacted by the Congress must be designed to facilitate the operation of whatever treaties the United States entered into.[130]

In lecture three Taft made his strongest plea for arbitration between nations, for "arbitration treaties that mean something," as he phrased it. With the treatment accorded his own efforts at arbitration fresh in his mind, the ex-president examined the problem from the viewpoint of *binding* arbitration.[131] Quoting from court decisions, he argued that binding arbitration was "no new thing" in American law, and it was well within the treaty-making power granted under the Constitution.[132] He cited historical examples as well, such as the *Alabama* claims against England in 1867, to show how a great sovereign nation might, with honor, submit to a judgment made against its interest.[133] The United States, as a great sovereign nation, should be prepared to do no less. This was the consideration Taft wanted to stress in his address: binding arbitration became meaningful only when there was a chance that the findings of the arbitration court might go against one. He marshaled considerable judicial and historical data to support his contention, showing a good knowledge and a rare perception of the realities of competition among nation-states.[134]

Professor Taft was at his scholarly best in lecture four. He undertook an examination of the experiments in federation that had served as a means of reconciling differences between peoples and countries. Beginning with the Achaian League in ancient Greece and proceeding from antiquity to the later Roman Empire, with a sidelong glance at the tribes of Israel, and then to the Holy Roman Empire from Otto to Napoleon, he proposed to show two things: the value of federations in providing a framework for peace, and the function of a court or a judge in taking up the difficult task of deciding the merits of a given disagreement. The latter consideration brought him into modern French and English history as he quoted authorities from Grotius to Lord Bryce.[135] Taft proposed reading the American Articles of Confederation and the Constitution in conjunction with examining European tendencies to demonstrate the psychology of compromise at work among civilized states and peoples. This final lecture was particularly the learned Taft speaking, persuasive on the need of modern nations to work out their disagreements peacefully as became peoples of intelligence. He deemed war unworthy of Western civilization in its early-twentieth-century stage of development. A poor prophet, Taft was an earnest advocate of peace.

From 1910, when as president he became associated with the American Society for the Judicial Settlement of International Disputes, William Howard Taft had high hopes for the peace movement. As long as he was president he made a number of statements and appeals for support of the process of peaceful arbitration, apart from his sponsorship of the 1913 Arbitration Treaties.[136] When war came to Europe the ex-president favored American neutrality and nonentanglement. The sinking of the *Lusitania* and the accompanying furor in the United States did not alter his opinion. When America entered the conflict in 1917 Taft was prepared to support President Wilson, in no small degree because of his awareness of the awesome responsibility thrust upon his successor. As the months went by, however, he thought it necessary to criticize Wilson for his conduct of the war as well as his preparations for peace. Taft was one of the promoters of the League to Enforce Peace, as distinct from and counter to Wilson's League of Nations and the mentality behind it. Without abandoning idealism, Taft believed his position was more realistic: after the war the victor powers would have to be in charge. Taft emerged as a powerful voice for some kind of enduring settlement of the problems of Europe and the world after 1918. He had given numerous speeches over the war years. They were addressed mainly to the plain citizen and appeared in the daily newspapers. Motivating both his actions and his words was a sense of history that told him—just as it spoke to many others of his generation—that the time to put down the foundations of a true and lasting peace was fast draining away. Now was the time to act, if any semblance of the old order was to be preserved. The alternative was chaos, the bane of any man of the law and especially of Taft, who had such great faith in liberty under law.[137]

In the history of the Supreme Court the chief justiceship of William Howard Taft is best and justly remembered as a period of major Court administrative reform.[138] Taft set about to bring the various federal circuit and district courts into a single, unified court system. The chief justice was to stand at its head and to manage the judicial personnel, including an increased number of federal judges, to facilitate the movement of cases through the system. Procedures in federal trials were to be simplified and the obligatory jurisdiction of the Supreme Court decreased by allowing it far more discretion in selecting cases for its docket. Taft recognized the need for these reforms as well as the cause of the problems. Federal courts were falling further and further behind in their work, while at the same time there was a steady growth in the number of congressional laws—the

Volstead Act was the prime example—under which suits were being brought. The package of reforms that Taft proposed was referred to as the "judicial conference," inasmuch as the deployment of judges, distribution of case loads, and assignment of cases were to be accomplished by the chief justice and the senior circuit-court judges conferring with the attorney general. An annual conference was to take place in Washington at which time schedules for each court were to be agreed upon.

Over stiff congressional opposition the controversial Judges Act of 1922 was passed and signed into law in September of that year. Taft had won a singular victory against strong odds. He had lobbied hard for the bill, appearing before the Senate Judiciary Committee, seeking support from the American Bar Association, and going public to the extent that his position and the interest of the average citizen in court reform would allow. He managed to make an important Progressive reform by this improvement in the machinery of the federal judiciary. Taft was, in fact, a remarkably active chief justice, a man very much in charge. He was determined to make the court efficient in its operation and conservative in its complexion by influencing presidents in the matter of judicial appointments. He was a close adviser to both Harding and Coolidge, but less effective with Hoover whom he pronounced a "dreamer." Taft was also determined to maintain the dignity of the Court at all times. The dignity of the law was keyed to the reputation of the Court. His fundamental intellectual commitment was to the law, a basis for and a guide to civilization.

There were four areas of constitutional law in particular in which Chief Justice Taft wrote case opinions designed to further his conception of the place and function of law in society. Each of these, involving complex legal considerations, spelled out his philosophy of law clearly and in a learned manner. Other cases might well be cited to show the contours of his judicial outlook, but his majority opinions in *Truax* v. *Corrigan* (1921), *Myers* v. *United States* (1926), *Bailey* v. *Drexel Furniture Company* (1922), and *Olmstead* v. *United States* (1928) were especially striking examples of Chief Justice Taft's conservative judicial philosophy.

In the first of these cases, *Truax* v. *Corrigan,* Taft sought to protect private property from state interference by invoking the clause of the Fourteenth Amendment providing for equal protection under the law. Taft's opinion was not noteworthy because he ruled against an Arizona court's failure to protect a restaurant owner from being harmed by boycotting, quoting Justice Field to strengthen his ruling. What was memorable was Taft's philosophical view of class legislation, which discriminated against some and favored others. He wrote at some length:

Classification is the most inveterate of our reasoning processes. We can scarcely think or speak without consciously or unconsciously exercising it. It must therefore obtain in and determine legislation; but it must regard real resemblances and real differences between things and persons, and class them in accordance with their pertinence to the purpose at hand. Classification like the one with which we are here dealing is said to be the development of philosophic thought of the world and is opening the door to legalized experiment. When fundamental rights are thus attempted to be taken away, however, we may well subject each experiment to attentive judgment. The Constitution was intended, its very purpose was, to prevent experimentation with the fundamental rights of the individual.

By insisting on "attentive judgment" to "legalized experiment" the chief justice was proposing to turn the flank of the sociological jurisprudence of his fellow justices, Holmes and Louis D. Brandeis. Experimentation was not allowed to become license.

Perhaps Taft's most erudite opinion was occasioned by *Myers* v. *United States,* the case of a postmaster suing for back pay because he had been dismissed from his position by President Wilson who had failed to consult the Senate in taking this action. Taft wrote a long opinion, invoking both history and the Constitution, to uphold the principle that a chief executive could not be limited in his dismissal of a subordinate. The historical portion was built chiefly on what the chief justice called the "decision of 1789." This "decision" took the form of a vote or a series of votes in the first Congress on the establishment of a department of foreign affairs. The House originally voted to create such a department under a secretary appointed by the president with the advice and consent of the Senate and removable by the president. After debate this bill was amended in two ways. A clause was added clearly implying the president's sole and unrestricted power of removal. Then the clause granting the power of removal to the president was stricken on the ground that such a clause inferred that without it the president would not have the power. The Senate concurred. According to Taft, Congress recognized and established the exclusive and untrammeled power of the president to remove executive officers whom he appoints. A mass of historical material, including the opinions of statesmen, was cited to show that this had been the accepted theory of the removal power throughout our history, save in one or two instances when "heated political difference of opinion between the president and the majority leaders of Congress" led to a different result, as in passage of the Tenure of Office Act of 1867. These exceptions, however, the chief justice deemed to be outweighed by the force of almost continuous practice. The constitutional grounds used to support the ruling in *Myers* v. *United States* need not be examined except to note that Taft held that the responsibility of the president to "take care that the laws be faithfully executed" made the power to dismiss subordinates freely a necessary presidential prerogative.[140]

The majority opinion in *Bailey* v. *Drexel Furniture Company,* written by the chief justice, proposed to limit the commerce clause as a source of federal police power. The case dealt with congressional law aimed at limiting child labor, one of the worst social abuses of the 1920s. Congress had placed a 10 percent excise tax on the annual profits of any establishment engaged in interstate commerce that employed children under the age of fourteen. The purpose of the regulation was both to tax and to penalize the firms in question. But Taft demurred on grounds that he judged the very nature of the Constitution. In part he wrote:

> It is the high duty and function of this Court in cases regularly brought to its bar not to decline to recognize or enforce seeming laws of Congress, dealing with subjects not intrusted to Congress, but left or committed by the supreme law of the land to the control of the states. We cannot avoid the duty even though it required us to refuse to give effect to legislation designed to promote the highest good. . . .
>
> Out of a proper respect for the acts of a coordinate branch of the government the Court has gone far to sustain taxing acts as such, even though there has been ground for suspecting, from the weight of the tax, it was intended to destroy its subject. But in the act before us, the presumption of validity cannot prevail, because the proof of the contrary is found on the very face of its provisions. Grant the validity of this law, and all that Congress would need to do hereafter, in seeking to take over to its control any one of the great number of subjects of public interest, jurisdiction of which the states have never parted with, and which are reserved to them by the Tenth Amendment, would be to enforce a detailed measure of a complete regulation of the subject and enforce it by a so-called tax upon departures from it. To give such magic to the word "tax" would be to break down all constitutional limitation of the powers of Congress and completely wipe out the sovereignty of the states.[141]

Alpheus Mason, the leading authority on the Taft Court and not always its friendly critic, has described the opinion in the Bailey case as "one of Taft's most cogent statements on federalism and judicial review."[142]

The rising crime rate in the United States in the 1920s, one reason for the crowded federal dockets, was especially disturbing to Taft. He was strongly of the view that no criminal must be allowed to escape punishment on some legal technicality or court fluke. His opinion, again for the majority, in the celebrated case of *Olmstead* v. *United States,* in which it was held that information obtained by federal agents through wiretapping was admissible evidence, was both vigorous and sophisticated. Taft ranged from statutes to past court decisions to American state and English cases to legal textbooks in order to substantiate his judgment. His summary statement spoke his mind on the legalities involved: "A standard which would forbid the reception of evidence if obtained by other than nice ethical conduct by government officials would make society suffer and give criminals greater immunity than has been known heretofore." In his own way and for his own purpose Taft had embraced a version of sociological jurisprudence in claiming that the community would be unnecessarily endangered if wiretap evidence was rejected.[143] This is an enduring irony inasmuch as the *Olmstead* decision is thought of as Taft at his most conservative and was one with which both Holmes and Brandeis sharply disagreed.

As with Theodore Roosevelt and Woodrow Wilson, the mind of William Howard Taft and the uses to which he put his learning were colored with ethical hues. They produced a different effect from Roosevelt to Wilson but fell mainly in the same area of the ethical spectrum. In 1922 Taft made a full statement of his public ethic in his lecture, "Liberty Under Law." It was an interpretation of the principles of American constitutional government, carrying a heavy ethical accent. Quoting from Matthew Arnold—"it is our relation to the Being, not to ourselves, which makes for righteousness"—he spoke of religion as "the great stay of morality," with "unselfishness as its cornerstone."[144] Theodore Roosevelt had mixed civic responsibility with a religious ethic just as easily and with as much reliance on the history of mankind to substantiate it. It was an attitude familiar, too, in the life of Woodrow Wilson.

Roosevelt and Taft remained remarkably alert in their last years, Roosevelt out of frustration and Taft out of satisfaction at being the chief justice. Their paths had diverged after 1910 but they continued to occupy the common ground of learned discourse, of articles and books written, and of ideas refined. Woodrow Wilson's final days were lugubrious. The promise of his youth, the success of his academic career, and his spectacular rise to power at home and adulation abroad, in each of which his learning had been elemental, ended in rejection and defeat. Indeed, the tragedy of Woodrow Wilson causes history to look at Wilson's learning for what it may reveal of the last of the learned presidents.

3
WOODROW WILSON
Righteous Scholar

In March 1911, while he was governor of New Jersey, Woodrow Wilson addressed a breakfast meeting of the Young Men's Democratic League in Atlanta. The previous day former president Theodore Roosevelt had spoken to the group, and that evening President Taft was to talk. Wilson was introduced as "the next president of the United States," as much a sign of local pride as of prophetic sense. This coincidental association in time and place comes as a reminder of how intertwined were the public careers of these three men and offers a suggestion of some commonality in their private lives.[1]

Born within three years of one another, they belonged to a generation that was supremely confident of the future of America. And there were also individual similarities among them. Roosevelt and Wilson were frail youths, plagued by poor health with which they had to contend in order to achieve. Like TR, Wilson held his father in the highest respect: "my incomparable father" was his phrase.[2] The Civil War touched each of them in meaningful but distinct ways. Despite his love for his father, TR was always somewhat uneasy that the senior Roosevelt had not served in the Union army, while Wilson was proud of his father's Confederate chaplaincy. Beyond this, the Roosevelt and Wilson families were divided by the war; TR's maternal uncles were ranking Confederate officers and two of Wilson's paternal uncles were Union generals. Wilson had serious reservations about the "economic man" of Roosevelt's view, believing that the practice of law for gain, for example, was "antagonistic to the best interests of the intellectual life."[3] Both of them had an abiding fondness for the literary heritage of the Anglo-American race.

There were strong resemblances between the Wilson and Taft families in the way in which family life had a nurturing effect on the young. The family circles were closely drawn and the sons appeared to receive much in the

way of counsel and to subscribe to it. Wilson and Taft took college very
seriously; for them it lacked the fashionable social dimension of Roosevelt's time at Harvard. Both had grandfathers who sat as Ohio judges, and
while Taft was utterly devoted to the law he did not practice it with much
more enthusiasm (although with considerably more pecuniary advantage)
than did Wilson. They were at one time university professors; Wilson was
professor of jurisprudence and politics at Princeton, and it is well to recall
that in the 1890s Taft was considered by a large number of Yale alumni as a
suitable university president. The formalities of education, along with the
substance, came naturally to both of them. A different decision here, a
missed opportunity there, and they might be remembered today as distinguished educators. Finally, all three presidents married remarkably able
and supportive wives, women who had definite and constructive places in
the public and private lives of their husbands.

Wilson's scholarly side may be illuminated in an initial way by relating
him to the first of the learned presidents, Adams, Jefferson, and Madison.
His intellectual instincts were strongly reminiscent of those of John
Adams, except that Wilson's were not so wide ranging, tending to be
concentrated on those considerations of history and politics that appealed
to him. Much as Adams had written the constitution of Massachusetts and
had expended considerable time and energy defending the constitutions of
the United States, Wilson was always ready to draft constitutions for the
university societies with which he was associated at Virginia, Hopkins,
and Wesleyan, and, eventually, for all peoples in a covenant for the League
of Nations. The minds of Wilson and Adams were grooved in much the
same way.

As a Princeton undergraduate Wilson moved in the shadow of James
Madison and the old Whig Society that Madison had helped to organize as
a debating club as long ago as 1769. Joining the society as a freshman he
remained active in it throughout his four years at college and was elected
Speaker of the Society in 1878, the highest position and honor it could
bestow. Wilson took pride and pleasure in the fact that he and Madison
were fellow Whigs, fellow Princetonians, and fellow Virginians.

After college Wilson studied law at Mr. Jefferson's university and came
to love the University of Virginia much as he loved the South. At Charlottesville he met Dr. John B. Minor, head of the law department, who was
his preceptor in legal studies as George Wythe had been Jefferson's guide.
Jefferson once referred to the law as a "dull old scoundrel," and Wilson
agreed with him. He confided to his friend, Charles Talcott, that the law
was "indeed a hard taskmaster," that it could get "as monotonous as that
other immortal article of good, HASH, when served with such endless
frequency."[4] They tended to endorse the verdict of the Autocrat of the
Breakfast Table, Dr. Holmes, who advised that if you can eat sawdust

without butter, be a lawyer. That neither Wilson nor Jefferson became practitioners of the law is not surprising. They were more concerned with what had given rise to law—man living in and governing himself according to society—than with legal technicalities.

Roosevelt, Taft, and Wilson have each received different and often divergent historical estimates, but Woodrow Wilson has invited the more comprehensive and controversial analysis. Lincoln Steffens once observed of Roosevelt that the inner man was not significantly different from the public TR. Taft's relative lack of complexity has made it possible for critics to identify only variations of a personality that was basically straightforward and at times rigidly so. Interpreting Woodrow Wilson defied any facile formula, however. The contrasts between his regional loyalties and his national outlook were sharp. Tension arising from the clash of a deep religious faith with the amorality of American politics troubled him. Wilson's striving for perfection and for power, his stubborn resolve and moral arrogance, have become the subject of literary psychoanalysis. Estimating Wilson as a scholar and a president involves dealing with the neurological disturbances that afflicted him, as well as measuring his intellectual prowess.

Woodrow Wilson remained a Southerner his entire life. "I am obliged to say again and again that the only place in the country, the only place in the world, where nothing has to be explained to me is the South." These were not the words of a homesick collegian or a young professor adjusting to life at Bryn Mawr or Wesleyan, but of a mature man of affairs.[5] Yet Wilson's origins were almost accidentally Southern. He was born in Virginia in 1856 and grew up in Augusta, Georgia, but forebears on both sides of his family were immigrants from the British Isles, Northern in persuasion. His father's father came to America from Northern Ireland in 1807, landing in Philadelphia and, within a few years, heading west, first to Pittsburgh and then to Steubenville, Ohio. There Joseph Ruggles Wilson, the future president's father, was born and raised. The family of Woodrow Wilson's maternal grandparents, the Woodrows, originated in England, though the grandparents were Scots by birth, arriving in Chillicothe, Ohio, by way of New York City and Canada early in the nineteenth century. Joseph Ruggles Wilson moved his family south shortly before Wilson's birth. His Southern patriotism was acquired rather than innate.

Until the age of twenty-one Thomas Woodrow Wilson, as he was christened, endured fateful days in the South. His earliest recollection of national events was hearing news of Lincoln's election and the threat of the war that all too surely followed. Augusta escaped the worst ravages of the fighting and was bypassed by Sherman's armies as they cut their historic swath through Georgia, but the war was real enough. Wilson's father was a staunch Confederate supporter and, briefly, a chaplain to troops. His church served as a hospital, and Union prisoners of war were kept in the nearby cemetery. Young Georgians marched off to war, many to return maimed, or not at all. Reconstruction also took its toll, and while the Wilson family suffered less disruption and privation than most, this tragic era was to be an influence on Wilson as a president and statesman. Years later when he uttered his famous lament that it was a terrible thing to lead this great nation into war, the ghosts of Civil War dead stood at his side.

Despite the war and its aftermath, Woodrow Wilson was an instinctive nationalist at a time when nationalism was a compelling force in American life. He was increasingly American as he came to manhood and never a champion of the Lost Cause, asserting once that "because I love the South, I rejoice in the failure of the Confederacy."[6] By that time (1880), he had come to see more clearly the worth of the political experiment launched in Philadelphia in 1787, and he rejoiced that it would go on.

Wilson dwelt on the essence of this paradox of genuine affection for the South and unalloyed attachment to the nation in his interpretation of Robert E. Lee, in an address delivered at the University of North Carolina in 1909. Lee's career, he thought, could be summed up perfectly as that of "a celebrated American general in the Confederate service." Lee was, in other words, a "national character who won his chief celebrity in the service of a section of the country but who was not sectionalized by the service, recognized now as a national hero." Wilson took special pride in Lee's postwar career as an educator, doing his "part in trying to make the young men of the country ready for the things that are yet to be done." In going to war Lee had expressed devotion to his native land; in helping to heal the wounds of war he was no less dedicated to peace. Each pursuit was a product of his conscience. This quality in Lee made it possible for the greatest of the Confederate generals to become a genuine national hero. For Wilson, regional affection and national aspiration merged in similar fashion. As the first Southerner to enter the White House after the Civil War, his policies were national in scope and purpose.[7]

One of the scathing terms of denunciation directed at Woodrow Wilson when he was president was his enemies' dismissal of him as "the Presbyterian priest." A curious insult, but one that was more than an alliterative catch phrase. His deep commitment to the theological tenets of covenant Presbyterianism guided him in his public and private life alike. But why priest? In religious invective, "priest" is often used as a word of contempt, one that easily shades into such terms as "priestcraft" and "priest ridden." A specific connotation of the word priest has been suggested by Lytton Strachey who, in *Eminent Victorians*, wrote of the "illimitable pretensions" of the priest. It was the "illimitable pretensions" of Woodrow Wilson—his absolute certainty of the rectitude of his policies, his vision, and his League of Nations, what his opponents derided as his moral arrogance—that have been called his glory and his shame. As "Presbyterian" indicated his status as one of the elect of God, one of his saints, so "priest" reinforced the impression of one who was ordained to renew God's work here on earth. All this suggests in a perverse way how vital were religious beliefs in President Wilson's conduct of affairs. Born of parents who were devout adherents of the teachings of Calvin and John Knox, and a member of an extended family noted for its piety and its learning respecting the things of God, Wilson prized his heritage and proposed to live by its precepts.

Woodrow Wilson's father was a highly respected and influential Presbyterian divine, and his maternal grandfather, Rev. Dr. Thomas Woodrow, was a scholar of Greek, Latin, and Hebrew as well as a preacher of the word of God. Faith and scholarship were represented in a natural and wholesome combination and the church was central to Tommy Wilson's upbringing. Each Sabbath Day he listened to his father's finely crafted sermons; in Sunday school he mastered the catechism; and every day he was made to feel the presence of God. Looking back to his boyhood the president recalled "the atmospheric pressure of Christianity the week through."[8] Yet in the teaching of Calvin no man was born to faith. He must freely accept it, finding God as a personal savior through a religious experience or conversion. For Woodrow Wilson this occurred in the summer of 1873 when, after a period of intense introspection, he came to understand that God had elected him. His father was a professor at the Presbyterian Theological Seminary in Columbia, South Carolina, at the time, and the young man applied for and was accepted into full membership in the First Presbyterian Church of that city. When he was president he returned to visit the chapel where he had prayed and had been converted, referring to it as "holy ground."[9]

The world that Wilson encountered as a young student, as a lawyer and academic, and especially later as a politician was an unconverted place. Like the saints of the primitive church he dwelt *in partibus infidelium*. Undaunted, he was all the more determined to make people and situations conform to his purpose and to his will. Elected by God for his service he saw himself as doing God's work, whether as president of a university or a nation. When he was unable to effect the desired ends, which were always cast in the shape of reform, Wilson's sense of moral superiority could contribute to his undoing. The tensions created by the clash of faith with a sinful world help to account for his alternation between euphoria and depression, between his vision of creating a new moral order and his blindness to the implausibility of the extensive changes his zeal demanded.

This sense of frustration with failure, as real as it was, can be overstated.

Wilson was sincere in his contention, for example, that Progressive democracy and Christianity could be properly identified one in the other. The war against human greed and exploitation of the weak might be won, and indeed was being won, he told a large audience of Protestant faithful in Denver, Colorado, in 1911, whenever and wherever Progressive laws were passed and put into effect.[10] To Woodrow Wilson, as to Theodore Roosevelt and a very broad segment of voting Progressives, progressivism was old-fashioned moral regeneration making use of new, pragmatic techniques and methods. The influence of his religious convictions is as important for measuring his political successes as it is for understanding his failures.

Woodrow Wilson's religious avowals were consistent with the strongly introspective side of his character. He dwelt often on the kind of person he was, once writing that "it isn't pleasant or convenient to have strong passions. . . . I have an uncomfortable feeling that I am carrying a volcano about with me. My salvation is being loved."[11] This same introspection fed Wilson's self-reliance. His well-known practice of appealing over the heads of state and national legislatures for vindication by the people was only one of numerous ways in which such confidence manifested itself. This self-esteem was part of his hubris, in the analysis of which certain of his biographers became a nemesis. Prominent among them were Sigmund Freud and William C. Bullitt in their book, *Thomas Woodrow Wilson: A Psychological Study.* Along with other students of Wilson's personality; Freud and Bullitt attempted to negotiate the perilous path of literary psychoanalysis.

The initial attempt to probe the Wilsonian personality was undertaken when he was still in the White House. In *The Story of a Style,* which was published in 1920, William Bayard Hale proposed to come to an understanding of the real Wilson by means of a painstaking examination of his language. He argued that it was in the use of language that "Wilson's real self will be revealed." Using numerous examples culled from Wilson's writings—the adjective count was a pet device employed by Hale—the investigation concluded that Wilson's style pointed to a person assailed by inner doubts that he struggled to banish, to someone troubled by contradictions that had to be resolved. Laying particular stress on Wilson's life of George Washington (thought by some authorities to be his weakest piece of major writing), Hale discovered Wilson to be pompous, artificial, proud, insecure, and given to exaggeration. Such conclusions amounted to a bitter attack on the president, one so novel in its methods and so relentless in its negativism as to be altogether suspect. As subsequent works were to demonstrate, it was only one of several efforts to expose the man within Woodrow Wilson.[12]

No less an authority than Sigmund Freud, in collaboration with the

American diplomat and student of public affairs, William C. Bullitt, under-took a further literary psychoanalysis of Wilson. Work done largely in the 1920s was not published until 1967. The nub of the Freud-Bullitt study was Wilson's relationship with his father. The father was represented as the great figure in Tommy Wilson's childhood. As a boy, the theory went, he found it necessary but difficult to reconcile his own wishes with his father's commands and expectations. Their egos clashed, the father over-powered the son, and young Wilson took a submissive, almost feminine attitude toward his parent. According to the Freud-Bullitt interpretation Wilson never grew beyond identification with his father. Reverend Wilson had his supreme moments when he was expressing himself in the pulpit, while President Wilson experienced his supreme moments in the political sermons he delivered from the White House. More telling still, according to this line of explanation, just as his father was not in the habit of devising the practical means to translate his pulpit principles into everyday life, so the president did not provide any really practical methods, for example, of compelling translation of the Fourteen Points into international practice. Wilson never deemed it necessary or found it possible to go beyond the model established by his father. To point out the way was judged by father and son to be sufficient; good men would follow their direction because the agents of an almighty God had spoken. Stated so plainly the Freud-Bullitt interpretation may sound grossly simplified, whereas it was im-mensely complex. The very defects in Wilson's personality, so these biographers contended, centered as it was in submission to the father, produced a reaction formation against it, driving Wilson to ceaseless activity at risk to his physical well-being. It demanded that he achieve the impossible. The conclusion was a harsh one: "The qualities of his defects raised him to power; but the defects of his qualities made him in the end not a great statesman but a great fiasco." What Freud and Bullitt had done in their study was to offer tantalizing rather than convincing judgments on Wilson in history.[13]

The lesson for Wilsonian biographers was clear, nonetheless; no serious account of his life could be devoid of some reliance on psychological data and their possible meaning, whatever the literary perils involved. In *Wood-row Wilson and Colonel House,* Alexander and Juliette George repre-sented Wilson's insistence on his unquestioned ascendancy, whether in an academic or a political test of wills, "as a rebellion against the domination of his father, whose authority he had never dared openly to challenge."[14] *He* must dominate, as his father had dominated him. Another biographer, John M. Mulder, in *Woodrow Wilson: The Years of Preparation,* acknowl-edged the powerful shaping effects of the clergyman father but insisted that the domination always was in terms of love and affection, that the father and son were companions and often coworkers. Furthermore, according to

Mulder, the parent's influence was positive: devotion to God, to principles, and especially to duty; a love for the South as a native land; and a commitment to covenant theology. To Rev. Joseph Wilson God was a "loving authority," a belief that Tommy Wilson, enraptured by his father's sermons, could hardly have failed to heed. The senior Wilson, in Mulder's judgment, was to accept the considerable achievements of his son as the completion of his own ambitions for greatness that never came to fruition.[15] Another variation on the father-son relationship was offered by Henry W. Bragdon in *Woodrow Wilson: The Academic Years*. He wrote that rather than dominate his son, the senior Wilson made many sacrifices contributing to his son's happiness and success. He gladly underwrote the costs of Wilson's graduate education at Johns Hopkins, for example, when many fathers would have insisted on financial self-reliance from a son of twenty-seven who was a practicing attorney.[16]

The biographer's debate over the formative years of the future president has been enlivened further by the interpretations of Edwin A. Weinstein's *Woodrow Wilson: A Medical and Psychological Biography*. The study mainly concerned Wilson's health and personality with a view to assessing the impact of his illnesses on major events in his adult life, but it paid considerable attention to the place of the youngster within the family and the larger social context. As a trained neurologist, Weinstein made assessments that command respect. He identified developmental dyslexia in Tommy Wilson, a condition undiagnosed by medical science until the 1890s, and considered its effects on the relationship he had with his parents and on his intellectual growth. Noting periods of depression (Wilson wrote that he often got "the blues"), Weinstein ascribed these moods to the stress associated with measuring up to the expectations of his parents, despite his physical limitations of which they could hardly have been aware. Weinstein also challenged some long-held beliefs about Wilson's life, representing him as a normally healthy boy rather than sickly. He suggested further that such illnesses as Wilson did endure were probably psychosomatic in origin. It remains, however, that Wilson's parents believed him to be sickly, his doting mother worried about him especially, and love and affection were showered on him.[17]

The developmental dyslexia that Wilson apparently suffered manifests itself in reading difficulty in a child of normal health with no brain damage who comes from a bookish, verbal family. The condition may have been caused, according to Weinstein, by "delay in the establishment of the specialized dominance of the left cerebral hemisphere of the brain for certain features of language." The effects were long range in character. Wilson remained a slow reader all his life. He spelled only fairly well and was weak in mathematics and, accordingly, lacked confidence in these areas. Dyslexia was not without some compensation. Weinstein suggested that it could have contributed to Wilson's skill in the use of auditory and visual imagery as a child, and to "his cognitive, linguistic style as an adult."[18] The influence of this condition on his family life was critical. He became the center of family attention and was conditioned to expect support from all those around him, an attitude typical of Wilson the domestic reformer and Wilson the international statesman. Failure to obtain approval might cause feelings of personal rejection and plunge him into fits of gloom verging on despair. At crucial junctures in his career Wilson was to know the pain of alienation from those he had been led to count on, and sometimes the results were adverse in the extreme. Weinstein's speculations added to the analyses offered by Freud and Bullitt, Hale, the Georges, Mulder, and Bragdon constitute an intriguing approach, persuasive without being fully satisfying. Dealing with the psyche, they tend to invite a consideration of the mind of Woodrow Wilson as manifested in his writings.

More tangible than the psychological considerations that have been used to render appraisals, and better suited to the purpose of showing credible connections between the inner self and the public man, is Woodrow Wilson's scholarship. He became the leading academic political scientist of his time. His presidency was that rare occasion when an authority on political institutions is raised to a premier public position and afforded the opportunity to wed theory and practice. Not even his religious convictions offer a richer source for understanding this philosopher-king. Wilson confessed that his chosen profession was politics, and when the profession he entered, the law, proved an unsatisfactory way of gaining political office, he moved in the direction of an academic career. "A professorship was the only feasible place for me," he concluded.[19] The writing and the lecturing entailed were essential ingredients in a parapolitical career that might, one day, become fully political. Wilson never abandoned the prospect of active politics. He did concede, however, that he might have to enter by a side door.

The household of Rev. Joseph Wilson was no stranger to serious secular literature or controversial ideas. Ultimately all issues were referred to Scripture and covenant theology, but the occasion remained to discuss the merits of free trade, the writings of Charles Lamb, or the meaning of Darwin's evolutionary theories for sinful mankind. Reverend Wilson introduced his son to favorite authors: Burns, Tennyson, Wordsworth, and Dickens. He was a regular reader of the *Edinburgh Review* and the New York *Nation,* and conveyed his views of the great public controversies to his son. He was his son's first and most influential teacher and lavished affection and discipline on him. The years of parental tutoring must have been trying for both parties. Young Wilson's dyslexia prevented him from learning to read until he was eleven years of age. The spoken word, of which his father was a true master, figured decisively in the boy's early intellectual formation and imparted a lifelong fondness for speaking. The dyslexia also accounts for his lack of a systematic education until the post–Civil War days.

Thomas Wilson first went to school in 1866, attending a "select school for boys" called the Houghton Institute that was conducted by Joseph T. Derry, a former Confederate officer. The usual school subjects were taught: Latin, history, spelling, grammar, arithmetic, and geography. Wilson's class at the Houghton Institute turned out to be a remarkable one as it included not only a future American president but a future Supreme Court justice, Joseph Lamar, as well as William Kenner, who was later to be dean of the Columbia University Law School. Wilson did poorly at the school and various reasons have been given in explanation: his eyesight was poor, he was slow to mature, he had no interest in subjects, and, of course, there was his dyslexia. These factors were counterbalanced to some degree by a supportive family that tried to inculcate in the reluctant schoolboy its own fondness for learning. When the family moved to Columbia, South Carolina, in 1870 where Reverend Wilson was appointed to teach in the Presbyterian Theological Seminary, Tommy attended Mr. Bramwell's private school and was taught the rudiments of Greek and Latin. Meanwhile, his reading disability now behind him, he began to devour the best books in his father's considerable library.

Wilson entered Davidson College in North Carolina in the fall of 1873. It promised much more than it was to yield and he left the school at the end of a year, his private world in disarray. Davidson was a sound Presbyterian institution, characterized by low tuition, primitive accommodations, strict discipline, and total dedication to its religious ideals. It appeared the perfect place for the boy of a Presbyterian clergyman who more than half expected his son to follow him into the ministry. That expectation was one of Tommy's difficulties at Davidson. Poorly prepared scholastically, he found it was necessary to drive himself to make respectable grades. Greek, Latin, and mathematics were especially trying, while he did well in composition and rhetoric. His deportment was exemplary, but his frail health was threatened by the regimen of study he set for himself. The physical breakdown that occurred in the spring of his freshman year must be attributed to the stress of courses complicated by his uncertainty about the choice of a life's work. To be or not to be a minister, that was the question. Spiritual turmoil subsided when he chose public life over the church as the place to make his mark. The demands of study and spiritual decision were so draining, however, that he was forced to leave Davidson. It was another fifteen months, time spent at home with his family, before he was well enough to enter the College of New Jersey at Princeton.

The Princeton years form the centerpiece of Woodrow Wilson's formal education. His year at Davidson was a serious preparation for higher study, while his time studying law at Virginia and political science at Johns Hopkins completed an edifice of learning, the foundations of which (and something of its superstructure as well) were constructed at McCosh's Princeton. Before the presidency of James McCosh, whose years in office ran from 1868 to 1888, the College of New Jersey was without great intellectual distinction. The Scots philosopher called from The Queen's University, Belfast was to change that. Under his imaginative leadership Princeton attracted a new and promising faculty, revised and modernized its curriculum, expanded library resources and scientific facilities, increased endowments, and constructed new buildings. More important than these considerable accomplishments, McCosh at the same time ignited the college intellectually. Learning became the new watchword in an atmosphere that promoted inquiry and advances in scholarship. Princeton graduates took their places alongside men of Harvard and Yale (and other emerging collegiate foundations as well) in positions of political trust. Wilson was the direct beneficiary of McCosh's work, and when he assumed the presidency of Princeton he thought of himself as consciously furthering the improvements to the university's life of the mind initiated by President McCosh.[20]

The claim that Princeton was the decisive intellectual experience in the shaping of Woodrow Wilson derives from his course of study, which, while traditional, included large elements reflecting scholarly advances in the 1870s, and from the various student activities in which he immersed himself almost from the start. As well as he performed in his subjects, and his record was commendable rather than sterling, Wilson blossomed intellectually by reason of his oratorical and debating successes, his editorship of the *Princetonian,* which he filled with many of his own essays and opinions, and through his first efforts at writing for publication beyond the university. The underpinning for his course work and extracurricular activities was an appetite for reading. Though not catholic in taste it was noted for an intensity that history has come to associate with Wilson. He left long, handwritten lists of his reading in a notebook, a sampling of which is useful to specify the areas and depth of his interests as a collegian. Among other reading material for 1876 were Milton's political writings, Macaulay's *Essays,* Boswell's *Johnson,* Dante's *Inferno,* Shakespeare's plays, and literary criticism. The next year he turned to the works of Daniel Webster, Carlyle's *French Revolution,* Burke's *Essays,* and the plays of Richard Brinsley Sheridan. The list of books read for 1878 shows a discernible and decisive trend. *The Federalist* papers, Walter Bagehot's *The English Constitution,* Earl Russell's *Recollections and Suggestions,* and John T. Morse's *Alexander Hamilton* reveal a bent clearly in favor of history and politics with an implied emphasis on the importance of individuals in growth and change. In his last Princeton year Wilson chose to study closely Carlyle's *Sartor Resartus,* Freeman's *Growth of the English Constitution,* Taine's *History of English Literature,* and Lieber's *Civil Liberty and Self-Government* and *Political Ethics.* Wilson's choice of reading indicates that he was consciously developing a special sophistication in government.[21]

Given his self-directed reading, the grades he received in his course subjects figure less importantly in assessing his undergraduate development. That he did reasonably well in formal courses is corroborated by the record; he ranked thirty-eighth in a class of 105. History was his strongest subject, followed by philosophy, which included logic, psychology, religion, and ethics. There were weak performances in the physical sciences and French. These results are interesting, if predictable, but they throw less light on the realities of Wilson's education than either his reading or his extracurricular writing and speaking. As a devoted member of the American Whig Society he had the opportunity for oratory and debate as well as the writing of speeches. The topics dealt with in the Whig were contemporary, enabling him to remain conversant with current issues. Wilson greatly improved his ability to think on his feet and to extemporize. Fondness for the spoken word, if inherited, nonetheless required refinement. Wilson remained aware that speeches were the means to an end and not ends in themselves, that they were designed to persuade others to adopt a stand or espouse a principle and were an indispensable tool for the successful politician. As editor of the *Princetonian* he enhanced his self-confidence and gained an outlet for the expression of many of his views. In his critique of Green's *History of the English People,* for example, he wrote: the "history of the English people is the history of the American people as well; it is a high and solemn thought that we as a lusty strain of a noble race, are by our national history adding lustre or stain to so bright an escutcheon."[22] A young Theodore Roosevelt could have said it no more boldly, or simplistically.

Wilson was the author of several noteworthy addresses and essays while an undergraduate, work that assumes an enlarged dimension because of his later accomplishments. Three orations stand out: "The Ideal Statesman," "Thomas Carlyle," and "Bismarck." There were three noteworthy essays: "Prince Bismarck" and "William Earl Chatham"[23] both appeared in the *Nassau Literary Magazine,* and "Cabinet Government in the United States" won notice for its author beyond the confines of Princeton when it was published in the highly regarded *International Review.*[24] The above titles show what emphasis Wilson was prepared to place on leaders in history and, by inference, on the conduct of contemporary affairs. Though it was important to argue in favor of a certain form of government, statesmen were needed to animate the form and render government effec-

tive. The essay on "William Earl Chatham" described Pitt as bold, pur-
poseful, self-reliant, and gifted with an ability to dominate other men. The
elements of greatness in a statesman such as Pitt "lay almost entirely
within himself."[25] This essay may be no more than an example of good
undergraduate writing, but the message must be linked to Wilson's celebrated piece on cabinet government to understand better a future president's overall political theory.

"Cabinet Government in the United States" was seminal. The essay
became the basis of Wilson's first book, *Congressional Government*. Later
he was to put his ideas to the test as New Jersey governor and president.
So accepted a practice as the president's appearance in person before a
joint session of Congress to deliver a State of the Union message, which
Wilson reintroduced on coming into the presidency, is traceable to "Cabinet Government in the United States." The idea had occurred to others as
well, but Wilson alone was to have the opportunity to make it a feature of
presidential government.

"Cabinet Government in the United States" was directly influenced by
Wilson's reading of Walter Bagehot's *The English Constitution*. Bagehot,
the foe of "checks and balances" in government, inspired the young
Princetonian's advocacy of merging the separate executive and legislative
functions in the national government as a matter of practicality. For
example, he proposed to allow cabinet officers a place in Congress. The
parallels between Bagehot's commentary on the English way of governing
and Wilson's proposals regarding the American Constitution frequently
have been commented on. In his strictures on the operation of the Constitution in the post–Civil War period, Wilson also deplored the rising tide of
democracy. Such passages in his essay are reminders of the views of
William Howard Taft, voiced about the same time in his graduation oration. Wilson was reflecting certain ideas advanced by Timothy Dwight
Woolsey of Yale in his book, *Political Science,* views doubtlessly familiar
to Taft and feeding his suspicions of mobocracy. At a comparable stage of
growth, Theodore Roosevelt was more optimistic about the voice of the
people but no less scornful of special interests and political corruptionists.

To Wilson the operation of the American government constituted a
vicious circle. The committee system of Congress fragmented responsibility and denied to those of ability the opportunity to become effective
leaders. Men of high caliber, possessing leadership potential, were accordingly discouraged from standing for election to the legislature. Congress
was left in the hands of "scheming, incompetent political tradesmen
whose aim and ambition are merely personal." Wilson's appeal for cabinet
officers in the legislature was designed to break the vicious circle by
providing opportunities for leadership in Congress. At the very least his
proposal would remove from office those cabinet officials to whom the

legislature would not respond positively, an American version of "no confidence." What offended Wilson, the budding theorist, was a pervasive irresponsibility in the exercise of power; power without responsibility was inimical to sound government.[26]

The totality of Wilson's undergraduate experience reflects the contours of a developing mind. College subjects, oratory and debate, and ephemeral essays and pieces of a substantial sort—all these undertakings were viewed by Wilson as the means to an end. That end was a political career. Leaving Princeton in 1879 he was hopeful that he would soon be able to enter actively into politics. As he spoke his farewells to the many friends he made in college he found it easy and natural to say to more than one of them: "When I meet you in the Senate I'll argue that out with you." Said in a spirit of good fellowship, it also indicated an earnest intention.[27]

Woodrow Wilson in the Senate of the United States was not to be. It is necessary to search no further than his study of law at the University of Virginia in the years 1879–80 to discover the reasons. The custom was time honored and proven: law opened the way to political preferment in America. But there were some hidden provisions. One had to be willing and able to use the law as a club or a key or a guise in pursuit of a public career, which required a certain cynicism respecting the lawyer's craft. Wilson was not so inclined. He came quickly to dislike the study of law, and to doubt its capacity to satisfy him intellectually or to be used in the quest for elective office. He rejected the law as a result.

Wilson's choice of the University of Virginia as a place to pursue legal studies was, however, fortunate. It enabled him to return to the South, to the state of his birth, and to Thomas Jefferson's foundation. Virginia at the time had a small, superior law faculty, headed by John B. Minor. Minor was a legal authority, an author of treatises on the common law, and a singular teacher. Wilson studied under him, admired his learning, and remained a lifelong friend. The future president's resistance of Minor's efforts to make the law an enchanting mistress may be the best measurement after all of his innate distaste for it.

Training at Princeton made Wilson eager to pursue an independent course at Virginia, whereas the rule of the law department would admit of no exceptions to the student's steady and thorough mastery of the subject in a prescribed method. In consequence Wilson struck out on his own and in familiar directions. He joined the Jefferson Debate Society and soon was one of its leading members, and he wrote scholarly pieces on men and government that appeared in the *Virginia University Magazine*. How much such endeavors advanced him beyond his level of achievement as a student is another matter. Debating is debating, and though membership in the Jefferson extended his experience and refined his skill it brought little in the way of intellectual gain. Much the same must be said about his published essays. The pieces on John Bright and William E. Gladstone broke no new ground. In some ways, in fact, they were retrogressive, lacking a sufficiently critical element and tending to eulogy. The essay on "Congressional Government" that he wrote after leaving Princeton, revisions of which he undertook while a first-year student at Virginia, was not published, though he was to draw upon its content and argument for his later book of the same title. In sympathy with the power of individuals to shape history—the tributes to Bright and Gladstone are reminders of this—and intensely interested in political theory—his proper métier—Wilson at Virginia grew but little yet remained very much alive.

The total mix at Virginia was not right. Wilson greatly missed the atmosphere and old friends of his Princeton days, and some at Virginia thought they detected in him a condescension toward them. Disliking the law, he had to plod along in order to attain some success. He experienced the ill effects of unrequited love in his unsuccessful pursuit of a first cousin, Harriet Woodrow. Finally, his physical condition became a source of worry to himself and his parents. The decision to leave Virginia in December 1880, without taking his law degree, symbolized the Virginia experience as surely as it predicted his disenchantment with a legal career. After a year and a half of living at home and some further reading in the law, he was admitted to the bar. His partnership with Edward I. Renick followed, but it did not prosper and was soon dissolved. Wilson was still looking for the low door in the wall, beyond which lay his enchanted garden that must flower intellectually for him to be happy.

Johns Hopkins University, which Wilson entered as a graduate student in 1883, rounded off the future president's formal education as at the same time it provided him an environment appropriate for writing *Congressional Government*. It should not be assumed, however, that the successes at Hopkins were inevitable. In light of the pre-1883 side of Wilson's life, the choice of graduate study can be seen as a near-desperate effort to decide at last on a career. Despite prior decisions Wilson might well have drifted into the ministry, had Hopkins proved hostile. An ex-lawyer and failed graduate student of Wilson's background and parental reliance could easily have become a clergyman in the absence of other options.

In the 1880s the history and political science programs at Hopkins responded to the leadership of Herbert Baxter Adams and the influence of the German school in general. Adams had been trained at Heidelberg and was infused with the German ideal of scientific fact-gathering as an indispensable preliminary to the grasp of history. For students under his direction no amount of research was too onerous, no document too obscure if an understanding of the past was to be advanced, admittedly inch by inch. Wilson was singularly cool to the prospect of such a regimen and within a month of his arrival was determined to "have it out" with

Adams regarding the approach he wanted to take in his studies. Adams had the good sense to allow Wilson his head, impressed by his publication of "Cabinet Government in the United States" and scenting, perhaps, a scholar of promise.

With the approval of Adams, Wilson set to work immediately on a series of essays, refining his previously published and unpublished ideas and adding much besides to complete his critique of American government. The result was *Congressional Government,* published early in 1885 before the author had completed two years of graduate work. It was a remarkable achievement considering Wilson's uncertain health, his involvement in the debate society at Hopkins, and his new love for Ellen Axson, whom he was to marry in 1885.

So large does *Congressional Government* appear in the body of Wilsonian scholarship that it tends to overshadow the total of his development during his two years of graduate school. At Hopkins he became acquainted with great minds and often enjoyed meeting the men behind such minds: Josiah Royce, the philosopher; Edmund Gosse, the literary critic; James Bryce, the British authority on government and law; and Richard T. Ely, the economics theorist, in addition to Adams, who stimulated his interest in public administration. Wilson and Ely were especially close. Greatly impressed by his performance in the graduate seminar, Ely invited Wilson and another student, David R. Dewey, to collaborate with him on a book dealing with the history of American economic thought. Wilson quickly completed his part of the assignment, in the course of which he read widely in the theories of a variety of Americans, including Francis Wayland and George Tucker. The book was never published as neither Ely nor, apparently, Dewey, was able to finish his portion of the task. Nonetheless Wilson profited markedly from a broadened economic perspective. Once again he moved in the shadow of Walter Bagehot, whose *Economic Studies* helped to direct him away from hypotheses to facts in order to get the best reading on economic realities. At Princeton Wilson had been confirmed in a strict laissez-faire faith. Working with Richard T. Ely, a good portion of his belief was eroded when a priori assumptions became less convincing than conditions as guidelines for shaping the economic future of society.[28]

It is a sign of Woodrow Wilson's maturity and self-confidence that after two years at Johns Hopkins he decided to leave the university before taking his degree and to accept an appointment at the newly founded Bryn Mawr College in Pennsylvania. Professionally he was well positioned to make the move. Few if any second-year graduate students could point to proven worth comparable to the authorship of *Congressional Government.* Personally, Wilson was impelled to find a position. His loving attachment to Ellen Axson must be fulfilled, and the Bryn Mawr appointment would provide him with income and the start of a career. His Ph.D. was granted the next year, 1886, through a special set of examinations. He submitted *Congressional Government* as his dissertation, among the most remarkable in the history of American graduate education.

Congressional Government, subtitled "a study in American politics," might well have been termed "a study in American history."[29] Consistently historical, some of Wilson's observations were acute, as, for example, his judgment that once the Constitution had been ratified most of its opponents "must have been not only conquered but converted as well."[30] The Constitution was likened to Magna Carta and the Bill of Rights, "only the sap-centre of a system of government vastly larger than the stock from which it has branched. . . ."[31] References to John Marshall, John Quincy Adams, and John Taylor appeared throughout the introduction, exhibiting the same historical impulse. Various events, theories, disagreements, crises, and personalities in the record were used to demonstrate how the Constitution with its checks and balances was altered by exigency and by purpose, rendering the U.S. government one dominated in reality by the legislature. Wilson's grasp of American history has to impress the modern reader quite as much as his style, with its dignified cadences only occasionally marred by special pleading. Regrets were expressed in the introduction about the eclipse of states' rights as a result of the Civil War, despite the assertion that *Congressional Government* was not commentary but an outspoken presentation of cardinal facts.

Wilson's dissatisfaction with what history had wrought was painfully evident when he dealt with the House of Representatives. Part of his account consisted of a series of deficiencies, malpractices, and blunders— and the list was by no means a short one—that could be identified in the functioning of the lower house of Congress. The House of Representatives had no leader, since the Speaker was lacking "formal or imperative power."[32] Members of that body had, instead, a multiplicity of leaders in the chairmen of the standing committees. Members had little chance to represent the views of their constituents, since their voices were muted by the ubiquitous committee system.[33] The effect of the standing committees, forty-seven in number, was disintegration rather than integration. The day-to-day routine of the chamber was time wasting, adjournments and holidays were frequent, and numerous absences by individual congressmen slowed work. At times even the fully initiated might be hard pressed to follow the labyrinth of House proceedings, so baffling and perplexing were they.[35] Furthermore, the committee system afforded no opportunity for debating the issues raised by proposed legislation; the very chamber in which the House met was too vast in dimension to render speeches audible. The constant undertone created by talk on the floor caused Wilson to liken making a speech there to "trying to address the people in the omnibuses from the curb stone in front of the Astor House."[36] These and many other flaws in the functioning of the House of Representatives were set off dramatically by a comparison with the procedures in the House of Commons, where debate, leadership, and party responsibility for action or inaction were the order.[37]

A close look at the "revenue and supply functions," as Wilson spoke of the work of the House Ways and Means Committee, prompted more harsh criticism. Wilson's quarrel began with the division of responsibility, reflecting an attitude no doubt derived from a strong Calvinistic sense of the responsibility that every man must bear for his behavior.[38] Such an intersection of private and public morality is not at all surprising. But Wilson's condemnation also was based on common sense: the committee that determined the money to be raised should also be the committee that controlled the disbursement of funds. In this way taxes and expenditures would be coordinated. The problem was no longer constitutional but a matter of efficiency. Wilson's idea corresponded roughly to the practice of the House of Commons.[39] The Commons thereby enjoyed consistent, coherent, and progressively continuous fiscal habits. The very opposite obtained in the House of Representatives, where committees often worked at cross-purposes, spurred on by corruption and pork barrel legislation.

It is apparent that Wilson evoked history and British parliamentary ways as standards for judging the American national legislature and applied his standards equally to the Senate and the House. He frankly admired the Senate in its great days of Calhoun, Webster, and Clay. The Senate was then an arena for discussion, for the formulation of views and the molding of public opinion. On balance the young scholar was less hostile to the Senate, even as he surveyed the dismal record of the upper house in the post–Civil War period. It was smaller than the House, more cohesive, more conscious of its dignity—traits that others might see as flaws but that Wilson termed strengths because they more closely accorded with his conception of what a legislative body should be. Ultimately, however, the Senate was found wanting because no formal provision had been made for its leadership, the majority leadership being a position of "anomalous insignificance and curious uncertainty."[40]

When the second president, John Adams, wrote his *Defence of the Constitutions of the United States,* he did so in response to Turgot's charge that America had sedulously aped the English constitution with a separation of powers between the upper and the lower houses. Bagehot, Wilson's great hero during his writing of *Congressional Government,* echoed Turgot.[41] It is of some interest, therefore, that in defending the idea of a bicameral legislature he broke with Bagehot and sided with John Adams. According to Wilson, Bagehot ignored the federalism embedded in the American situation. The states were of necessity to be represented in the national legislature as states, and as the sum of the people of the states. Bagehot had mistaken the Senate as representing the upper classes. But Wilson insisted: "The Senate and the House are of different origins but virtually of the same nature."[42] Separated by twenty-five presidencies, Wilson and Adams seemed united by a common perspective on the Constitution.

It may be unfair in reading Wilson's analysis of the executive to seek clues to illuminate his presidency. After all, the event was nearly thirty years in the future and he was to alter many positions and judgments with the passage of time and the accumulation of experience.[43] Some of the ideas he advanced, however, may have worked to impart to the presidency certain features it was to exhibit shortly before and long after 1913. Wilson showed himself sensitive to the force of change through history, offering as an example the method of choosing presidential candidates via party conventions. Moreover, the power of the Congress had made the duties of the president mere administration. Wilson concluded that the best preparation for a president was the governorship of an important state.[44] As for the cabinet, it deserved limited attention as it lacked responsibility either to the legislature or to the people. Wilson believed that the separation of powers as well as the checks and balances ordained by the Constitution "have proved mischievous just to the extent to which they have succeeded in establishing themselves as realities."[45] It was virtually written between the lines that should he ever have an opportunity, he would try to undo some part of the mischief. Quoting both Roger Sherman, a member of the Constitutional Convention, and Tocqueville, he acknowledged that the executive was the servant of the legislature, but whereas Toqueville merely observed it and Sherman approved it, Wilson decried it. History did show that on occasion a cabinet officer such as Hamilton or Gallatin had risen above the confines of the Constitution, but "as the legislature is the originating force," the Congress generally prevailed.[46]

The formal conclusion to *Congressional Government* is not noted for any extension of arguments made in the main body of the study, but for the skill of language and the heavy debt owed Walter Bagehot. The whole was marked by an awareness of the historical process to which, true to the habit of his age, Wilson accorded a scientific inflection. He exhibited a willingness to interpret American history as a phase of the broader Anglo-American experience, and an intention, covertly present, to educate a generation of Americans to the need for responsible government. Despite an intense factualism there was less of the remote scholar and more of the dedicated public man in *Congressional Government*. The lessons of politics from the end of the Civil War—weak presidents, wayward congresses, plundering spoilsmen, and plumed knights—were such as to warn of the perils of a governing instrument that was not responsible to the masses or often to the classes but always to itself. Congressional government was synonymous with professional politics, and the political party was its own raison d'être. *Congressional Government* was both praised and damned. Lauded by men like James Bryce for its wisdom, it was condemned by spoilsmen stung by its strictures. Wilson had written a book that brought learning to bear on public life and had taken the first steps in the direction of the profession he preferred, better prepared to enter politics by the side door.

Meanwhile he had settled in at Bryn Mawr College and was leading the unspectacular life of an academic. The college was new, the student body was female, and the educational style preferred by the dean, the indomitable M. Carey Thomas, was not to the young professor's taste. At Princeton and Virginia, Wilson had been used to building on well-established traditions and had not much interest in launching new ones at Bryn Mawr. He discovered that teaching women by means of colloquy was much less satisfying than the lecture method in which he believed he could excel. And, as he was to write after leaving Bryn Mawr, "I have been for a long time hungry for a class of men."[47] Some of his unhappiness stemmed from a lack of intellectual companionship on the small faculty, and as is typical with teaching novices, he spent long hours preparing class notes and lectures. In his teaching two familiar themes were evident: the importance of leaders in history and the growth of legal and political institutions as organizing concepts for a pursuit of historical understanding.

Lecturing aside, Wilson managed time to write important essays during his time at Bryn Mawr. One of these was "The Study of Administration," published in the *Political Science Quarterly* in 1887.[48] The article packed a punch. It assumed and at the same time deplored that governmental administration in America, whether at the national, state, or local level, was inept. Wilson noted that it was not until the nineteenth century, by which time governments had grown more complex in response to the requirements of fully evolved societies, that administration attracted much attention.[49] But by the 1880s, he argued, Americans had no choice but to take seriously the challenges of proper governmental administration, to appreciate its essentiality and thus to perfect its machinery. The conduct of government had replaced the constitutionality of government as the leading public concern, as he had iterated in *Congressional Government*.[50] Though the United States might not follow the example of European nations in buying and building railroads and telegraphic facilities, "no one can doubt that in some way it must make itself master of masterful corporations." As he explained, Europe had developed proficiency in administration as governments there, more independent of the people, had to govern more actively; the ruling classes, furthermore,

sought to make their rule more palatable through smooth administration.[51] To Wilson administration was neutral; it was as essential to a
democratic republic as to a Napoleonic France. Getting done efficiently
what the law called for was the heart of good administrative practice.
Unfortunately, as experience so well demonstrated, America was not
immune to the baleful influence of politics. "Administrative questions are
not political questions," he insisted.[52] The people did have a role to play;
public opinion was the "authoritative critic" in the execution of administration. Wilson's real worry was too much public input, not too little.
"Self-government does not consist in having a hand in everything," however much public opinion was useful to thwart domineering and illiberal
officialdom.[53] Wilson believed it was necessary to attack directly the
widely held American conviction that as we were a people of political
genius, administration would take care of itself. ". . . Mere unschooled
genius for affairs will not save us from blunders."[54] It may be assumed
from the stress the future chief executive placed on the study and practice
of administration that he was beginning to move away from criticism of
congressional government and heading toward an overall concern for
responsive rule, which offered more constructive scholarly and practical
prospects. The American challenge was all the more impressive because of
the intricacies of the federal system of government and the need to
synchronize the actions of the state and the national authorities. This
consideration prompted Wilson to close his essay on a farsighted, almost
prophetic note. He deserves to be quoted with the reminder that these
sentences were set down in the late 1880s.

> If we solve this problem we shall again pilot the world. There is a
> tendency—is there not?—a tendency as yet dim, but already steadily
> impulsive and clearly destined to prevail, toward, first the confederation
> of parts of empires like the British, and finally of great states them-
> selves. Instead of centralization of power, there is to be wide union with
> tolerated divisions of prerogative. This is a tendency towards the Amer-
> ican type—of governments joined with governments for the pursuit of
> common purposes, in honorary equality and honorable subordination.
> Like principles of civil liberty are everywhere fostering like methods of
> government; and if comparative studies of the ways and means of
> government should enable us to offer suggestions which will practically
> combine openness and vigor in the administration of such governments
> with ready docility to all serious, well-sustained public criticism, they
> will have proved themselves worthy to be ranked among the highest and
> most fruitful of the great departments of political study. That they will
> issue in such suggestions I confidently hope.[55]

Wilson the scholar and the idealist were mutually supportive.

A second valuable essay of the Bryn Mawr years was "Character of

Democracy in the United States," which appeared in the *Atlantic Monthly* in 1889.[56] The piece contained any number of the leading ideas of the day, including those on science, inductive history, and socialism as a challenge to laissez-faire economic theory, the Teutonic origins of the common law, and, of course, a pronounced social Darwinism. The contentions were colored throughout by a concern for morality in public life; "politics was a sphere of moral action." "Character of Democracy" was basically a historical inquiry, however, as it was from history that Wilson sought to extract a true philosophy of government. His study of the past underscored the evolution of legal and political institutions as they tended to progress toward a form of polity that was both representative and democratic. Democracy was the adult stage in political growth; when successful, it combined freedom with restraint. The foundation of democracy was moral because it comprised moral agents, the people. The people were crucial to its well-being. They must display the adult virtues, self-reliance and self-control, at the same time they enjoyed liberty and the freedom to choose. In so saying Wilson was arguing for, perhaps preaching is the better word,[57] a synthesis of traditional values and scientific imperatives, a reflex action common to his age that was no less evident in a man like Theodore Roosevelt.

In 1888 Woodrow Wilson was appointed professor of history and political economy at Wesleyan University in Connecticut. His stay was to be brief, only two years, but the position was altogether congenial. He plunged immediately into college life, reorganizing the debate club as the Wesleyan House of Commons and helping to coach the football team. He taught his classes of young men with zest and with good effect. Within the year Wilson also completed one of his most important books, *The State,* published in the autumn of 1889.[58]

The State was at first glance a textbook on governments and on government, subjects that had occupied Wilson since 1886. It suggests beyond doubt that while Wilson's Bryn Mawr years were marred by unhappiness and complaints about lack of opportunity for scholarly writing, neither his mind nor his pen was in repose. Wilson had an ambivalent attitude toward *The State,* the subtitle of which was "Elements of Historical and Practical Politics, A Study of Institutional History and Administration." He referred to it as a "dull fact book" but was glad enough to have it in print, hopeful that sales would earn him royalties. But he also admitted that in writing *The State,* "a great deal has gone out of me into it. . . ."[59] He was justly proud of his accomplishment, both for what it had taught him and what he believed it would teach others.

In keeping with the view that political theory was to be understood largely from actions taken in the past, Wilson introduced his study of the state by observing that "the probable origin of government is a question of fact, to be settled, not by conjecture, but by history."[60] The investigation relied on research into the earliest forms of government, from Greco-Roman civilization to the present, with attention paid to the Celts, the Aryans, and the Semites. Family structure was judged to be especially critical; the role of the father was that of head of the family and acknowledged leader. This leadership had figured in tribal and then in nation-state development, the leader having been recognized without question as an authority figure.[61] In this respect the successful state would resemble the successful family or tribe, even as it extended the meaning of possession from homestead or tribal grounds to territory, land held by the state. Wilson's contention that theory must arise from fact caused him to reject the social compact idea because it lacked historical foundation. The state was not artificial or ideological in origin; it was organic and therefore evolutionary. To quote Aristotle, as Wilson did, man was a political animal and it was his choices and decisions as a political being that had brought forth the state.[62] These determinations, furthermore, could hardly have been sustained without the ties of blood, the link of language, the support of religion, the force of custom, and the utility of the legal and political institutions that emerged.[63] Facts taken from antiquity, the Middle Ages, and the early modern era served to concretize Wilson's estimate of the state.

Considering nature and forms, Wilson conceded that all governments in their exercise of authority rested ultimately on force. "Government, in its last analysis, is organized force." By "force" he did not intend mere armed power, but the will of the few or the many or the community to realize its own purposes.[64] The machinery of government consisted of the instruments proper to achieving its ends. Once again Wilson accommodated himself to the demands of science while working to avoid its most undesirable implications for mankind. The rights of a minority could be imperiled even when a modern government rested on the will of the people, just as they were threatened in times past under emperors and kings. Wilson was convinced that in the remote past, authority was accepted by the members of a family or a tribe or a nation-in-the-making because to do so was inbred, "born of the habit of the race." Contemporary governments were found to be much the same; laws were obeyed as a result of "inculcated approbation." Furthermore, there was a "large amount of drift" involved.

Continuing to explore the nature and forms of government Wilson distinguished between ancient and modern states by emphasizing two great historical events. The rights of the individual did not obtain in ancient times, when "man existed for society. . . . The State was the only Individual."[65] The birth of Christianity and the rise of Teutonic institutions altered the course of history. Christianity "gave each man a magistracy over himself," while in Teutonic custom the individual bound himself to his leader by a pledge of personal service.[66] The interaction of Christian faith and Teutonic custom explained the irradicable strain of individualism in Western civilization, whence most of the great nations of the late nineteenth century derived the nature and forms of their governments.

The textbook properties of *The State* came through in the consideration given the functions of government. The tone and substance of these passages suggest a lecture. Wilson broke down functions into two parts: constituent (e.g., the rule of contract) and ministrant (e.g., regulation of industry and labor). The history of governmental function was reviewed briefly but usefully, from the ancients to the moderns, on the basis of which Wilson identified similarities from epoch to epoch.[67] The differences he found stemmed from policy and not principle. In other words the question was what *ought* to be the function of government, since the power of government was a historical constant. Noting the two extremes, laissez-faire and the ubiquitous state, Wilson looked into the historical foundations of each, studying in the process how the rights of the individual clashed with the requirements of society. His purpose was to reach and to defend a middle ground. Society was greater than government and there were natural limits to state action. His summary statement was explicit. "The end of government is the facilitation of the objects of society. The rule of government action is necessary cooperation. The method of political development is conservative adaptation, shaping old habits into new ones, modifying old means to accomplish new ends." Wilson had come to political pragmatism early.[68]

Wilson's estimate of the place of law in the practice of political rule invites comparison with the ideas of William Howard Taft and with the whole school of legal realism. Wilson judged the law to be mutable, growing out of customs that were always forming and always being discarded in the life of a people. ". . . We can say with assurance that it [custom] becomes Law only when it wins the support of a definite authority within the community."[69] Through religion and the judiciary the law had been kept and should be kept conservative; the best from the past must be preserved. Courts helped to make the law "a living system of thought and practice."[70] Much taken with the unfolding of law in history, Wilson was concerned with testing the power of the community that must stand in support of the law. Law was both a "body of principles" and "an active force, an expression of will." It was more than mere opinion. It was the mirror held up to reflect and display a national character. For all the differences in law from nation to nation that this statement implied, Wilson insisted that there were features common to the laws of diverse peoples, including the sacredness of human life, the sanctity of the family, and the obligation of promises made. But did law have moral properties? Oliver Wendell Holmes, Jr., had argued that the law did not see man as God sees him, that is, from within, but rather from without, judging behavior by the effects it had on society. Wilson wrote in like vein. "Law plays the role neither of conscience, nor of Providence." Instead, it creates "a new class of wrong relative to itself alone: *mala prohibita,*" or things that are wrong because they are forbidden.[71] For Wilson, however, this highly scientific theory of morality was designed to implement rather than supplant the old moral law, which was not the view of many legal realists.[72] As were most writers of his era, he was prepared to fall back on the use of force in order to ensure that the laws as supported by the community were obeyed. The state alone was sovereign. *The State* marked the maturity of Wilson as an important scholar and political commentator and facilitated his move from Wesleyan to Princeton in 1890.

Woodrow Wilson's return to Princeton as professor of jurisprudence and politics was to be as central to his career as a scholar as his attendance there had been in the progress of his higher education. Had he never become president of Princeton, with all that followed from his tenure in that post—its triumphs and defeats—he would still have regarded Princeton as his birthright. He was happy there and enjoyed his years as professor hugely. Popular with the students, Wilson sided with the younger liberal segments of the faculty that were keen to see the College of New Jersey become a modern university. It was Wilson who delivered the Sesquicentennial Address in 1896 when the institution formally became Princeton University. At the same time he promoted himself as a public speaker, as a political commentator, and a senior scholar. From 1890 to 1902, the years of his time as a professor, he published *An Old Master and Other Political Essays* and *Division and Reunion,* both in 1893; *Mere Literature and Other Essays* and *George Washington,* both in 1896; *When a Man Comes To Himself* in 1901; and *A History of the American People* in 1902, to cite only his books. All the while he was writing briefer accounts on history and politics for prestigious periodicals, including the *Review of Reviews* and the *Atlantic Monthly,* as he had done in the past and would continue to do after he assumed the leadership of Princeton.

During these years Wilson was also maturing his idea of a university. At the Chicago World's Fair in 1893 he gave a resounding "yes" to the question of whether a liberal education was a proper preparation for medicine, law, and the ministry, the three leading professions of the time.[73] In the course of numerous addresses he brought forward the social duty that the university and its graduates had to fulfill. Theodore Roosevelt was soon to elaborate his "stewardship" theory of pubic service; Wilson, as early as 1894, had written: "It is the object of learning, not only to satisfy the curiosity and perfect the spirits of individual men, but also to advance civilization."[74] The best minds and the best men were taking different roads to reach the same objectives, animated by the same spirit of service to others. One of the major results of this new dedication was the restored presidency, in the accomplishment of which Taft, along with Roosevelt and Wilson, had a part to play. It comes as a sobering reflection that these three men, who had so much in common and whose paths had intersected in previous years, came to collision in the Armageddon that was 1912. It is more sobering still to realize how sharply and totally the paths of the three diverged thereafter, marked by bitterness and hostility that not even a love of learning could soften. Looking back from 1919, 1924, or 1930—years of death—the audiences in Atlanta in 1911 that had heard each of them speak positively about politics might savor the memory of that occasion and regret the tragedy that followed.

The most important of Wilson's books written in the 1890s were *Division and Reunion* and *George Washington*. In them he again demonstrated that his scholarship was historical as well as concerned with aspects of political science. The two volumes showed also that as a historian Wilson was much taken with the growth of political and legal institutions and the influence of individuals on their development. By standards of a later day neither book should be highly regarded, but contemporary estimates of them varied widely. *George Washington* was much the weaker of the two both in scholarship and style. Initially written to be serialized in *Harper's Magazine,* one of Wilson's biographers has dismissed it as a potboiler.[75] *Division and Reunion,* in contrast, was widely praised at the time of its publication. Distinguished authorities such as Frederick Bancroft and Frederick Jackson Turner, while rejecting certain of Wilson's interpretations, on the whole praised the book.[76] It was a successful synthesis of a period in American history, 1829–89, that did not readily yield to a unified presentation. *Division and Reunion* was, in fact, an objective account of the middle years of the nineteenth century when the country was torn by sectional passions. If Wilson was more kindly in his treatment of his Southern homeland than critics thought justified, the book nonetheless, marked the further emergence of the Southerner as historian in the post–Civil War generation.

Division and Reunion was the third and final volume in the Epochs of American History series under the general editorship of Albert Bushnell Hart. Wilson was in fine company. Reuben Gold Thwaites had been asked to do volume one on the colonial period, and Hart himself wrote the second volume on the formation of the Union. Wilson gained much from his association with Hart, who was a demanding editor, and from exchanges with Turner whom he had known from his Hopkins days. As Theodore Roosevelt had consulted with Turner when he was writing the later volumes of *The Winning of the West,* the historian of the frontier is another link in the chain of persons and events that brought together the future presidents and antagonists. In the first paragraphs of *Division and Reunion* describing "a new epoch," Wilson wrote of the success of the young republic after forty years.[77] "It had once more proved the capacity of the English race to combine strength and bold initiative that can subdue a wilderness with those self-controlling habits of ordered government that can build free and permanent states."[78] Roosevelt had written in the same vein in the opening statement of *The Winning of the West*. The advance of the English-speaking race meant progress for mankind in the judgment of the gifted amateur and the professional scholar alike.

Optimism characterized Wilson's interpretation of American history after 1829, years certain to test a positive view of the affairs of an increasingly troubled nation. Wilson saw how government under the Constitution was tried in numerous ways and at numerous times by the rise of the common man, contests over the bank and the tariff, fallout from Manifest Destiny, and the debate over the future of slavery in the Union, culminating in the ultimate test that any government can face, civil war. The Union was sustained and though the South was defeated, Wilson wrote plainly that the survival of the United States was best for all sections and for the people of all sections. A Confederate victory would have run counter to the entire evolutionary process as it applied to the American experience. It would have been intellectually inconsistent with the thrust of modern history as conceived by the Whig historians, Wilson among them.

Another distinguishing feature of *Division and Reunion* was the heavy emphasis placed on presidents, from Jackson through Lincoln and on to Grover Cleveland, and on a host of other public notables including Clay, Calhoun, Webster, Marshall, and Douglas. It was a person-oriented account of the division and then the reunion of the United States, Wilson agreeing with one of his historical mentors, Edmund Burke, that "great men are the land-marks and guide posts of the state." Wilson's awareness of personality was often astute. Of Jackson he wrote: "The character of Jackson created everywhere its own environment, bred everywhere conditions suitable to itself and its own singular, self-willed existence. It was as simple and invariable in its operations as a law of nature. He was wholly a product of frontier life."[79] His estimate of Stephen Douglas was equally penetrating and unreserved. Referring to Douglas's decision to bring forward the Kansas-Nebraska bill, he observed that "no one but Douglas would have dared to offer it. . . . Douglas with his strong, coarse-grained, unsensitive nature, his western audacity, his love of leading boldly in the direction whither as it seemed to him there lay party strength. . . ."[80] More briefly, of the controversial John Brown after the raid at Harper's Ferry, he wrote: "his plan had been one of the maddest folly, but his end was one of singular dignity."[81] Wilson's estimate of Lincoln, which must be considered at length, was the most interesting of all his character sketches. Lincoln was great because he had been determined to uphold constitutional government, with or without slavery:

> His task as President was "more difficult than that of Washington himself had been," as he had said to his neighbors with solemn solicitude for the future. There was a sentiment to create and a party to compact; and these things were to be done by a man comparatively unknown as yet. He meant to respect the Constitution in all things. It was in the oath that he took as President, he said, that he would to the best of his ability preserve, protect, and defend the Constitution; and he did not feel that he might "take oath to get power, and break the oath in using that power." Neither did he feel, however, that he could be said even to have tried to preserve the Constitution if, "to save slavery or any minor matter," he should "permit the wreck of government, country, and Constitution all together." He sought to follow a course of policy in which firmness and conciliation should be equally prominent, and in which he could carry the plain people of the country with him.[82]

As much as celebrating Lincoln, whom he called the "supreme American in our history," Wilson was a spokesman for the great-man theory of history. Disraeli once advised: "Read no history, only biography, for there is life without theory." Very probably Wilson would never have endorsed this extreme, but he would readily have agreed with the inspiration of Disraeli's advice, that it is the character of great men that often makes the historical difference. On the eve of his entrance into public life he declared that his contemplation of the lives of Lee and Lincoln "set me very seriously to meditating upon the responsibilities and character of my own particular task in life," an affirmation of his faith in the place of the hero in history.[83]

Though he was to choose a worthy subject through whom to explore the great-man thesis more thoroughly, Wilson's *George Washington* was successful neither as history nor biography.[84] It was in the tradition of Parson Weems, the faultless and bloodless hero. To read the book today is to wonder about both the unrealness of the subject and the unreality of the author. As it was not the product of any wide research, it is necessary to look elsewhere to discover its merits, and, lacking such, to consider its uses for appraising the learned Wilson. Wilson frequently considered himself a man of letters, and in fact protested that he was not only not a scholar, but did not want to be one. The kind of scholarship he had in mind was the long-suffering research of the German school that he had encountered and rejected while at Hopkins. Among other things, such history was dull. To Wilson literary grace and historical awareness were equally important. In the case of *George Washington*, style became a preoccupation. But he was roundly criticized for it. He adopted a deliberately archaic mode of expression, intending to evoke an era. He distorted the character of Washington in the effort, without leaving any memorable or convincing impression of the times.

A second look at *George Washington* shows, however, how thoroughly Wilson believed in heroes. Washington was a Southerner, a Virginian, a gentleman of purpose and integrity; and therefore it served no good use to belittle him by reference to his failings. Belittlement was the literary equivalent of political obstructionism. How much or how little of himself Wilson discovered in Washington is impossible to say. Weinstein flatly asserts that Washington's personality as described "bears a close resemblance to Wilson's self-image."[85] He did possess certain of the attributes that other biographers have duly noted in Washington: *gravitas*, the desire for the well-merited applause of his fellow citizens, and the belief that all right-minded men should give him allegiance because he judged his actions to be righteous.

The year before the publication of *George Washington*, Wilson had made a case for history as literature in an article in *Century Magazine*, "On the Writing of History."[86] The biography of Washington appeared to be an effort to carry out his own mandates. Truth, he asserted in the *Century* article, "is a thing ideal, displayed by the just proportion of events, revealed in form and color, dumb till the facts be set in syllables, articulated into words, put together into sentences, swung with proper tone and cadence."[87] Further along he contended that "a trifle too much knowledge will undo" the historian, "it will break the spell of his imagination."[88] Finally, he said that the task of the historian "is radically different from the task of the investigator. The investigator must display his materials, but the historian must convey his impressions."[89] The impression the reader was to gain from *George Washington* had become Wilson's all-important purpose. Unfortunately that impression was a pale one, popular enough with the masses but unhistorical.

The two sets of essays that Wilson brought out in the 1890s, *An Old Master and Other Political Essays* and *Mere Literature and Other Essays*, are convenient collections for examining aspects of his thought and learning that lent themselves to expression in a brief form. In addition Wilson wrote any number of articles and reviews that have not been gathered but that are to be found in *The Papers of Woodrow Wilson*, the magisterial and still ongoing compendium of his life's work. Consideration of some of his collected essays will show how relentlessly he chose to pursue certain issues, how much a man of letters he was, and how his thinking adumbrated his outlook once he came to politics.

"An Old Master," the title essay of the 1893 collection, was designed to do for the art of lecturing what Wilson's essay on administration had intended for that much neglected aspect of government, namely, to remind the indifferent of its value.[90] Wilson selected Adam Smith as his model of an old master, based on the period when Smith was lecturing at the University of Glasgow where he occupied the chair of Moral Philosophy. According to Wilson, Smith's success "was due to two things: the broad outlook of his treatment and the fine art of his style." "He was no specialist, excepting *in the relation of things.*" Wilson pointed out that Smith worked largely from secondary sources, borrowing many of his ideas directly from the Physiocrats (much as John Adams had borrowed from Smith's writings for his *Discourses on Davila*). Originality was less valuable than meaning gained through synthesis. "But no matter who mined the gold," Wilson quipped, Smith "minted it." For Wilson, the great teacher and the great statesman shared the need to know a multitude of things and to conclude from them a bold synthesis, "lest all knowledge and all thought fall apart into weak analysis."[91] This was a prescription for a learned leader, even a learned president.

In "Government Under the Constitution," one of the political essays, Wilson returned to an early favorite theme, criticism of a national government dominated by the Congress.[92] His complaint was the want of "ministerial responsibility" in the American constitutional system. Admitting that the establishment of this feature would require important changes, he expressed himself "strongly of the opinion that such changes would not be too great a price to pay for the advantages secured."[93] Many of the reasons he advanced to support his views and much of the comparison and contrast of the American and the British models were well known to readers of *Congressional Government*. What was interesting about "Government Under the Constitution" was the expression of a philosophy of rule that he laid down in the opening passages. The form of government depended ultimately for its success or failure on "the men who became governors and upon the people over whom they are put in authority." "Definition of legal provision," Wilson warned, "has no saving efficiency of its own." "The vitality of such provisions consists wholly in the fact that they receive our acquiescence," the "constitutional morality of our race." The Constitution had endured not because it was brilliantly contrived by the ablest of men drawing on the best ideas of a remarkable age, but because "we are self-restrained" as a people.[94] In so saying Wilson was rounding out further his conception of government in the larger sense. The intangibility of "constitutional morality" was more central than the tangibility of the framework of the Constitution. What was lacking, and Wilson came to this point only indirectly when he lamented the dependence of the executive on the legislature, was a national leader who could move the nation because as a leader he had gained the backing of Congress.[95] The characteristic Wilsonian formula was, to say the least, intimated: a moral leader, a responsive legislature, and a self-restrained people interacting to bring about improvements in society, at home or abroad.

Woodrow Wilson was not necessarily dreaming of his own presidency in all this. He may well have had in mind his fellow Democrat, Grover Cleveland. He wrote two articles dealing with Cleveland's presidency, "Mr. Cleveland's Cabinet," [96] which appeared in *Review of Reviews* in 1893, and "Mr. Cleveland as President," [97] published in the *Atlantic Monthly* in 1897. In the former he urged that given the high caliber of men in Cleveland's cabinet, that body should have taken a more assertive part in the functioning of the national government. Its work should have centered in building a door in the wall that divides the legislative and the executive branches. After an elaborate series of arguments and much analysis this was Wilson's conclusion: "The natural connection linking [the Congress and the President] is the cabinet."[98] Four years later Wilson addressed himself to the presidency of Grover Cleveland, just as it passed into history. In the discussion, two aspects of his time in office were emphasized. First, Wilson stressed that Cleveland was a man of force and character, derived from his origins and breeding. Wilson described it this way:

Mr. Cleveland had a very definite home training: wholesome, kindly, Christian. He was bred in a home where character was disciplined and the thoughts were formed, where books were read and the right rules of life obeyed.[99]

Cleveland's leadership was a second important consideration, examples of which were many: the tariff, veterans' pensions, the money question, Hawaiian annexation—Cleveland's handling of these and other problems won Wilson's praise. He thought that as president Cleveland had "made policies and altered parties after the fashion of an earlier age in our history."[100] In print and in private Wilson in the 1890s pondered more and more the nature of the presidential office and the need to resuscitate its failing health by restoring its authority, not as an end but as a means of achieving better government. With the coming of the Progressive era, the purposes to which better government was to be put readily turned to economic and social reforms.

Not far removed from Wilson the historian and political scientist, and integral to his work in each capacity, stood Woodrow Wilson the man of letters. Long evident in his approach and style, the literary man came swiftly to the fore in the 1890s and for a while had full play. *Mere Literature and Other Essays* was not only a persuasive statement of Wilson's literary disposition, it was a stirring defense of literature as a field of learned endeavor against the philistine scientist.[101] The origin of the phrase "mere literature" is interesting in itself. Wilson wrote the essay as a rejoinder to a comment made by Professor James Wilson Bright, a well-known philologist at Johns Hopkins who was heard to dismiss a work as "mere literature." Wilson wrote in answer and attacked as pedantic philological studies in particular and purely scientific studies of man's personal or social behavior in general.[102] He was in deadly earnest. In the first sentence of his essay he described the phrase "mere literature" as "the irreverent invention of a scientific age." "I suppose that in Nirvana," he added, "one would speak in like wise of 'mere life.'" Literature "is not an expression of form, but an expression of spirit."[103] It could not be counted or categorized or reduced to tactile experience. Great passages in literature, Wilson thought, had a beauty and a meaning that rendered context often unimportant—a value "almost independent of subject matter." As science was the study of form, literature was "the study of the essences in man." Why, he asked, do some books live and others die? Enduring books transcended form and force of passion to express the ultimate nature of reason and mankind. "Mere literature is made of spirit." Nor was Wilson above giving a direct reproach to Bright. "The language which the philologist sets out before us with such curious erudition is of little use as a vehicle for the essences of the human spirit." As for the historian, it was both a privilege and an opportunity to invoke constructive imagination in writings about the past. "Scholarship gets into literature by becoming part of the originating individuality of a master of thought. . . ."[104] "Scholarship is material, it is not life. It becomes immortal only when it is worked upon by conviction, by schooled and chastened imagination, by thought that runs alive out of the inner fountains of individual insight and purpose." In contrast, "literature in its essence is mere spirit and you must experience it rather than analyze it too formally."[105]

Having written this much and more in the name of "mere literature," Wilson was not willing to fall silent. He included two other literary essays in the collection, apart from five pieces dealing with politics. The latter group included his essay on Walter Bagehot, "Bagehot a Literary Politician."[106] The two literary essays were "The Author Himself"[107] and "An Author's Choice of Company."[108] In the first of these Wilson explained how it was possible to discern the person of the author in the book he had written. Having read a memorable book, one has, so to speak, come face to face with a memorable person. Such works of literature were noteworthy further because they possessed a certain character. On coming to a bit of political analysis one is apt to exclaim: "Why, only Bagehot could have written that!"[109] In lasting literature the author has entered into and taken temporary possession of the reader's mind. The power of literature is that of stimulation, whereas that of the scientist is only to order and to organize. The author himself interprets nature in human terms, but such an author can not rely merely on learning. "Learned investigation leads to a good many things," Wilson argued, "but one of these is not great literature, because learned investigation commands as the first condition for its success the repression of the individual."[110] The individual man of learning must see things for himself.

In the second essay, "An Author's Choice of Company," Wilson voiced much the same message from a fresh perspective. A great author was not likely to be a man of fashion, he thought. Fashion was a harness and a restraint; a great writer would be an innovator who went beyond fashion and its conventions—not that an author could ever be completely free. He was likely to reflect the spirit of his age, but he should not do so at the sacrifice of his individual vision. After all, "the present age is transient," so that to be "timely" might ill-suit an author's purpose unless his work was intended merely as useful.[111] In Wilson's scheme of things there existed a community of letters. To belong to it was not simply to write well but to see the "permanent element in things—the acts which display the veritable character of men."[112] Life was to be understood through literature, not through logic. In his literary essays Wilson made a challenging case for that proposition.

When Woodrow Wilson was elected president of Princeton University it was none too soon. The promise the College of New Jersey exhibited in the hands of James McCosh went unfulfilled under the successor regime of Francis Patton. Simply stated, Patton was "a wonderfully poor administrator" and a wonderfully poor educator as well. His indifference to academic standards was predicated on the belief that undergraduates were not capable of serious learning. Efforts by the faculty to push Princeton in the direction of further educational improvement had little support from Patton, and Princeton languished accordingly. Wilson's election was intended to begin anew the work undertaken by McCosh, to put Princeton on a par with the leading institutions of the day. The scholar who for so long had written of the need for leadership in government, as history had demonstrated that need, now had become a statesman, albeit an educational statesman, and a leader in his own right.

The changes this new status brought to Wilson's life of the mind were substantial. They meant that, once and for all, he had to abandon his plan for a magnum opus, a study he had been planning at least since 1889 and that he had wanted to call "The Philosophy of Politics." That such a book would have included an emphasis on leadership in a democracy and on evolutionary development in law and government—illustrated by means of historical references and examples—and in the end proclaimed the accomplishments of Western Civilization and especially of its Anglo-American component, could be readily predicted. Just how these large themes and countless smaller threads would have been woven into a grand pattern one can but surmise. "The Philosophy of Politics" was the only significant scholarly endeavor on which Wilson did not follow through.[113] He had planned to get down to the serious business of writing the book in the summer of 1902, only to be elected to the Princeton presidency in July.

As though to mark an end and a beginning, October of that year saw the publication of *A History of the American People,* a five-volume generalized account of the American past.[114] Designed to do for the history of the United States what John Richard Green's *History of the English People* had done for its subject, Wilson fell well short of the standards set by his model. *A History of the American People,* as John Spencer Bassett once told Ray S. Baker, "is not history but what Woodrow Wilson thought about history."[115] Some years after publication Wilson admitted to a public gathering that "I wrote it not to instruct anybody else, but to instruct myself. I wrote the history of the United States to learn from it."[116] The *History* has been variously characterized as unresearched and unbalanced, superficial and one-dimensional, and hastily written and pretentiously packaged—all with some justification. More pertinent, however, is to determine what Wilson thought about the history of his country. In this respect *A History of the American People* was consistent with Wilson's prior judgments. The excellence of American institutions was first of all based on their English origins, the values and traditions of the mother country. From these beginnings the American people had evolved their own unique and superior civilization. In the process the influence of the frontier, as interpreted by Frederick Jackson Turner, was a paramount factor, but it was a frontier opened and developed by a remarkable people under remarkable leadership. Granting that much of what Wilson wrote was a story retold, he chose to stress certain aspects of the story that bear on his political philosophy. He greatly enlarged the role of Andrew Jackson (one reason why the book was deemed out of balance), finding in Jackson both a frontiersman and a democrat. Jackson was the first national leader to understand, at least dimly, the power of group dynamics and the importance of leaders, both interacting with and providing direction to the great body of the citizenry. Wilson was fascinated with the Jackson presidency for just such reasons. The influence of the frontier persisted through Wilson's account of the history of his people. In the final volume, as the frontier closed, his attention shifted to the new frontier of Progressive democracy. Critical to what he sensed was coming over America was the changing nature of the presidency:

> The President seemed again to be always in the foreground, as if the first days of the government were to be repeated,—that first quarter of a century in which it was making good its right to exist and to act as an independent power among the nations of the world. Now, full grown, it was to take a place of leadership.[117]

What needs to be added is that the learning of the presidents, from the early years of the Republic down to the time of Roosevelt, Taft, and eventually Wilson himself, was a key element in their exercise of the leadership that the author of *A History of the American People* called for so consistently.

The presidency of Princeton placed innumerable demands on Wilson, largely nonscholarly in character; even then educational executives could be far removed from the processes of learning. It was a position of power and responsibility that Wilson greatly enjoyed; his friends intimated that until 1906, at any rate, he was never happier in his work. Popular with students, faculty, and alumni and genuinely devoted to the building of a new Princeton, he was reluctant to forsake his scholarly pursuits altogether. Lord Acton had asked him some years before to ready an entry dealing with the United States in the period 1850–61 for inclusion in the *Cambridge Modern History,* and Wilson brought the task to completion in the early weeks of his new position. The result was as fine a piece of historical writing as Wilson ever produced.[118] His mature judgments on the critical decade combined impressively with a clear, unaffected, masculine prose. As he had done before, Wilson regretfully noted the passing of the senatorial giants—Calhoun, Clay, and Webster—and the way in which their places were taken by men less astute and less patriotic. The failure of politics in the 1850s was not a failure of party but of leadership. The presidents' cabinets, many of the members of which had served in the legislature, continued to be denied "a place on the floor of the Congress" where the laws were voted. Neither a private nor a public connection had been encouraged.[119] Wilson showed himself sensitive to the rising force of American nationalism, noting its deplorable outbreak in know-nothingism and the impulses that brought on territorial expansion. An aptitude for character delineation was evident in his treatment of Buchanan. Buchanan's "chief fault, if it was a fault, was not that he yielded to improper influences as his opponents unjustly believed, but that he did not act and judge for himself. He was weak; and weakness was under the circumstances fatal."[120] Finally, in his summing up of the meaning of the Civil War, Wilson reached out for and succeeded in touching historical ultimates:

> For the whole country it was to be the bitterest of all ordeals, an agony of struggle and a decision by blood; but for one party it was to be a war of hope. Should the South win, she must also lose—must lose her place in the great Union which she had loved and fostered, and must in gaining independence destroy a nation. Should the North win, she would confirm a great hope and expectation, establish the Union, unify it in institutions, free it from interior contradictions of life and principle, set it in the way of consistent growth and unembarrassed greatness. The

South fought for a principle, as the North did: it was this that was to give the war dignity, and supply the tragedy with a double motive. But the principle for which the South fought meant standstill in the midst of change; it was conservative, not creative; it was against drift and destiny; it protected an impossible institution and a belated order of society; it withstood a creative and imperial idea, the idea of a united people and a single law of freedom. Overwhelming material superiority, it turned out, was with the North; but she had also another and greater advantage: she was to fight for the Union and for the abiding peace, concord, and strength of a great nation.[121]

No sounder judgment, expressed in so brief a compass, had ever been offered by one so close to the war and so much an unlikely benefactor of its outcome.

Two or three additional examples drawn from Wilson's learned essays sustain the impression of his appreciation of the influence of ideas on events and the need of a busy university executive to express himself in learned discourse. "Politics 1857–1907," "The Tariff Make-Believe," and "Hide-and-Seek Politics," all of which appeared in important periodicals between 1906 and 1910, revealed uses of history in pursuing contemporary issues. As the titles plainly show, Wilson was increasingly attracted to a consideration of practical affairs rather than abstruse matters when he found it possible to break away from the tasks and worries of office.

To mark the occasion of its fiftieth year of publication, the *Atlantic Monthly* invited Wilson to write an essay that would link the years 1857 and 1907 in some special and historically meaningful fashion. The result was an interesting if only partially convincing effort to identify common elements between the great debate over slavery in the territories that was raging in 1857 and the still-pending answer to the question of the rights of corporations in the America of 1907.[122] Wilson ingeniously argued that just as Stephen Douglas had contended that the territories "formed the great corporate bodies of the East . . . [and] must be free corporately to form their lives and practices as they pleased," he concluded, "the industrial corporations must continue their ways of business at their pleasure and their peril, and that law can only deal with them . . . as an organizing power to be regulated in its entirety."[123] Guided by history, Wilson judged the state of affairs in 1907 as Lincoln faced the issues of 1857: "by a flat denial that there can be any such thing as corporate morality . . . which is lifted out of the realm of individual responsibility."[124] There were proponents of two schools of thought, according to Wilson: those who wanted government big enough to regulate corporations through the instrumentality of the expert commission, and those who stood for the older and simpler method that "prefers courts to commissions." Wilson favored the latter, not so much because he distrusted the new instrumentalism, but because moral responsibility figured more prominently in the commands of the courts.[125] The courts must insist that corporations assume a moral responsibility based on individual behavior. Wilson's support of the traditional approach to the problem of the corporations is not surprising, whether based on his theology or historicism. These two sources, in fact, appeared to be mutually supportive, rendering Wilson's conviction fully persuasive in his own view.

In dealing with two other contemporary problems, the tariff and machine politics, Wilson put forth proposals that grew out of his scholarly investigations of history and government. He was almost bitter when he wrote of the House Ways and Means Committee's specifying tariff schedules, with public debate virtually precluded when it came time for a floor vote. It was a policy of "silence and secrecy." The high tariff rates represented "entrenchments of Special Privilege." His proposals to reform the tariff he thought "Hamiltonian" in the purest sense. Hamilton was not a protectionist. He had advocated a tariff policy that would work for the benefit of the many and not for the few. Special interest was not part of Hamilton's thinking. Nonetheless, reform of the tariff could not be sudden or drastic; as it had evolved, so it must be revised downward, step by step. There must be about the new tariff a "moral soundness," which applied to individual actions, business practices, and the connections between the corporations and government. "Honest men" were required to determine a tariff of "moral soundness" and to put such a wholesome law into effect.[126]

Wilson attacked machine politics in "Hide-and-Seek Politics," appearing in the *North American Review* for May 1910. He pleaded for a return to truly representative government by means of which the public would get what it wanted: "good men in office, sensible laws adjusted to existing conditions, conscience in affairs, and intelligence in their direction." The machine politics of the era discouraged honest men from taking up public life, thereby denying the voter a proper leadership. Political parties were essential to the functioning of government, but political machines were the enemy of good government. The power of the machine was pronounced "secret and sinister"—in a word, immoral. Wilson went on to praise Theodore Roosevelt as president because Roosevelt was open and aboveboard, believing that the people had a right to be informed on matters of public concern. Because Roosevelt trusted the people and scorned secret deals the people trusted him as their leader. Wilson added quickly that the problem of machine politics was too deep and pervasive to be solved by any one man. He called for a reform movement that was a "thoughtful artisan of genuine democracy."[127]

What these and similar forays into print and from the lecture platform held for Woodrow Wilson's future was problematic. He continued to think and act as a political animal in the context of Princeton. Defeat there on the issues of the graduate school and the eating clubs rendered continuance as president at least difficult and probably unthinkable. The governorship of New Jersey became an attractive alternate possibility. Election as governor in 1910 put the presidency of the United States in his sights in 1912. Meanwhile, before taking leave of Princeton, Wilson published his last scholarly book, *Constitutional Government in the United States.*

Constitutional Government was a book much like *Congressional Government* and *The State,* a scholar's effort to understand and to make intelligible to others the actualities of American government during the Progressive years.[128] Given on the Blumenthal Foundation as a series of lectures at Columbia University, the talks were delivered from notes that Wilson used afterward as the basis of the book. It was published by Columbia University Press in 1908. More than twenty years separated it from *Congressional Government,* during which time the reality of rule in America had changed. Wilson's perceptions kept pace with such developments. The fresh promise that government under the Constitution then appeared to hold out lent to the book an optimism befitting the presidency of Theodore Roosevelt, who was in office at the time.

After rehearsing salient features of English constitutional history from the days of Magna Carta to the eighteenth century, which provided a link between England and America, Wilson discussed the step-by-step growth across the years and across the continent of constitutional government in the United States. In the process the nation became "a country not merely constitutionally governed but also self-governed." Wilson dramatized his point by reference to the political situation in the Philippine Islands. The United States could provide constitutional government for the Filipinos and had done so. But the American government could not give the Filipinos self-rule, which, were that possible, would be "an unprecedented operation, reversing the process at Runnymede."[129] This and other general propositions regarding constitutional government made up the introduction to the book. Chapters were given over to the president, the House, the Senate, and the courts. Two final chapters dealt with states' rights and the place of parties in American government.

Nothing had more substantially changed his understanding of the operation of American government, Wilson announced, than the new and modern presidency. This judgment was not the result of a rethinking of the second article of the Constitution, but of observing and responding to the emergence of a different kind of office. That such a change had taken place was due fundamentally to the theory that government is not a machine (as with Newtonians) but a living thing (as with Darwinians). "It falls not under the theory of the universe, but under the theory of organic life."

"Government," Wilson added, was "not a body of blind forces. . . . [but] a body of men with highly differentiated functions."[130] It was officers with special constitutional assignments who made the whole system work. He quoted Bagehot approvingly to the effect that it was not proof of the excellence of the Constitution that Americans had operated it with success, because Americans could operate any constitution successfully.

In discussing the executive office, Wilson felt it was easier for him to write of the president—the man—than the presidency—the theory. The men who had held office, and especially Lincoln, Cleveland, and Roosevelt, had made the position more than a "legal executive," as called for by the strict Whig theorists of the eighteenth century. "Greatly as the practice and the influence of the Presidency has varied, there can be no mistaking the fact that we have grown more and more inclined from generation to generation to look to the Presidency as the unifying force in our complex system."[131] One manifestation of this was that the president had become the party leader, of necessity with the growth of the political party system. The president, Wilson thought, was "at liberty, both in law and in conscience, to be as big a man as he can." Not that he sanctioned the abuse of power. "Nothing in a system like ours can be constitutional which is immoral or which touches the good faith of those who have been sworn to obey the fundamental law." In such a passage Wilson was working to bring power and morality together as characteristics proper to a modern president. Looking to this fusion he wrote that "we can never hide our President again as a mere domestic officer. We can never again see him the mere executive he was in the thirties and forties. He must stand always at the front of our affairs, and the office will be as big and as influential as the man who occupies it."[132] As it has turned out, such a statement becomes a fairly accurate description of the presidency in the whole of the twentieth century.

Part of the new status was bound up with a modern president's conduct of foreign affairs, in the analysis of which Wilson offered remarks made doubly meaningful by events in his own presidency. In 1908 he wrote:

> One of the greatest of the President's powers I have not yet spoken of at all: his control, which is very absolute, of foreign relations of the nation. The initiative in foreign affairs, which the President possesses without any restriction whatever, is virtually the power to control them absolutely. The President can not conclude a treaty with a foreign power without the consent of the Senate, but he may guide every step of diplomacy, and to guide diplomacy is to determine what treaties must be made, if the faith and the prestige of the government are to be maintained. He need disclose no step of negotiation until it is complete, and when in any critical matter it is completed the government is virtually committed. Whatever its disinclination, the Senate may feel itself committed also.[133]

In Wilson's view it was now no longer necessary for an American president to function in some way as a British prime minister. The presidency had become a unique and powerful office. To be derivative was not enough, and imitation was no longer appropriate. The Constitution and the presidency had matured together.

Wilson's estimate of the presidency tended to soften some of his previously expressed strictures of the House of Representatives. He stated explicitly, for example, that the work of the House had to be taken as part of a living organism of government, and he observed that the power of the Speaker was not really that of a Czar. The House of Representatives could unmake a Speaker the way the House of Commons could unmake a government. His conclusion was that the House of Representatives was much less powerful than it might have become, again with the Commons as a comparison. One does not have to look far to discern the reason for this: the house lacked *executive* leadership.[134]

Wilson strongly defended the Senate in its origins—representative of all areas of the country, however sparsely settled—and its peculiar role as both a coordinate branch of the legislature and a body with a special relationship to the executive. A senator, Wilson wrote, "is not a mere legislator. He is directly associated with the President in some of the most delicate and important functions of government. He is a member of a great executive council. He is brought into very confidential relations with the President in matters which often times call for not a little discretion and very important judgments—judgments not to be drawn from public opinion. . . ."[135] As though to chart his own problems in the years to come, Wilson went on to note "the unmistakable condescension with which the older members of the Senate regard the President of the United States. Dominate the affairs of the country as he may, he seems to them at most an ephemeral phenomenon. . . . A member of long standing in the Senate feels that he is the professional, the President an amateur."[136]

The discussion of the courts in *Constitutional Government* amounted to a quick review of the work of the judiciary, in which the courts were described as "the balance-wheel of our whole constitutional system." In the building up of the system from an English base John Marshall was given major credit—"no other name is comparable with his in fame or honor in this singular field of statesmanlike judicial control,—a field of our own marking out and creation, a statesmanship peculiar to our annals." At times Wilson could be overborne by history. His statement that "Marshall, putting the oath of office to Jackson, was repeating in quiet modern form the transaction of Runnymede" was simply excessive, verging on gush.[137]

The final chapters of *Constitutional Government* dealt with federal-state relationships and with party government. Wilson chose to express his considered concept of states' rights by denying the constitutionality of a

1906 bill seeking to outlaw child labor by means of the commerce clause. He repudiated the proposal on two grounds: the bill was an unwarranted extension of the meaning of the commerce clause, and it was unwise to attempt uniform regulation of economic conditions in a country so vast and so varied as the United States. Such police power rightly belonged to and should be maintained in the hands of the states. "It would be fatal to our political vitality to strip the States of their power and transfer it to the federal government." States' rights were an expression of local option. The Constitution was not "a mere legal document" but a "vehicle of life" that the rights of the states helped to keep healthy and effective. Wilson put it directly: "centralization is not vitalization," asserting that decentralization in power ought to be maintained in federal-state relations.[138]

His treatment of party government was matter of fact. He traced American parties back to the Whig and Tory factions of English history. But party machinery in the United Stated was especially complicated because of the federal system. It was further distinguished by the separation between party management and administrative responsibility. Americans alone made the distinction between politicians and statesmen. Nonetheless, party machinery was essential to the operation of government. The efforts of statesmen depended on the ability of politicians to provide a unified party to face the great issues of the day. The parties were, in Wilson's view, "our veritable body politics." This he did not approve, expressing the hope that the legislature and the executive would become the real body politic. Were that to come about, "Americans would have to think less of checks and balances and more of coordinated power, less of separation of function and more of synthesis of action."[139]

Constitutional Government was a sound, scholarly book. Wilson confirmed his reputation as a first-rate political scientist, knowledgeable of theory and conversant with practice. It was, furthermore, a positive study, in contrast with the tendency of *Congressional Government* to be negative. Its author no longer yearned for a cabinet government for the United States, wise enough to appreciate that the American system had grown according to environment and pressures. Wilson's last scholarly book had given some good advice to the American people. Since the advice was spoken by an academic voice, however distinguished, there was no guarantee that it would be taken. Four years were to change all that. Wilson became president and, it can be assumed, was guided by his own advice. In the process his conception of a modern president was put to the severest test.

The New Freedom, a collection of 1912 campaign addresses, is the best place to begin to consider the presidency of Woodrow Wilson. The addresses represented an honest effort to translate political theory and historical study into the language of the electioneering platform. Much of his learning was cut away in order to keep the message clear and simple, but enough of Wilson the scholar remained to give *The New Freedom* a learned flavor. The collection was first published serially in *World's Work* in early 1913 and was brought out in book form that same year. Today *The New Freedom* is remembered as an important American expression of classic liberalism.[140] Wilson intended his speeches for the audiences of his day as statements of a political philosophy and a plan of attack on the evils of American life. The core of his position was opposition to paternalism and rejection of government protection of business and industry and government provision of social welfare. As there was present in America a good deal of the former and rather less of the latter, Wilson's obvious target was the industrial trust. His advocacy of tariff reduction was premised on the belief that high tariffs fueled the engines of the trusts. Wilson was a strong advocate of free enterprise, however. "If America is not to have free enterprise then she can have freedom of no sort whatever." With equal vigor and fine impartiality he also identified with the people: "I feel the intensity of the common man." Wilson's progressivism was middle of the road.

One of the prominent motifs of *The New Freedom* was change, change of which neither government nor society had been sufficiently aware. "We shall have to run until we have caught up with our condition," Wilson told one gathering.[141] "The old political formulas do not fit the present practices," which had forced him, as he put it, to become a Progressive. In "The Old Order Changeth" Wilson deplored the impersonality of the modern day, a marked difference from previous times when "in the ordinary course of life . . . men dealt freely and directly with one another." "In this modern age," he went on, "we find that our laws with regard to the relations of employer and employee are in many respects wholly antiquated and impossible. They were framed for another age. . . ." Since they did not take note of this new state of affairs, the laws, Wilson insisted, must be changed to give a constructive relationship to existing conditions. Progressivism was designed to achieve that objective. But such things could be accomplished without revolution; "America is not given to the spilling of blood in political conflicts." As life is organic so changes must be as gradual as growth. Nonetheless there should be a quickening of the ordinary processes of development, what Wilson termed a "silent revolution."[142]

If the presence of social evolution spiced with reform Darwinism was discernible in Wilson's understanding of change, the influence of Whiggery was no less evident in his treatment of "What Is Progress?" There must be a distinction maintained between change and improvement, to begin with. Progress was not properly associated with ancient or medieval civilization but with modern man: "Progress, development,—these are modern words," and especially popular in America. In a search for progress America was born in revolution and in the new government that followed. The men who wrote the Constitution were "only following the English Whigs, who gave Great Britain its modern constitution."[143] By the twentieth century a dramatic transformation had occurred. Twentieth-century men could no longer think in eighteenth-century ways. The Newtonian visualization of the universe as a machine had been replaced by an understanding of life and law in Darwinist terms. There were immense possibilities for improvement in America, where the Whig view of history and the Darwinist interpretation of life combined naturally to spell Progress.

Other elements of the learned Wilson surfaced readily in *The New Freedom*. Celebration of agrarian virtues owed as much to Turner's frontier thesis as to Jefferson's *Notes on Virginia*. Referring to the "parliament of the people," Wilson insisted that there must be open debate on the great issues. From his earliest years he had valued free discussion—as a debater at Princeton, Virginia, and Hopkins and as a critic of the committee system of the House of Representatives in *Congressional Government*. Opinions on the tariff were shaped by an understanding of Hamilton's proposals for a tariff in the 1790s. Opposition to monopolies stressed that they were but parts of the whole and should be treated accordingly. Big business, Wilson admitted, was to a large extent "necessary and natural." Monopolies were another matter. When big business became a monopoly or a trust it could no more be allowed to rule the country than, in the 1850s, the wishes of the people in a territory could be allowed to determine the attitude of the entire nation toward slavery.[144]

Once he was in office, Wilson appeared to abandon as impractical many of the *New Freedom* proposals regarding public policy. What he actually did was to scrap a plan of campaign while retaining a philosophy of government. He continued to believe that the law must be brought into line with prevailing conditions, that conditions would improve by an intelligent use of the means at man's disposal as registered in the Whig and Darwinist rationales of history, that the spirit of the frontier was an enduring element in American life, that special privilege must be rooted out for the welfare of the many, and that "free men need no guardians."[145] In these and other ways the learned Wilson walked hand in hand with the moral Wilson from 1913 to 1921.

In office Wilson chose to be guided by the old adage, "the way to lead is to lead." As he proceeded to act in matters of state, the leadership he exercised appeared to merge the two great models of executive style to which his knowledge of history had exposed him: the English prime ministry and the American presidency. In spite of his recognition, as recorded in *Constitutional Government,* that the presidency had achieved a new dynamic, he continued to sense a need to overcome, in informal fashion at least, the separation of the two political branches as laid down in the Constitution. He conceived of his own presidency as part of a historical process, only lately begun, that might eventually give the executive a commanding influence over the legislature. He had a keen sense of commitment to this outcome. Discussions of the presidency in *Constitutional Government* demonstrated, however, that quite apart from the lessons to be drawn from the English constitution, the American presidency had taken off in a new direction under stimuli peculiar to the environment of the new century. The office had become "the unifying force in our complex system," as he had written, attributable in part no doubt to America's great-power status. No modern president coming into office, before or after Wilson's time, had given so much consideration to the nature of the office or attention to its needs, its problems, and its potential. Wilson's handling of reform proposals during 1913 bears this out. The first of these was the issue of the tariff.

Downward revision of the protective tariff had long been a demand of farmer and consumer groups (broadly defined), yet somehow the tariff escaped unscathed and became more and more entrenched. Theodore Roosevelt had avoided grasping the rose of tariff reform because the nettles were too sharp and politically dangerous. William Howard Taft made the mistake of endorsing the Payne-Aldrich act, to the enduring fury of tariff reformers. Wilson, for his part, met the problem head on. It was the first item on his legislative agenda. He intended it as an early test of his presidency.

As though to dramatize his leadership intentions Wilson called Congress to meet in special session in April 1913 and appeared before a joint session of the legislature, the first president to do so since John Adams. Arthur Link has written that Wilson wanted Congress "to think of him as a colleague in the great work of tariff reform they were about to undertake." The Underwood tariff proposal, which reduced the overall rates by some 25 percent and placed many important products on the free list, passed the House of Representatives easily enough but encountered the traditional stiff opposition in the Senate. It was at this point that President Wilson swung into action. He wrote letters to key senators and conferred in person with others. He publicly denounced the special interests and their lobbyists in a fashion that won wide and favorable coverage in the press. With the assistance of Senator LaFollette, the members of the Senate, some of whom figured to profit from continued high tariff rates, were brought to disclose their stock holding in various corporations. Having assembled in April, Congress finally passed the reform measure in October, and Wilson signed it with undisguised satisfaction. Both the nation and the politicians had responded to Wilson's leadership. There were other lessons as well. The need for party loyalty had been evident throughout the struggle. Wilson had to crack the whip to maintain discipline, especially with regard to some disgruntled southern senators. A tightly run party was one practical means of uniting the executive and the legislature in a single cause. Wilson believed that the distinction between the statesman and the politician that he found common to American public life and that he frankly deplored had been diluted by this first exercise of presidential leadership.

The president had a less conspicuous hand in the battle over a new banking system, another item high on the agenda of the reformers. Both conservative financiers and Progressive leaders expected the Democratic administration to step into the bank muddle and clear the air, though each side had a vastly different version of the remedy the situation required. Unlike the tariff, which the average citizen felt he understood and which had been used so flagrantly by the plutocracy, banking reform sounded, and indeed was, highly technical. Wilson's leadership was therefore less public in character. To someone who had made a lifelong study of rule by Congress, the whole process of moving a controversial proposal of major consequences through a bicameral legislature was fascinating. The political scientist in Wilson was involved only slightly less than the public official. But by no means was Wilson a mere interested observer. He consulted Carter Glass of Virginia, a leading member of the Senate Banking Committee, and H. Parker Willis, a private expert, some days before his inauguration. The banking community, Wilson learned firsthand, preferred a highly centralized banking system, with banks responsible for issuing the currency. Though this proposed system called for fifteen branches across the country, control of the banking business would remain rooted in Wall Street. The reformers demanded a decentralized system, with currency issued only by the federal government and control resting in a governmental agency or commission to be created by the law.

Wilson had few preconceived notions and he easily assumed the position of the honest broker. Initially, he was to keep negotiations between rival factions in the Congress from bogging down while countering the influence of outside interest groups. This was no easy matter since the infighting was intense. There was real danger, furthermore, that differences could grow and split the Democratic party, compounding the disaster of an aborted banking bill. In pursuit of an acceptable law and a united party the president addressed the Congress and entered fully into the fight through a series of personal appeals to House and Senate leaders. He tried to maintain the consistent impression of a disinterested arbiter of opposing arguments. The pressure on Wilson was enormous, but it appeared from press accounts and public discussion that he continued to enjoy the reputation of a neutral even as he kept Congress at the task of finalizing a law that would satisfy his conservative instincts and Progressive expectations. The struggle over the banking law surged one way and the other, Wilson vowing to keep the Congress in session until a law was written. Final action came just before Christmas, when the President signed the Federal Reserve Act. With the tariff and banking measures safely on the books, Woodrow Wilson came away from his first year in office almost the model president described in *Constitutional Government,* that is, an executive who had fused political power and moral responsibility.

There is more involved in playing the game of politics than most scholars even dream, and Woodrow Wilson experienced an unsettlingly complex political situation as he faced 1914. He was basically a conservative caught in a web of Progressive importunities and political realities. His leadership became distinctly shaky in the face of demands for further reforms. Labor wanted immunity from prosecution under antitrust laws, farmers expected the federal government to furnish capital for rural bank credits, social workers were outspoken in seeking a federal child labor law, women insisted on a suffrage amendment—to list major Progressive expectations. Additional pressure was felt by the Wilson administration because of controversies over immigration, maritime working conditions, and deprivation of the rights of Negro citizens. In the mind of the true Progressive each of the foregoing problems required strong action by the national government—action that would break down the distinction between the new nationalism and the new freedom. Wilson proposed to stand firm in his conviction that no class or vested interest, whether it be business, labor, or the farmer, should be the beneficiary of government protection, opposition to which was at the heart of the new freedom philosophy. The question that came inevitably to the surface was, What kind of Progressive does this make Woodrow Wilson?

The Clayton Anti-Trust Act and the Federal Trade Commission Act became law in 1914, each being consistent with if not fully satisfying Progressive requirements. What was Wilson's contribution to the passage of these laws, and what use did he make of presidential prestige and power? He huddled with legislative leaders and went before the Congress again to address a joint session, the fifth time he had done so, in order to explain in detail the administration's antitrust proposal. The fact was, however, that neither Wilson nor the Democratic leadership in Congress could agree on the bill's particulars. It was a perfect opportunity for Wilson to take charge, but the most he was prepared to do was remain stoutly opposed to the exemption of labor from the operation of the antitrust law. The uncertainty forced the president to ponder his ideological future. Louis Brandeis is usually credited with drawing Wilson in the direction of government regulation of big business, especially in his draft version of the Federal Trade Commission Act, a prophetic indication of Wilson's later reorientation. In 1914 all this appeared more a case of drift.

At the end of that year Wilson announced himself convinced that the passage of the four critical laws dealing with the tariff, banking, the trusts, and interstate trade had fulfilled the reform program. Many moderate Progressives were less sure: advanced Progressives were dismayed. Wilson had preached reform and laws had been enacted, but he seemed unaware that more steps would have to be taken for the new laws to take hold and make a difference in society. His appointments, to the Federal Reserve Board, for example, were men of conservative outlook. As was his preacher father before him, Wilson was convinced that sound directives were enough. The laws would somehow produce the intended results.

The longer Woodrow Wilson remained in politics the more of a politician he became. During 1915 his progressivism had been subordinated to serious foreign policy matters; 1916 was an election year, however, and Wilson's concern with Progressive issues suddenly revived. To win the presidency again would require the construction of a coalition of old-line Democrats and dedicated Progressives, of eastern workers and western farmers, of urban dwellers and small-town voters. The year 1916 began on a controversial note when the president nominated Brandeis, the doctrinaire liberal, to the Supreme Court and immediately exercised his privilege of leading the contest for confirmation. The nomination connoted morality and Wilson warmed easily to the fight. Soon the president announced himself converted to the long-pending scheme for rural credits and executed a remarkable *volte-face* on child labor by pushing for passage of the Keating-Owens bill. In the matter of a child labor law Wilson displayed both force and skill as he persuaded a number of southern senators to agree to accept the idea. Continuing to speak the advanced Progressive line he advocated acceptance of the Jones bill, which enhanced the opportunities for self-rule in the Philippines. While the final version of this law contained no definite promise of independence, Wilson had demonstrated his own brand of anti-imperialism. The president agreed to the Adamson Act, limiting the hours of railroad workers to eight a day, as readily as he had to the revision of the tariff in 1913. These various initiatives appealed directly to the components of the ad hoc Democratic, or better still, Wilsonian coalition.

Political ambition, which he had never disguised, had become a powerful it not a dominant impulse in Wilson's conduct of domestic affairs in 1916. The effort to unite the politician and the statesman seemed complete. Wilson's newly reworked progressivism was only part of the 1916 election success, however. The war in Europe required the president to enunciate United States policy regarding the conflict and the combatants.

His position on neutrality was cast in an irresistible slogan: "He kept us out of war." A highly popular set of reform measures combined with a highly popular neutrality policy to return Woodrow Wilson to the White House.

In the conduct of foreign policy it could be assumed that President Wilson would be greatly influenced by morality and by learning. Those who have studied Wilsonian diplomacy have been quick to agree that deeply rooted ethical commitments go far to explain triumphs and failures alike. The argument from the moral stance is convincing, without being complete. In setting forth the argument from the viewpoint of learning the purpose is not to challenge the place or the primacy of morality in Wilson's policies but to complement it, much as morality and learning were complementary throughout the course of his private and public life.

The president was anything but preoccupied with problems of a diplomatic nature at the outset of his administration. Nineteen thirteen was the last year of peace among the powers, but few if any anticipated the catastrophe that was to engulf Europe in 1914. Wilson was no exception. Concerned with problems of tariffs and trusts, banking and big business, he was content to name William Jennings Bryan as his secretary of state. The veteran Democratic politician and perennial presidential hopeful was expected to do little harm. The most prestigious of cabinet posts became something of a sinecure, a sign no doubt that the president had abandoned, in practice, any intention of introducing a variation of the cabinet system. Bryan's appointment was purely political. As Wilson was to continue to discover, political theory gave way to precedent in any number of ways and it became both necessary and prudent to fit into the mold rather than attempt to break it. Bryan was cut to the measure of midwestern isolationism, but his limited diplomatic activity as secretary of state seemed unlikely to mean much. Besides, if international affairs were to turn ugly, Bryan's pacifism would find support from the President.

That Wilson continued to ponder the nature of the presidency, believing it an office still to be fully evolved, was attested to by his letter to A. Mitchell Palmer just a month before he was sworn into office. The presidency was "passing through a transitional state," he thought, which "must lead eventually to something very different."[146] The president had become both a national leader and a party leader. "He must be prime minister, as much concerned with the guidance of legislation as with the just and orderly execution of law." Wilson went on in the letter to Palmer to argue that the president was "the spokesman of the nation in everything, even the most momentous and most delicate dealings with the governments of foreign nations."[147] Such ideas were common enough in Wilson's books and articles on government. His analysis of the power of the chief executive in *Constitutional Government* had been especially forthright. He had called the president's control of diplomacy "very absolute," suffering no restrictions, requiring "disclosure of no step in negotiation until it is complete." The most constitutional of men, Wilson appeared to interpret the power of the president in matters of diplomacy as virtually without restriction. Since he himself possessed no great public office at the time he wrote *Constitutional Government* and there was in 1908 little prospect that he would ever exercise the power of the president of the United States, it is appropriate to inquire about the source of these notions. The answer lies in Wilson's conception of evolving government in general and of the presidency in particular. As a scientist in the political laboratory, Wilson saw that times were changing, that the environment in which governments functioned would shape new understandings of old institutions, and that the Constitution of the United States was open ended. The presidency of Theodore Roosevelt was also on Wilson's mind as he studied the evolution of the office, adding a new dimension to the exercise of executive power. He had often displayed a sympathy for the great-man theory of history that now combined with an instrumentalist assessment of the Constitution to effect a new dynamism in the presidency.

It was "the irony of fate," to employ his own phrase, that Woodrow Wilson was required to pursue an active foreign policy almost from the start of his eight years in the White House. The ultimate irony was that his diplomacy would bring about a final defeat. In 1913 and early 1914 Secretary Bryan pushed hard for treaties of conciliation and eventually enlisted twenty-nine signatory powers, including Great Britain and France, to accept the principles of conciliation. These were simply "cooling off" arrangements that were expected to prevent war by substituting delay and diplomacy for a resort to force. Morally such treaties were consistent with the new president's outlook. The learned Wilson also had expressed endorsement. In *The State* he had written that "the end of government is the facilitation of the objects of society. The rule of government action is necessary cooperation."[148] William Howard Taft's version of such treaties had been rejected by the Senate; Theodore Roosevelt had very serious doubts about "indiscriminate arbitration" understandings, however. In his view some nations simply could not be trusted, which meant if the United States were bound by treaty to conciliate, one day the nation might find itself in the unacceptable position of having to arbitrate "being slapped in the face." Woodrow Wilson's morality and learning led him to disagree with Roosevelt and to agree with Taft.

"Missionary diplomacy," as Arthur Link has referred to Wilson's foreign-policy efforts in the western hemisphere, was highlighted by American misadventures in Mexico. The president sought to shape the Mexican Revolution of 1913 into a pattern of his own design. Its most prominent features were moralistic and constitutional, the latter derived from his long study of government. Moral and constitutional elements figured generally in missionary diplomacy and were, in fact, inextricably linked together. If the lives of people in the Americas were to be improved and the well-being of society promoted, Wilson (and Bryan) believed that constitutional governments, which were the most moral form of government, had to be supported strongly. In the Caribbean area, however—in Nicaragua, the Dominican Republic, and Haiti, where Wilson committed United States forces in unusual displays of American intervention—the people were not prepared to assume the kind of self-rule that Wilson held up as an ideal. Other factors, including inherited commitments, military-naval strategies, financial involvement, and the desire for personal gain on the part of some American officials, had to be figured into any comprehensive explanation of United States interference in the Caribbean states. What made the whole of the package palatable to Wilson was the presence of the moral and constitutional elements that the president hoped to promote by American influence. Contemplation and admiration of representative government gave him an ill-founded confidence that, through conscious effort, any people could measure up to the responsibilities of self-government. This was quite apart from whether vested interests in the country or grasping and corrupt leadership would permit self-rule to come about. For all his learning Wilson had little awareness of the Latin American political sense or of the history of the Latin American states. For this reason he blundered time and again during U.S. involvement in the Mexican Revolution from 1913 to 1917.

At first the president was morally revulsed by the coup in Mexico whereby Victoriano Huerta, in the process of coming to power by a forceful overthrow of the established government, murdered the deposed president, Francisco Madero. Second, the President moved to support the anti-Huerta movement led by Venustiano Carranza because Carranza promised his followers to support the reforms instituted by Madero and to do so through a new constitutional government. The Carranza party called itself the Constitutionalists. Brushing aside the prior question of whether the United States should directly intervene in the politics of a sovereign nation, however noble the intention, Wilson was soon entangled in a rapidly shifting power struggle in Mexico. Had his interference not been prompted by his obsession with a moral and constitutional outcome, it is doubtful that he could have been drawn so deeply into Mexican affairs.

The study of history guided Wilson's Mexican policy in still another way. He believed passionately that good men made the difference between good and bad government. The form of the polity was less critical than the quality of the individuals who carried on the affairs of a nation. The president had his share of historical heroes, Lincoln and Gladstone among them, men of integrity and high resolve. At one point in the Mexican crisis the British diplomat, Sir William Tyrrell, asked the president what exactly his Mexican policy was. The reply was a telling one, an unguarded response for the biographer to prize because it revealed Wilson's deepest convictions: "I am going to teach the South American republics to elect good men."[149] A further question must be asked: What made a public man good, in Wilson's judgment? A man who was sternly honest in his conduct and a staunch advocate of constitutional government would have been Wilson's unhesitating response, based as it was on his own moral sense and on his study of history and government.

The conduct of policy between the United States and Mexico—with Caribbean affairs, the Chinese loan question, differences with Japan over discrimination against the Japanese in California, and negotiations over tolls charged at the Panama Canal thrown in for added measure—would have been more than enough to keep the State Department busy. Larger problems, of course, were to come with the outbreak of hostilities in Europe in the summer of 1914, less than a year and a half after Wilson came into office. The war would be an increasing worry for the president and his advisers until the United States entered the conflict in the spring of 1917.

Woodrow Wilson's scholarly concerns had centered on the phenomenon of government and on the history of the people and leaders of the United States. A dedicated student of the British constitution as well, he had gained much knowledge of and insight into human affairs from his reading and writing over the years. In these enterprises, however, he had not become well or widely acquainted with international politics. The history of other countries was viewed from the lofty perch of Anglo-American constitutional success and with little sustained attention given to diplomacy. Wilson displayed hardly any feel for geopolitics, though it was a subject much discussed at the close of the nineteenth century. There was no sense of Captain Mahan's ideas about his outlook and not much appreciation of the need for a *Weltpolitick* along the lines suggested by Brooks Adams. Wilson's travels abroad were limited largely to friendly climes where the culture was much the same as his own. He had no foreign experience similar to William Howard Taft's sojourn among the Filipinos, much less Theodore Roosevelt's wide acquaintance with the world beyond the United States. Comparable experiences would have enlarged Wilson's understanding of foreign countries and various peoples. He had depended heavily on his book knowledge of government and history to guide him in his presidential political moves at home. Although as a highly educated man, he had amassed a great deal of information about the world beyond America, his lack of studious attention to international affairs over a long period of research and writing made for a deficiency in his preparation to be the main architect of American foreign policy. Wilson had to learn the diplomatic ropes and to learn them quickly. This he did readily enough but they were lessons learned from experience rather than from contemplating theory and studying history, which were his natural habit.

On the other hand the rules of politics can be much the same at home and abroad, in peace and in war: protect the rear and the flank, keep the opposition off balance and guessing, maintain a unified command and a set purpose, and, in wars fought by democratic nations, be certain of support from the rear areas, namely, the people. If Wilson's foreign policy respecting the war in Europe succeeded from 1914 to 1918, first in the effort to keep America neutral, and then in the timing of the decision to ask for a declaration of war, it was because the president was able to observe and implement the tactics common to domestic and diplomatic politics.

When World War I commenced Wilson openly favored a neutral position: "neutrality in thought, word and action." By no means disinterested in the outcome, along with a majority of his countrymen he could discover no vital American interests involved. When the British and the Germans proceeded in their respective ways to make the path of neutrality a difficult one to walk, Wilson reproached both governments. The difference was that while British measures disrupted American shipping, German submarines brought death and destruction. The sinking of the *Lusitania* in May of 1915, which deeply shocked Wilson, was not enough to force a break in diplomatic relations with Germany. He resisted as well the preparedness advocates who had in mind American entry into the war on the side of the Anglo-French. There was such a thing as a "nation being too proud to fight" in Wilson's judgment, and public opinion was with him. The *Sussex* Pledge, whereby the Germans in 1916 agreed to restricted submarine warfare, was a diplomatic triumph. It appeared to ensure American neutrality. Wilson was reelected in 1916 in no small part because he had kept the nation out of the conflict. The president had carefully abided by the advice to presidents he had offered in *Constitutional Government*. As leader of the nation and the party he had remained responsive to the will of the people. Since he kept them out of war, the people preferred him to be their leader for the next four years. German resumption of unrestricted submarine warfare in early 1917, constituting a violation of the *Sussex* Pledge, moved both the American people and Wilson closer to active participation. The Zimmermann Note, the German effort to incite a Mexican attack on the southwest, caused as much uproar along the Potomac as the Rio Grande. But there was to be no stampede; the president moved deliberately from neutrality, to armed defense of shipping rights, to a nation in arms.

President Wilson's wartime leadership exhibited a sure touch. Taking advantage of the mood of the country and the Congress he got almost all he wanted or needed to support the war at home, in the factory, and at the front. "A war to end all wars" and "making the world safe for democracy" had anything but a hollow sound when the president and the Committee on Public Information repeated these wartime objectives again and again. Wilson exceeded even himself with the Fourteen Points—and that dramatic beginning, "open covenants for peace, openly arrived at"—as a basis for peace and security in the twentieth century. On the battlefield Allied armies were bolstered by Wilsonian idealism and, more significantly, by American men and matériel. The Germans were demoralized by the onrush of revitalized armies opposing them and by American propaganda. Four years after the start of the Great War American entry promised to bring it to an end. As German armies retreated the Kaiser abdicated and Germany sued for peace. Wilson had emerged as the leader without peer, at the head of an American nation (and a Democratic party) that had been determined to achieve a wartime objective consonant with the requirements of an exhausted Europe: peace without victory.

If, indeed, there is a tide in the affairs of men, Wilson's fortune began to recede almost at the hour of his greatest strength, as he made mistake after mistake. The appeal to elect a Democratic Congress was an ill-advised tactic in the off-year election of 1918 and it backfired. If the Allied leaders were tempted to conclude that Wilson did not have a unified electorate behind him, there was some justification. The president's determination to attend the Paris Peace Conference in person, while understandable in light of his Calvinist sense of the election of certain men to do God's work, may have weakened his bargaining position. His refusal to take any senators with him to Paris, much less any Republican senators, flew directly in the face of both common sense and constitutional reality. His learning in the field of politics served him poorly in all these decisions. Wilson had admired Washington and had studied Gladstone, but in dealing with Clemenceau and Lloyd George he would have been better equipped had he studied Machiavelli and admired Talleyrand. His performance at the sessions of the Big Three was simply inept. By making concession after concession in order to win support for the League of Nations, concessions that vitiated the spirit and in some instances the clear intention of the Fourteen Points, Wilson left himself no option but to insist on ratification of the Versailles treaty exactly as he had brought it back from France. No one knew better than he that the Senate could block ratification. No one knew better than the senators that the president had blithely ignored them in the treaty-making process. Wilson's version of the presidential treaty-making prerogative requires no restatement. Whether this interpretation of the president's power was a viable one would depend to a large extent on events; events were the outward manifestation of the environment that would continue to shape the evolution of the office.

Plunged into the real world of fierce national rivalries at the peace conference Wilson abandoned his prior position of peace without victory to endorse a treaty that he was to characterize as severe but no more severe than the defeated enemy deserved. The most certain feature of the proposal was that it was Woodrow Wilson's treaty and therefore it must be accepted by the Senate unaltered by amendment, unsullied by other hands. Wilson had spoken. The rest was not silence, however. After a brief period a storm of controversy was generated by opponents of various stripes. The irreconcilables led by Senator Borah, faithful Republicans, and moderate nonpartisan skeptics alike indicated that the treaty as it stood should not become law. Henry Cabot Lodge, the senator from Massachusetts who led the fight against the treaty, offered amendments known as the Lodge Reservations that were designed to protect American sovereignty. Wilson's response was characteristic and predictable: an appeal to the people. As he undertook his arduous speech-making western tour in the late summer of 1919 it seemed that he had moved to gain control of the situation. His addresses won applause and support, which makes his physical breakdown in the midst of the tour all the more tragic. It may be hard to fault the policies of a sick man in all that followed. In one sense, learning relative to the Constitution had led Wilson astray, and lack of learning about international affairs prevented him from getting on track. When the battle was fairly joined on Capitol Hill the president was back on familiar ground, and he felt he might yet win the single most important provision of the treaty, the League of Nations, with the United States a member.[150]

It was not to be. Voting on the Versailles treaty first took place in November 1919. Both the treaty with the Lodge Reservations and the treaty without the reservations were rejected by the Senate. The irreconcilables, the utter opponents of the treaty, voted with the Democrats to defeat the treaty with reservations; the same hardliners joined the moderate Republicans to reject the unamended version. In the absence of any long schooling in the history and the ways of international treatymaking, Wilson courted disaster. A believer in the great-man theory of history, he now embraced the evil man, the devil theory, to explain his failure. Had Wilson been well read in modern international relations and the history of treaty making, his moral resolve might have been tempered. If he had taken a long view of treaty arrangements, something history could have taught him, he might have been able to see the Lodge Reservations for what they were (irrespective of the senator's intention)—modifications that would not have fundamentally altered the American commitment to collective security through the League. Such scholarly preparation might have enabled him, further, to depersonalize his attitude toward Lodge and other moderate opponents. Had he been as conversant with the history of the negotiations at Utrecht, Paris, and Vienna as he was with the growth of self-government in England, his opponents would have appeared to him less as villains and more as rivals across the diplomatic chessboard. When the final negative vote on the treaty with the Lodge Reservations was recorded in March 1920, Woodrow Wilson paid the price not alone of blinding self-righteousness but of an untutored comprehension of the inner workings of historic international agreements. In the modern period, from the Peace of Augsburg to the Congress of Vienna, history had demonstrated, but unfortunately not to the president, that it was sometimes the imperfect but practical instrument that produced the best results.

One can only speculate on the history of Europe and the world after 1919 had the United States become a League member, Lodge Reservations and all. It is not necessary to speculate, however, on how the failure of the League, and the rejection of the Versailles treaty of which it was a part, led to the greatest war the human species has ever waged against itself. If Woodrow Wilson is to bear any blame for what came about, the learned Wilson must in some way be implicated. His was a pitiless destiny.

When first enunciated, "the learned presidency" displays a certain novelty. It cuts across the grain, challenges a given, and seeks to falsify the truism that, historically, men of action have been best suited to occupy the office. Yet the intellectual qualities of John Adams, Thomas Jefferson, and James Madison have long been celebrated. And there is nothing especially startling in stressing the scholarship of Wilson's connection with the work of Frederick Jackson Turner and the common effort of the men to appreciate the meaning of the American frontier.[151] Only recently John M. Cooper termed Wilson the premier political scientist of his day.[152] John Higham, in discussing professional historical scholarship in America, placed Roosevelt on a level with Moses Coit Tyler, John Bach McMaster, and James Ford Rhodes, respectable company by any standard.[153] In his sweeping description of the American mind Henry Steele Commager grudgingly admitted that had TR never become president, students would still read *The Winning of the West* and *The Naval War of 1812*.[154] Only Taft has not been duly recognized for his jurisprudence, though a fair estimate of the Taft Court will show that as chief justice he often dominated the widely acclaimed dissenters, justices Holmes and Brandeis. In any number of opinions Taft displayed an impressive grasp of legal theory and legal history, never more tellingly, according to one leading constitutional authority, Robert E. Cushman, than in *Myers v. United States*, where his arguments were persuasive in large part because of their depth of learning.[155]

By linking in a single, unified statement the considerable intellectual accomplishments of Roosevelt, Taft, and Wilson the proposition, "the

learned presidency," sheds its novelty and identifies an important characteristic of the premier public office in America. Why has this been a
neglected aspect of the presidency? Not because of any failure to honor
the individual genius, be he a Jefferson or a Wilson, but rather by treatment of learning as restricted to the man, and not with the high office he
came to hold. What a close consideration of Roosevelt, Taft, and Wilson
yields is not only learned presidents but "the learned presidency." Because it is viewed in a new light the post takes on a new dimension. A
quasi-biographical examination of the writings of these presidents imparts
a learned proportion to the office, revealing their exercise of its powers in a
fashion influenced by their scholarly awareness of both the past and the
present.

There are numerous reasons why the American presidency has been
held in high esteem, but rarely has the yardstick of learning been utilized
to measure its greatness. Perhaps this is attributable to the American trait
of preferring results to theories. As Harold Laski has pointed out, "action
is the essence of the American spirit."[156] Applied to the presidency this
rule highlights achievement at the expense of thought, concealing the
learned feature of the presidency in the process. Roosevelt, Taft, and
Wilson, by reason of their scholarly preparation and deep respect for the
life of the mind, did much to part the clouds obscuring this important
quality of what Alexander Hamilton described as an office whose occu-
pant should be such as "desired by a enlightened and reasonable people."

The presence of Roosevelt, Taft, and Wilson in the presidential office
demonstrates that Americans have not always been satisfied with mere
results, but have on important occasions insisted on honesty and wisdom,
and on intellectually defensible methods of achieving results. At the very
least, the American character as it developed in the early years of this
century displayed an uncommon respect for men of the mind in the
election of these three chief executives. There is no need to make a
comparison, for example, with the heads of state in either Great Britain or
France during the same period to underscore the acceptance by the
American electorate of learned men in public life. Just as the Puritans of
the seventeenth century had insisted on a learned clergy to lead them, so
the Americans at the beginning of this century preferred learned political
leaders, not as a matter of chance but as a by-product of the maturing
American spirit. And there was something of the Puritan in all these men.
Roosevelt's respect for and admiration of Cromwell, Taft's New England
heritage, and Wilson's covenant diplomacy were all signs of the Puritan
strain that figured in their leadership and stewardship. To be learned was
not un-American, as the Puritans and these presidents testified.

Roosevelt, Taft, and Wilson were Progressive presidents. The Progressive climate was agreeable to a man of letters, a jurist, and a profes-

sional scholar serving as head of state. A learned presidency, which would have been slightly absurd as well as irrelevant for the Gilded Age—neither Hayes nor Garfield was typical of those years—was compatible with two decades of Progressive ascendancy. Henry May claimed it as a new Augustan Age in which culture and learning gained fresh respect even from the two established political parties lately given over to bosses and bossism. All three candidates for the presidency in 1912 were "custodians of culture," and among them there was a fundamental belief in the system, though as Progressives they differed in the degree of their commitment to reform. Barrett Wendell, the Boston Brahmin, has been described as "comforted by the thought" that all the candidates were gentlemen from the Ivy League and acquaintances of his.[157] In casting their votes the people were secure in the belief that America was unlikely to go wrong, irrespective of who was elected, because of the candidates' common morality, which was the morality of America.

The learned presidency was consistent with and contributed to what Richard Hofstadter has termed "the Progressive impulse."[158] If Roosevelt, Taft, and Wilson were not all strictly urban in background, neither were they rural or rustic. They were all urbane, however. More pertinent still, they embraced the "realism" of the age, and as Hofstadter well said, "the dominant note in the best thought of the Progressive Era"[159] was realism: realistic institutions, realistic laws, and realistic policies. At the same time these three presidents were intellectually Protestant, and "the Progressive mind was preeminently a Protestant mind."[160] The sense of personal responsibility properly associated with the Protestant mentality figured prominently in the new nationalism, the new freedom, and in William Howard Taft's version of reform. Finally, the broad intellectual currents that swept the Progressive historians, Frederick Jackson Turner, Charles A. Beard, and Vernon L. Parrington, to the forefront of their profession might be seen as having an analogue in the Progressive presidents. The same attitudes of mind that marked the Progressive historians—a lively curiosity, a persistence of scientifically inspired doubt, a demand for empirical evidence, and a rigorous pursuit of answers to troubling questions that combined these traits with old-fashioned honesty and integrity—were also recognized elements in certain of the writings of Roosevelt, Taft, and Wilson. The Progressive historians and the Progressive presidents were intelligible to one another as the American mind and character revealed an increasing complexity under the impact of Progressive ideas and actions. Max Lerner, for example, has judged that American civilization has often been a matter of the "relation between power and idea, between science and conscience."[161] To understand the learned presidency in this way is to appreciate it not as a freak or fashion but as a significant expression of that civilization.

EPILOGUE

"High office does not a learned president make"

The question emerges that has troubled students at least since the day of Plutarch: Do the times give rise to the man, or does the man make the times? The experience of the American presidency tends to show that the times shape the man and his mind. The Age of Reason explains many of the distinctive ideas found in the writings of the first presidents. Adams, Jefferson, and Madison are spoken of as "men of the Enlightenment," a phenomenon of which they and their revolution were a lasting part. One hundred years later ideas and their ethical implications were transformed by the onrush of the scientific method, which imparted new dimensions to history and literature as well to theology and philosophy. In their thinking, Roosevelt, Taft, and Wilson were all scientific, though in each there was a unique mixture of the traditional and the scientific, the old and the new. In a final accounting, it may not make much difference whether the times give birth to ideas, or ideas determine events. Such a question is asked in the first place as a means of "getting at" Jefferson and the Enlightenment, or as a device to probe the feasibility of splitting the atom of the historical Theodore Roosevelt between his mind and his era.

The prospects for a learned presidency between the age of Jackson and the days of McKinley were poor, in part because there was no generally understood intellectual movement that encouraged response or participation. Learned presidents have not existed apart from their times. If this assumption holds true, the technological learning explosion of the twentieth century may be expected to touch future presidents by the twenty-first century. To say that it has not happened is not to say that it will not happen. Approximately sixty years elapsed between the deaths of Jefferson and Adams and the rise of Theodore Roosevelt. The present hiatus in the learned presidency could be ended within the next score of years. Time has been a critical ingredient in the process of developing a learned presidency—time to transmit the philosophy or science from the pure thinker to the man of action who is nonetheless a man of thought.

The office may again be occupied by individuals, men or women, who are learned according to the standards of a new age. To date, two men have been presidents whose technical or scientific training was central to their education, Herbert Hoover and Jimmy Carter. Carter's time in office was marked by an earnest and consistent concern for human rights, at home and abroad, but there was little evidence of the technically trained Carter. Herbert Hoover, educated as a geologist and experienced as an engineer, was one of the great humanitarians of the World War I period, however much his reputation in this regard suffered thereafter. Except for the economic disaster that overcame his presidency, Hoover's conduct of affairs might have registered his experience as a technocrat.

There was in Herbert Hoover and his presidency considerable promise of a significant development in the character of the high office. Despite elements in his background and experience, and in his interests and his vision that were reminders of Roosevelt, Taft, and Wilson, he appeared to be a new kind of president when he took office in 1929. According to Arthur Krock, "party politics did not interest Hoover as such; he was surely no professional."[1] He appeared to reverse the dictum of Wilson; experienced in government, he was removed from politics. Had the learned presidency taken a new direction?

Hoover was a learned man. Though his Stanford education was scientific, he brought to it and continued to nourish a traditional sense of learning. Not unlike TR he had a natural disposition toward books. Marriage to Lou Henry in 1899 reinforced and widened his appetite for learning. They collaborated on the first English translation of *De Re Metallica,* written by Agricola and originally published in 1556. Because the Latin employed words that had no contemporary meaning, Hoover often had to work out experiments before an accurate translation could be achieved. He explained these experiments in footnotes, wrote an introduction, and drew up a bibliography. Mrs. Hoover was responsible for the Latin text in general. The whole of the project was completed and published in 1912. Meanwhile, Hoover had delivered a series of lectures on mining at Columbia University and at Stanford, and he brought these together in a short, impressive work, *Principles of Mining* (1909). Though concerned largely with the technical side of the industry he took occasion to stress qualities of honesty, creativity, and diligence as appropriate to success in the mining business. Hoover was no more likely to divorce character from intelligence than was Theodore Roosevelt.

By the time of World War I, Hoover had achieved recognition as a very able international businessman, an occupation curbed by the war. His organizational skill was put to effective use in a position as head of the

Belgian Relief Commission in 1914, and in 1917 he became chief of Food and Relief Administrations under President Wilson. In 1920 his reputation as a humanitarian and an administrative genius was well deserved and widely acknowledged; John Maynard Keynes noted that he was the only major figure to emerge from the Paris Peace Conference with enhanced stature. He accepted an appointment as secretary of commerce in the Harding cabinet, and in 1922 *American Individualism* was published.

American Individualism was a simple and forthright statement of Herbert Hoover's public philosophy. While it will not bear favorable comparison with the similar efforts of Woodrow Wilson, nonetheless he was serious and earnest in what he wrote. The book is intellectually respectable and at the same time has the strongly hortative qualities common to a sermon. But as Herbert Hoover was not a natural preacher, *American Individualism* remains a work for study rather than inspiration. Its incentive was the record of individual success in America; its occasion was the threat offered to individualism by the post-1918 chaos in Europe that could infect America with foreign isms. Central to *American Individualism* was Hoover's understanding of equality of opportunity:

> While we build our society upon the attainment of the individual, we shall safeguard to every individual an equality of opportunity to take the position in the community to which his intelligence, character, ability and ambition entitle him. We shall stimulate efforts of each individual to achievement; through an enlarging sense of responsibility and understanding we shall assist him in this attainment; while in turn he must stand up to the emery wheel of competition.[2]

In so saying Hoover believed that he was rejecting alike Adam Smith and Charles Darwin. He was also spurning the assumption that having been created equal, all men should enjoy equal rewards in life. His individualism has been likened to that of Walt Whitman's "I" in *Song of Myself,* that is, supremely confident of self yet leading others to meet the challenges of life. In Hoover's public philosophy, individualism included a call for service to mankind, insisting all the while on maximum opportunity for individual fulfillment. If this led to an accumulation of goods and property, Hoover could only applaud. Good Puritan that he was, he thought of men as worldly creatures. And as a good engineer he believed inefficiency was waste that had to be rooted out of the processes of production and distribution. This in turn depended on individual freedom to experiment. The duty of government was not to be indifferent to the fate of the individual but to rule and to regulate in a fashion most conducive to individual opportunity. Such was the special responsibility of the American government, for in America the individual enjoyed nearly optimum conditions for advancement and prosperity. The more Hoover became absorbed in public affairs, the more important *American Individualism* became for understanding and estimating his policies. The book marked his coming of age as a public man.

Standing at the threshold of the presidency, Hoover combined much of the best from the old and the new. He was a collector of books and a voracious reader; he prided himself on his collection of scientific first editions, and his personal library has been described as enormous. Hoover also displayed an uncommon affection for Stanford University, serving on its board of directors, donating his war documents as the basis of the Hoover Library, and occupying a house, one of his several homes, on the university campus.

As old-fashioned as all this makes him seem, it must be recognized that Hoover was genuinely scientific in his style. He believed that ceaseless experimentation by experts was a necessary preliminary to change. He retained a great respect for the specialist, provided he remained in his field. He was reluctant, nonetheless, to reverence learning for its own sake. Hoover was "the thoughtful man of action" who preferred practical to theoretical solutions. What made him an attractive presidential prospect was technical competence; he was "the great engineer," according to the 1928 slogan.

The best face possible to put on the Hoover presidency is that it was an understandable failure. Hoover proceeded as he did because of his belief in a self-adjusting economy, in the operation of which individualism was an article of faith. This attitude did not necessarily prolong the depression, which continued well after Franklin Roosevelt took office. The New Deal did not solve the economic problem, but it did turn the nation around psychologically, a task that was beyond the personal attributes of Herbert Hoover. His exile in the Siberia of American politics was a long one, as undeserved as it was self-explanatory. As many exiles do, Hoover took the occasion to think and to write. He published *The Challenge to Liberty* in 1934, a reassertion of the themes of *American Individualism* but highly defensive in tone as it condemned New Deal policies. With war clouds thickening in Europe in the late 1930s, he turned his attention to world politics and in 1942 brought out two books, *America's First Crusade* and *The Problems of a Lasting Peace,* the latter with Hugh Gibson. Statesmanlike in purpose, these books, because of their timing, identified Hoover with isolationism in an era of growing internationalism. *The Basis of a Lasting Peace,* also with Gibson, came out in 1945. In it he warned that "we must be on guard against setting up a purely mechanical body without a soul. However ingenious a new world charter may appear on paper it cannot succeed unless it is based on the great principles of the rights of nations and of individuals."[3] *The Basis of a Lasting Peace* did much to rehabilitate Hoover's reputation as an elder statesman. His

Memoirs were published in three volumes in 1951–52, followed by *The Ordeal of Woodrow Wilson* (1958), a knowing account of Wilson (and Hoover) at the Paris Peace Conference. In these several books Herbert Hoover displayed a sense of history, a knowledge of human beings, and hopes for a better world. It is both interesting and surprising that after he left the presidency there was only occasional indication of the technical side of Hoover in his various writings, and overwhelming evidence of the public man concerned for the welfare of the race. In sum, he was much more the classic liberal than the futuristic technocrat.

Apart from Hoover, professional politicians, some of whom were trained in the law, have been the most frequent occupants of the White House since the departure of Woodrow Wilson. Warren Harding was pure politico and Calvin Coolidge was a political accident. Franklin Roosevelt, a cultivated and cultured gentleman and the product of an upper-class background and schooling, was pragmatic without knowing much about William James. Harry Truman loved American history, read it without stint, and prided himself on his knowledge of his country, but he would have scoffed at being called learned. The one general who became president, Dwight Eisenhower, was a man of intelligence but a doer, not a thinker. John F. Kennedy had pretensions to learning but there are serious doubts about the authorship of *Why England Slept* and *Profiles in Courage*. History is left with the impression that Kennedy deemed it important, or at least useful, that presidents be perceived as writing books. Lyndon Johnson was a politician's politician, a good country boy who respected the school teacher the way he respected the preacher, but whose overriding ambition was to wield power.

Lawyers have been especially disappointing for the reputation of the learned presidency in this century. The training of Richard Nixon and Gerald Ford, at two of the best law schools in the country, rendered them potentially learned. However, the education Nixon received at Duke and Ford got at Yale was a specialized training in the technicalities of the law. Given their political ambitions it was unlikely that either would aspire to be legal philosophers. They were very unlike William Howard Taft, for whom the law in its majesty was the bulwark of free political institutions, a proposition Taft strove consciously to animate. For Nixon and Ford the law was an instrument to settle a dispute or to launch a political career.

Richard Nixon's efforts at literary expression, aside from his memoirs (the sort of historical record-*cum*-apologia that presidents from Hoover to Jimmy Carter have issued), deserve passing recognition. *The Real War,* termed both self-serving and sobering, acknowledges Nixon's respect for the power of the written word. *Leaders,* a collection of essays on certain notables of his time that includes reflections on the nature of leadership, is a reminder of Theodore Roosevelt's compulsion to write in order to explain himself. If his total output is limited and falls well below the standards set by other presidents, there is some evidence of a learned instinct that, had it been nurtured, might have grown. Neither book, however, owed very much to Nixon's technical training in the law.

There is some reason to believe, after all, that the highly technical learning associated with the twentieth century may not directly touch the American presidency. Learning has become increasingly specialized in the law and in all intellectual disciplines. The universal genius so long admired has become the dilettante. Specialists are experts called upon to consider a specific problem and to propose solutions. Knowledge is valued most insofar as it is immediately useful in getting things done—now. At the same time knowledge has become increasingly technical it has become accessible to fewer and fewer people. Voltaire was supposed to have said that while many spoke of Newton and his work, few had read him because to read Newton one must be learned. Much the same observation may be offered of the rarefied technology of today. The great desideratum is the application of scientific know-how to situations that puzzle mankind. Learning nowadays is less reflective, less integrating, than it was fifty years ago. Its function in society has changed and so, there, has its impact on the presidency.

But if the future belongs to the technocrat, can the presidency escape the future? Or, ironically, has the office already become the preserve of a species of technocrat, the contemporary professional politician? Except for Eisenhower, only professional politicians have been in the White House since Herbert Hoover. Franklin Roosevelt's rare personal magnetism made him a supreme politician, someone for chief executives to emulate. Post-FDR presidents have relied heavily on the mass media, in the use of which Roosevelt was the pioneer. They have projected their personalities and sold their images, calling on the special devices of mass communication to win and hold office. As the environment has become saturated with instantaneous information and a steady bombardment of "news," the professional politician has responded to these conditions by expert utilization of radio and television. The results in terms of the quality of national leadership have been mixed, but the dominance of the new political specialists, worthy successors to the party bosses of old, is hardly debatable. Woodrow Wilson had urged a merging of the national leader and the party leader in the president, and the mass media have greatly facilitated the fusion. They have also produced a new kind of chief executive.

The signs indicating a revival of the learned presidency are mixed, but the prospects may be considered at least as favorable as they were in 1900. That year McKinley defeated Bryan, and neither man threatened the office with learning. McKinley was the victim of a madman's bullet and, quite unexpectedly, Theodore Roosevelt, much more a booklover than a "crazy cowboy," was president. The exact character of a neo-learned presidency remains unclear. The general proposition of learning as scientific and technical is in place. What elements from the past world of knowledge will be retained and in which fashion and in what combinations—these considerations, as with all future events, are beyond calculation. Yet the possibilities are as intriguing as they must have seemed long ago when the office came alive in response to the learning of the first presidents. Meanwhile, the nation has chosen to honor John Adams, Thomas Jefferson, and James Madison by naming the three great buildings that comprise the Library of Congress complex after them, a fitting recognition and a faithful reminder of the historic link between learning and the American presidency.

NOTES

Prologue

1. *The Federalist* (New York: Random House, Inc., 1941) no. 69, pp. 441–51; p. 444.

2. Tom Paine, *The Writings of Tom Paine,* Moncure D. Conway, ed. (New York: G. P. Putnam's Sons, 1894), 1:83, 99.

3. *The Federalist,* no. 67, pp. 436–44; p. 436.

4. Ibid., no. 77, pp. 496–503; p. 502.

5. Jefferson to Walter Jones, quoted to J. G. deH. Hamilton, ed., *The Best Letters of Thomas Jefferson* (Boston and New York: Houghton Mifflin Company, 1926), p. 188.

6. Jack Shepherd, *The Adams Chronicles* (Boston: Little Brown and Company, 1975), p. 221.

7. Jefferson to W. F. Gardner, quoted in Merrill D. Peterson, *Adams and Jefferson A Revolutionary Dialogue* (Athens: University of Georgia Press, 1976), p. 16.

8. V. L. Parrington, *Main Currents in American Thought* 3 vols., (New York: Harcourt, Brace and World, Inc., 1927) 1:312; 325.

9. John R. Howe, *The Changing Political Thought of John Adams* (Princeton: Princeton University Press, 1966), pp. 106–7.

10. Jefferson to Richard Lee, 8 May 1825, *Writings,* Merrill D. Peterson, ed., (New York: Viking Press, 1984), p. 1501.

11. Jefferson, "A Summary of the Rights of British America," ibid, p. 11.

12. Jefferson, "A Bill for Establishing Religious Freedom," ibid, pp. 346–48.

13. Jefferson, "Essay on the Anglo-Saxon Language," pp. 855–82, Saul K. Padover, ed., *The Complete Jefferson* (New York: Duell, Sloan and Pearce, 1943), p. 863.

14. Quoted in Charles Warren, *Jacobin and Junto* (Cambridge: Harvard University Press, 1931), p. 50.

15. Jefferson, "First Inaugural Address," Peterson, *Adams and Jefferson,* p. 91.

16. Adrienne Koch, *Jefferson and Madison The Great Collaboration* (New York: Alfred A. Knopf, 1950), pp. 291–92.

17. Ibid., p. 260.

18. Garry Wills, *Explaining America* (Garden City, N.Y.: Doubleday and Company, 1981), pp. 3–12.

19. Quoted in Harold S. Schultz, *James Madison* (New York: Twayne Publishers, 1970), p. 77.

20. Ibid.

21. Edward McNall Burns, *James Madison Philosopher of the Constitution* (New Brunswick, N.J.: Rutgers University Press, 1938). Madison as the "philosopher" is the theme throughout the book.

22. Schultz, *Madison,* p. 21.

23. *The Federalist,* no. 10, pp. 53–63, p. 54, p. 55, p. 59.

24. Quoted in David C. Mearns, "Mr. Lincoln and His Books," pp. 45–88, in *Three Presidents and Their Books* (Urbana: University of Illinois Press, 1955), p. 64.

25. Ibid., p. 88.

Chapter 1. Theodore Roosevelt

1. Theodore Roosevelt, "Biological Analogies in History," in *The Works of Theodore Roosevelt,* Memorial ed., 24 vols., ed. Hermann Hagedorn (New York: C. Scribner's Sons, 1923–26), 14:65–106 (hereafter cited as *Works*).

2. Roosevelt to James Bryce, 27 November 1908, quoted in David H. Burton, *Theodore Roosevelt and His English Correspondents* (Philadelphia: American Philosophical Society, 1973), p. 12.

3. Henry F. Pringle, *Theodore Roosevelt: A Biography* (New York: Harcourt Brace, 1931), p. 71.

4. Roosevelt, "Biological Analogies in History," p. 71.

5. Ibid., p. 102.

6. Ibid., p. 104.

7. Roosevelt, "The New Nationalism," *Works,* 19:10–30; George F. Mowry, *Theodore Roosevelt and the Progressive Movement* (Madison: University of Wisconsin Press, 1946), p. 146.

8. Roosevelt, "The New Nationalism," p. 13.

9. Ibid., p. 15.

10. Ibid., p. 16.

11. Ibid., p. 17.

12. Ibid., p. 26–27.

13. Roosevelt, "Speech at Sioux Falls, S.D.," 5 September 1910, quoted in Hermann Hagedorn, *Roosevelt in the Bad Lands* (New York: Houghton Mifflin, 1912), p. 2.

14. The characterization offered by Richard Hofstadter in *The American Political Tradition* (New York: A. A. Knopf, 1948).

15. Roosevelt, "History as Literature," *Works,* 14:3–28, 9–10.

16. Carleton Putnam, *Theodore Roosevelt: The Formative Years, 1858–1884,* (New York: Charles Scribner's Sons, 1958), pp. 71–128.

17. Roosevelt, *An Autobiography* (New York: Charles Scribner's Sons, 1925), p. 22.

18. Edmund Morris, *The Rise of Theodore Roosevelt* (New York: Coward McCann & Geoghegan, 1979), p. 92: Roosevelt, "one of the best twenty five in a very brilliant class."

19. Edward Wagenknecht, *The Seven Worlds of Theodore Roosevelt* (New York: Longmans, Green, 1958), p. 43.

20. Roosevelt, *The Naval War of 1812, Works,* 7:7.

21. Ibid., p. xxviii.

22. Roosevelt, "The Influence of Sea Power on History," *Works,* 14:306–16.

23. Roosevelt, "The Influence of Sea Power on the French Revolution," *Works,* 4:317–25.

24. Roosevelt, "The Life of Nelson," *Works,* 14:326–33.

25. Putnam, *Theodore Roosevelt,* pp. 86–87.

26. Roosevelt, "Manhood and Statehood," *Works,* 13:317–27, 322.

27. Roosevelt to Brander Matthews, 5 October 1888, quoted in Pringle, *Theodore Roosevelt,* p. 115.

28. Roosevelt, *Hunting Trips of a Ranchman, Works,* 1:3–297.

29. Ibid., p. 225.

30. Ibid., p. 228.

31. Ibid., p. 118.

32. Roosevelt, *Ranch Life and the Hunting Trail, Works,* 6:361–585.

33. Ibid., pp. 368–69.

34. Ibid.

35. Roosevelt, *The Wilderness Hunter, Works,* 2.

36. Ibid., p. xxxi.

37. Roosevelt, *The Winning of the West, Works,* 10, 11, 12:3–414.

38. Roosevelt to Frederick Jackson Turner, 15 December 1896, *Letters of Theodore Roosevelt,* 8 vols., ed. Elting E. Morison et al. (Cambridge: Harvard University Press, 1951–54), 1:571 (hereafter cited as *Letters*).

39. Roosevelt, *The Winning of the West,* pp. 391–414. passim.

40. Ibid., 10:3.

41. Roosevelt to Turner, 4 November 1896, *Letters,* 1:364–65.

42. Roosevelt to Turner, 10 April 1895, *Letters,* 1:440.

43. Roosevelt, *Thomas Hart Benton, Works,* 8:1–269.

44. Roosevelt to Henry Cabot Lodge, 27 March 1886, *Letters,* 1:95.

45. Roosevelt, *Gouverneur Morris, Works,* 5:273–544.

46. Ibid., p. 369.

47. Roosevelt, *Oliver Cromwell, Works,* 13:287–461.

48. Arthur Hamilton Lee (Viscount Lee of Fareham), in "Cromwell and Roosevelt," *Works,* 13:266.

49. Roosevelt to John St. Loe Strachey, 27 January 1900, *Letters,* 2:1144.

50. Roosevelt, *Cromwell,* pp. 296–98.

51. Roosevelt, "Productive Scholarship," *Works,* 14:340–54, 340.

52. Hermann Hagedorn in *Works,* 1:x–xi.

53. Brander Matthews, "Theodore Roosevelt as a Man of Letters," *Works,* 14:ix–xxiii.

54. Roosevelt, "Social Evolution," *Works,* 14:107–28.

55. Ibid., p. 119.

56. Ibid., p. 128.

57. Ibid., p. 110.

58. Roosevelt, "The Children of the Night," *Works,* 14:360–64.

59. Ibid.

60. Roosevelt, "The Ancient Irish Sagas," *Works,* 14:384–401; see also, "The Irish Players," ibid., 14:402–4.

61. Ibid., p. 391.

62. Ibid., p. 401.

63. Roosevelt, "Dante and the Bowery," *Works,* 4:439–47.

64. Ibid., p. 439.

65. Ibid., pp. 439–40.

66. Ibid., p. 447.

67. Ibid., pp. 440–41.

68. Roosevelt, "The Law of Civilization and Decay," *Works,* 14:129–50.
69. Ibid.
70. Roosevelt to Lodge, 23 September 1901, *Letters,* 3:150.
71. Roosevelt, *An Autobiography,* p. 84.
72. Roosevelt, "Men of Action," *Works,* 13:417–635.
73. Ibid., p. 419.
74. Ibid., p. 428.
75. Ibid., pp. 436, 438, 444.
76. Ibid., pp. 445–50.
77. Ibid., p. 502.
78. Ibid., pp. 521, 525.
79. Ibid., p. 550.
80. Ibid., pp. 559–60.
81. Ibid., pp. 566–67.
82. Ibid., p. 570.
83. Roosevelt to W. Murray Crane, 22 October 1902, *Letters,* 3:360.
84. Roosevelt, "True Americanism," *Works,* 15:15–31, 16, 18.
85. Roosevelt to Owen Wister, 19 November 1904, *Letters* 4:1037.
86. William H. Harbaugh, *The Life and Times of Theodore Roosevelt,* (New York: Collier Books, 1963), p. 304.
87. Roosevelt, "The Forest Problem," *Works,* 18:127–34, 131.
88. Roosevelt, "Forestry and Business, *Works,* 18:135–44, 135.
89. Roosevelt, "The Puritan Spirit and the Regulation of Corporations," *Works,* 18:90–101.
90. Ibid., p. 94.
91. Ibid., p. 95.
92. Ibid., p. 99.
93. Roosevelt to Arthur Hamilton Lee, 6 October 1909, *Letters,* 7:32.
94. Roosevelt, "The Origin and Evolution of Life," *Works,* 14:29–37, 36.
95. Roosevelt, "History as Literature," *Works,* 14:3–38, 9.
96. Roosevelt to Oliver Wendell Holmes, Jr., 21 October 1904, *Letters,* 4:989.
97. Roosevelt, "Biological Analogies," pp. 82, 89–90.
98. Roosevelt to William Howard Taft, 12 March 1901, *Letters,* 3:11.
99. Roosevelt to William H. Hunt, 26 September 1901, *Letters,* 3:151.
100. Roosevelt, "First Annual Message to Congress," *Works,* 17:93–160, 128.
101. Roosevelt to Lodge, 30 April 1906, *Letters,* 5:1362.
102. C. A. Spring Rice to Roosevelt, 6 August 1896, quoted in Burton, *Roosevelt and His English Correspondents,* p. 7.
103. Roosevelt to Lee, 25 July 1900, *Letters,* 2:1362.
104. Roosevelt to William Howard Taft, 21 August 1907, quoted in Ralph E. Minger, *William Howard Taft and United States Foreign Policy: The Apprenticeship Years 1900–1908.* (Urbana: University of Illinois Press, 1975), p. 162.
105. Roosevelt to Speck von Sternburg, 12 July 1901, *Letters,* 3:116.
106. Roosevelt to Kermit Roosevelt, 4 November 1903, *Letters,* 3:644.
107. Frederick S. Marks, *Velvet on Iron,* (Lincoln: University of Nebraska Press, 1981), pp. 140–41; see also Howard K. Beale, *Theodore Roosevelt and the Rise of America to World Power,* (Baltimore: Johns Hopkins University Press, 1956) for the most thorough analysis of Roosevelt's foreign policy.
108. Roosevelt to Sir George Otto Trevelyan, 1 October 1911, *Letters,* 7:348–416.

109. Pringle, *Theodore Roosevelt: A Biography*, p. 473.
110. Roosevelt, "Tolstoy," *Works*, 14:411–17 passim.
111. Roosevelt, "History as Literature," pp. 3–38.
112. Ibid., p. 16.
113. Roosevelt to John St. Loe Strachey, 28 November 1908, *Letters*, 7:1388.
114. Roosevelt, "History as Literature," pp. 11–15.
115. Ibid., p. 23.
116. Ibid., p. 28.
117. Ibid.
118. Roosevelt, "A Layman's View of an Art Exhibition," *Works*, 14:405–10.
119. Ibid., p. 405.
120. Ibid., p. 406.
121. Ibid., pp. 409–10.
122. Roosevelt to Emily Carow, 4 January 1913, *Letters*, 8:689.
123. Roosevelt, *African Game Trails*, *Works*, vol. 5.
124. Ibid., pp. 291–92.
125. Ibid., p. 295.
126. Roosevelt to Lodge, 10 September 1909, *Letters*, 7:30.
127. Roosevelt, *Through the Brazilian Wilderness*, *Works*, 6:1–370.
128. Roosevelt, "Racial Decadence," *Works*, 14:151–66.
129. Ibid., 164–66 passim.
130. Roosevelt, "Woman in Science," *Works*, 14:179–84.
131. Ibid., p. 184.
132. Roosevelt, "Our Neighbors, The Ancients," *Works*, 14:52–57.
133. Roosevelt, "The Origin and Evolution of Life," pp. 29–37.
134. Ibid., p. 36.

Chapter 2. William Howard Taft

1. There is no unified collection of the writings of William Howard Taft. The Taft *Papers* are available on microfilm, Library of Congress. Specialized collections, such as *The Presidential Addresses and State Papers of William Howard Taft* (New York: Doubleday, Page, 1910) and *Political Issues and Outlooks* (New York: Doubleday, Page, 1909) have come into print.

2. Taft's most important judicial writings are in *United States Reports* for the years 1921–30.

3. Taft's books on politics and government include: *Four Aspects of Civic Duty* (New York: C. Scribner's Sons, 1907); *Popular Government* (New Haven: Yale University Press, 1913); *The Anti-Trust Act and the Supreme Court* (New York: Harper and Row, 1914); and *The President and His Powers* (New York: Columbia University Press, 1924).

4. Taft's books on war and peace include: *The United States and Peace* (New York: C. Scribner's Sons, 1914); *World Peace* (New York: George H. Doran & Co., 1917); and *Taft Papers on the League of Nations* (New York: MacMillan Company, 1920).

5. Henry F. Pringle, *The Life and Times of William Howard Taft*, 2 vols. (New York: Farrar & Rinehart. 1939), pp. 3ff. Pringle's study superseded both Herbert S. Duffy, *William Howard Taft* (New York: Minton Balch, 1930) and Edward Cotton, *William Howard Taft: A Character Study* (Boston: Beacon Press, 1932). Judith I. Anderson, *William Howard Taft, An Intimate History* (New York: Norton, 1981) has not displaced Pringle as the standard. The most recent study concentrating on

Taft as a public man is David H. Burton, *William Howard Taft In the Public Service* (Malabar, Fla.: Robert E. Kreiger Publishing Company, 1986).

6. There is much useful and much trivial information about Taft's family in Ishbel Ross, *An American Family: the Tafts* (Cleveland: World Publishing Co., 1964).

7. Harris E. Starr, *William Graham Sumner* (New York: Henry Holt & Co., 1925), pp. 77–95; for a somewhat different view of events see Brooks Mather Kelley, *Yale: A History* (New Haven: Yale University Press, 1974), pp. 235–39.

8. Pringle, *Life and Times,* p. 34.

9. Starr, *Sumner,* p. 465.

10. Yale College Class Book of 1878, Yale College Records, Yale University Archives.

11. Horace Dutton Taft, *Memories and Opinions* (New York: 1942), p. 107.

12. Yale College Records, Yale University Archives.

13. For a recent evaluation of Holmes see David H. Burton, *Oliver Wendell Holmes, Jr.* (Boston: Twayne, 1980), pp. 51–69.

14. Pringle, *Life and Times,* pp. 102–5.

15. Ibid., pp. 100–101.

16. Ibid., pp. 117–18.

17. 45 *Federal Reporter,* pp. 730–45.

18. 62 *Federal Reporter,* pp. 802–23.

19. 79 *Federal Reporter,* p. 561.

20. 96 *Federal Reporter,* p. 928.

21. 85 *Federal Reporter,* pp. 278–302.

22. Taft, *Four Aspects of Civic Duty,* (New Haven: Yale University Press, 1906).

23. Ibid., pp. 6–7.

24. Ibid., p. 7–8

25. Ibid., p. 8.

26. Ibid., p. 10

27. Ibid., p. 11.

28. Ibid., p. 12.

29. Ibid., p. 13.

30. Ibid., p. 15

31. Ibid., p. 17

32. Ibid., p. 25

33. Ibid., p. 20

34. Ibid., pp. 23–24.

35. Ibid., pp. 28–29.

36. Ibid., p. 35.

37. Ibid., pp. 36–37.

38. Ibid., p. 39.

39. Ibid., p. 40.

40. Ibid., pp. 40–45. passim.

41. Ibid., p. 46.

42. Ibid., p. 48.

43. Ibid., p. 50.

44. Ibid., p. 54.

45. Ibid., p. 59.

46. Ibid., pp. 60–89.

47. Ibid., pp. 65ff.

48. Ibid., pp. 78–80.

49. Ibid., pp. 87–88.
50. Ibid., p. 93.
51. Ibid.
52. Ibid., p. 95.
53. Ibid., p. 96.
54. Ibid., pp. 100–102.
55. Ibid., pp. 104–5.
56. Ibid., p. 102.
57. William Howard Taft, *Present Day Problems* (New York: Dodd, Mead and Co., 1908) contains fifteen representative writings by Taft on issues of the day. While informed, they should not be thought of as "learned" in any special way.
58. Duffy, *William Howard Taft,* p. 228.
59. Alpheus T. Mason, *Bureaucracy Convicts Itself* (New York: The Viking Press, 1941) deals with the Ballinger-Pinchot controversy fairly and fully.
60. Taft's presidency is taken up in Donald F. Anderson, *William Howard Taft: A Conservative's Conception of the Presidency* (Ithaca: Cornell University Press, 1973) and Paolo E. Coletta, *The Presidency of William Howard Taft* (Lawrence: University Press of Kansas, 1973).
61. Taft's foreign policy is discussed fully in Walter V. Scholes and Marie V. Scholes, *The Foreign Policies of the Taft Administration* (Columbia: University of Missouri Press, 1970), while useful background is to be found in Ralph E. Minger, *William Howard Taft and United States Foreign Policy: The Apprenticeship Years 1900–1908* (Urbana: University of Illinois Press, 1975).
62. Quoted in Anderson, *Taft: A Conservative's Conception,* p. 277.
63. Archibald Willingham Butt, *Taft and Roosevelt: The Intimate Letters of Archie Butt,* 2 vols. (Garden City, N.Y.: Doubleday, Doran & Co., 1930), 2:635.
64. Helen H. Taft, *Recollection of Full Years* (New York: Dodd, Mead, 1915), pp. 38ff. Her recollections close with the exit from the White House and so, apparently, does her interest in her husband's public life.
65. Taft, *Popular Government* (New Haven: Yale University Press, 1913).
66. Ibid., p. 2.
67. Ibid., p. 6.
68. Ibid., p. 9.
69. Ibid., p. 10.
70. Ibid., pp. 11–12.
71. Ibid., p. 17.
72. Ibid., p. 22.
73. Ibid., pp. 26–29.
74. Ibid., p. 34.
75. Ibid., p. 38.
76. Ibid., p. 64.
77. Ibid., p. 66.
78. Ibid.
79. Ibid., pp. 67–70.
80. Taft, *The Anti-Trust Act and the Supreme Court* (New York: Harper Brothers, 1914).
81. Ibid., pp. 4–5.
82. Ibid., p. 2.
83. Ibid., pp. 6ff.
84. Ibid., p. 11.
85. Ibid., p. 13.
86. Ibid., p. 17.

87. Ibid., p. 24.
88. Ibid., pp. 25–40.
89. Ibid., pp. 53–57.
90. Ibid., p. 76.
91. Ibid., pp. 85–88.
92. Frederick C. Hicks, *William Howard Taft, Yale Law Professor and New Haven Citizen* (New Haven: Yale University Press, 1945), pp. 80–81.
93. William Howard Taft, *The President and His Powers* (New York: Columbia University Press, 1924).
94. Nicholas Murray Butler, in Taft, *The President and His Powers,* p. vi.
95. Ibid., pp. 2–3.
96. Ibid., p. 4.
97. Ibid., p. 5.
98. Ibid., p. 9.
99. Ibid., p. 14.
100. Ibid., p. 18.
101. Ibid., p. 19.
102. Ibid., p. 23.
103. Ibid., p. 31.
104. Ibid., p. 32.
105. Ibid.
106. Ibid., p. 34.
107. Ibid., pp. 40, 41.
108. Ibid., p. 50.
109. Ibid., p. 66.
110. Ibid.
111. Ibid., pp. 78–81.
112. Ibid., p. 87.
113. Ibid., p. 93.
114. Ibid., p. 96.
115. Ibid., p. 97.
116. Ibid., pp. 105–9.
117. Ibid., p. 129.
118. Ibid., p. 139.
119. Ibid., pp. 104–41.
120. Ibid.
121. Ibid., p. 143.
122. Ibid., p. 144.
123. Ibid., pp. 150–52.
124. Ibid., p. 157.
125. William Howard Taft, *The United States and Peace* (New York: Charles Scribner's Sons, 1914).
126. Ibid., pp. 15–25 passim.
127. Ibid., p. 15.
128. Ibid., p. 16.
129. Ibid., p. 43.
130. Ibid., pp. 4–88 passim.
131. Ibid., p. 94.
132. Ibid., p. 100.
133. Ibid., pp. 97–99.
134. Ibid., pp. 115–17.
135. Ibid., pp. 145–46.

136. Ibid., pp. 133–51. passim.

137. Taft's theme in *Liberty Under Law: An Interpretation of the Principles of Our Constitutional Government* (New Haven: Yale University Press, 1922) in which he wrote (p. 20): "ours is the oldest popular government in the world and is today the strongest and most conservative because it stresses individual liberty."

138. Alpheus T. Mason, *William Howard Taft: Chief Justice* (New York: Simon and Schuster, 1965), pp. 193–235.

139. *Truax vs. Corrigan* 257 United States 312 (1921).

140. *Myers vs. United States* 272 United States 52 (1927).

141. *Bailey vs. Drexel Furniture Company* 259 United States 20 (1922).

142. Mason, *Taft: Chief Justice,* pp. 244–45.

143. *Olmstead vs. United States* 277 United States 438 (1928).

144. Taft, *Liberty Under Law,* p. 49.

Chapter 3. Woodrow Wilson

1. Woodrow Wilson, "An Address to the Southern Commercial Congress," 10 March 1911, *The Papers of Woodrow Wilson,* ed. Arthur Link et al., 51 vol. to date (Princeton: Princeton University Press, 1966–), 22:491–98 (hereafter cited as *Papers*).

2. Wilson to Joseph Ruggles Wilson, 16 December 1888, *Papers,* 6:30.

3. Wilson to Robert Bridges, 13 May 1883, *Papers,* 2:356.

4. Wilson to Charles Talcott, 31 December 1879, *Papers,* 1:591.

5. Wilson, "An Address on Robert E. Lee," 19 June 1906, *Papers,* 18:631–45, 631.

6. Wilson, "John Bright," *Papers,* 1:618.

7. Wilson, "An Address on Robert E. Lee," pp. 632, 634.

8. Wilson, "Address Before The Pennsylvania State Sabbath Association," 17 October 1904, quoted in Ray S. Baker, *Woodrow Wilson: Life and Letters,* 4 vols. (Garden City, N.Y. Doubleday Doran, 1925), 1:66.

9. Ibid., p. 67.

10. Wilson, "An Address on the Bible," *Papers,* 23:12–20, 18.

11. Quoted in Henry W. Bragdon, *Woodrow Wilson: The Academic Years* (Cambridge: Harvard University Press, 1967), p. 119.

12. William Bayard Hale, *The Story of a Style* (New York: B. W. Heubech, 1920).

13. Sigmund Freud and William C. Bullitt, *Thomas Woodrow Wilson: A Psychological Study* (Boston: Houghton Mifflin, 1967), p. 131.

14. Alexander and Juliette George, *Woodrow Wilson and Colonel House: A Personality Study* (New York: J. Day and Company, 1956), pp. 4–13, 11.

15. John M. Mulder, *Woodrow Wilson: The Years of Preparation* (Princeton: Princeton University Press, 1978), p. 35.

16. Bragdon, *Wilson: Academic Years,* pp. 6–7.

17. Edwin A. Weinstein, *Woodrow Wilson: A Medical and Psychological Biography* (Princeton: Princeton University Press, 1981), pp. 17–21.

18. Ibid., 18.

19. Mulder, *Wilson: The Years of Preparation,* p. 74.

20. Bragdon, *Wilson: Academic Years,* p. 21.

21. Wilson, *Papers,* 1:78, 442, 443.

22. Ibid., pp. 374–75.

23. Ibid., pp. 241–45, 280–81, 328–29, 307–13, 407–12.

24. Ibid., pp. 493–510.
25. Ibid., p. 408.
26. Wilson, *Cabinet Government in the United States, Papers,* 1:493–510.
27. Quoted in Baker, *Wilson: Life and Letters,* 1:104.
28. Wilson's career at Hopkins is admirably stated in Bragdon, *Wilson: Academic Years,* pp. 101–23.
29. Wilson, *Congressional Government, Papers,* 4:13–179.
30. Ibid., p. 4.
31. Ibid., p. 17.
32. Ibid., p. 43.
33. Ibid., p. 44.
34. Ibid., p. 46.
35. Ibid., p. 52.
36. Ibid., p. 57.
37. Ibid., p. 63.
38. Ibid., p. 78ff.
39. Ibid., p. 102.
40. Ibid., pp. 110ff.
41. Ibid., p. 123.
42. Ibid., pp. 124–25.
43. Ibid., pp. 134ff.
44. Ibid., p. 140.
45. Ibid., p. 156.
46. Ibid., pp. 148, 164.
47. Wilson to Robert Bridges, 28 August 1888, in Bragdon, *Wilson: Academic Years,* p. 162.
48. Wilson, *Papers,* 5:359–80.
49. Ibid., p. 360.
50. Ibid., p. 362.
51. Ibid., p. 366
52. Ibid., pp. 370–71.
53. Ibid., p. 374.
54. Ibid., p. 377.
55. Ibid., p. 380.
56. Wilson, *Papers,* 6:221–39.
57. The gist of the article was given first as a speech to the Owl Club in May 1888.
58. Wilson, *The State* (Boston: D. C. Heath, 1889).
59. Bragdon, *Wilson: Academic Years,* p.174; see also David D. Anderson, *Woodrow Wilson* (Boston: Twayne, 1975), p. 54.
60. Wilson, *The State,* p. 1.
61. Ibid., p. 4.
62. Ibid., p. 13.
63. Ibid., p. 5.
64. Ibid., p. 26.
65. Ibid., p. 21.
66. Ibid., p. 37.
67. Ibid., pp. 41ff.
68. Ibid., p. 68.
69. Ibid., p. 70.
70. Ibid., p. 71.
71. Ibid., p. 83.

72. Ibid., p. 84.
73. Wilson, "An Address at the World's Columbian Exposition," *Papers,* 8:285–92.
74. Wilson, "An Essay on Education," *Papers,* 8:587–96, 589.
75. Bragdon, *Wilson: Academic Years,* p. 244.
76. Ibid., p. 239.
77. Wilson, *Division and Reunion* (New York: Longmans, Green, 1893).
78. Ibid., p. 2.
79. Ibid., p. 24.
80. Ibid., p. 193.
81. Ibid., p. 212.
82. Ibid., pp. 227–28.
83. *Mulder,* Wilson: The Years of Preparation, p. 254.
84. Wilson, *George Washington* (New York: Harper & Bros., 1896).
85. Weinstein, *Wilson: Medical and Psychological Biography,* p. 139.
86. Wilson, *Papers,* 9:293–305.
87. Ibid., p. 296.
88. Ibid., p. 300.
89. Ibid., p. 304.
90. Ibid., pp. 444–54.
91. Ibid., p. 454.
92. Ibid., 8:254–70.
93. Ibid., p. 269.
94. Ibid., p. 254.
95. Ibid., p. 262.
96. Ibid., pp. 160–78.
97. Ibid., 10:202–19.
98. Wilson, "Mr. Cleveland's Cabinet," *Papers,* 8:178.
99. Wilson, "Mr. Cleveland as President," *Papers,* 10:103.
100. Ibid., p. 119.
101. Wilson, "Mere Literature," *Papers,* 8:11, pp. 240–53.
102. Editor's Note, "Mere Literature," pp. 238–40.
103. Ibid., p. 241.
104. Ibid., p. 249.
105. Ibid., p. 252.
106. Ibid., 6:335–54.
107. Ibid., 5:635–45.
108. Ibid., 9:338–47.
109. Wilson, "The Author Himself," *Papers,* 5:637.
110. Ibid., p. 643.
111. Wilson, "An Author's Choice of Company," *Papers,* 9:637.
112. Ibid., pp. 344–45.
113. For some ideas respecting Wilson's plan for the book see, *Papers,* 9:129–32.
114. Wilson, *A History of the American People,* 5 vols. (New York: Harper & Bros., 1903).
115. Quoted in Baker, *Wilson: Life and Letters,* 2:126.
116. Ibid., p. 119.
117. Wilson, *Papers,* 5:299.
118. Wilson, "State Rights, 1850–1860," *Papers,* 11:303–48.
119. Ibid., p. 323.
120. Ibid., p. 338.

121. Ibid., p. 345.
122. Wilson, "Politics, 1857–1907," *Papers,* 17:309–25.
123. Ibid., p. 323.
124. Ibid., p. 324.
125. Ibid., p. 324.
126. Wilson, "The Tariff Make-Believe," *Papers,* 19:359–80. William Diamond, *The Economic Thought of Woodrow Wilson* (Baltimore: Johns Hopkins University Press, 1943) provides background.
127. Wilson, "Hide-and-Seek Politics," *Papers,* 20:192–207.
128. Wilson, *Constitutional Government, Papers,* 18:69–216.
129. Ibid., p. 104.
130. Ibid., p. 106.
131. Ibid., p. 109.
132. Ibid., p. 121.
133. Ibid., p. 120.
134. Ibid., pp. 123–42
135. Ibid., p. 149.
136. Ibid., p. 155.
137. Ibid., pp. 162–82
138. Ibid., pp. 182–99
139. Ibid., pp. 199–216.
140. Wilson, *The New Freedom* (Englewood Cliffs, N.J.: Prentice-Hall, 1961).
141. Wilson, "What is Progress?" in *The New Freedom,* p. 35.
142. Wilson, "What is Progress?" p. 21.
143. Wilson, "What is Progress?" pp. 39–41.
144. Wilson, "The Parliament of the People," in *The New Freedom,* pp. 65–74 passim.
145. Wilson, "Freemen Need No Guardians," in *The New Freedom,* pp. 42–64 passim.
146. Wilson to A. Mitchell Palmer, 5 February 1913, *Papers,* 27:98–101.
147. Ibid., p. 100.
148. Wilson, *The State,* p. 68.
149. Wilson to Sir William Tyrrell, 22 November 1913, quoted in Burton J. Hendrick, *The Life and Letters of Walter Hines Page,* 3 vols. (Garden City, N.Y.: Doubleday, Doran & Co., 1924–26), 1:204.
150. Arthur S. Link, *Woodrow Wilson,* 5 vol. (Princeton: Princeton University Press, 1947) gives the most thorough appraisal of Wilson, the public man.
151. In addition to Richard Hofstadter, *The Progressive Historians* (New York: A. A. Knopf, 1968), pp. 60–61, see also George Osborn, "Woodrow Wilson and Frederick Jackson Turner," vol. 74 of *Proceedings* of the New Jersey Historical Society, 1956, pp. 218–22 and Wendell H. Stephenson, "The Influence of Woodrow Wilson on Frederick Jackson Turner," *Agricultural History,"* 19 (1945):250ff.
152. John M. Cooper, "Woodrow Wilson: The Academician," *Virginia Quarterly Review,* 58 (spring, 1982): 38.
153. John Higham, *History of Professional Scholarship in America* (Baltimore: Johns Hopkins University Press, 1983), p. 157.
154. Henry S. Commager, *The American Mind* (New Haven: Yale University Press, 1950), p. 347.
155. Robert E. Cushman, *Leading Constitutional Decisions* (New York: Appleton, Century Crofts, 1955), pp. 236–37.
156. Harold J. Laski, *The American Democracy* (New York: Viking Press, 1948), p. 42.

157. Henry F. May, *The End of American Innocence* (New York: Knopf, 1959), pp. 107–17.

158. Richard Hofstadter, *The Age of Reform* (New York: Vintage, 1960), p. 174.

159. Ibid., p. 198.

160. Ibid., p. 204.

161. Max Lerner, *America as a Civilization: Life and Thought in the United States Today* (New York: Simon & Schuster, 1957), p. 73.

Epilogue

1. Arthur Krock, *Memoirs* (New York: Funk & Wagnalls, 1968), p. 133.

2. Herbert Hoover, *American Individualism* (New York: Doubleday, Page, 1922), p. 9.

3. Herbert Hoover (with Hugh Gibson), *The Basis of a Lasting Peace* (New York: D. Van Nostrand & Co., 1945), p. 37.

SELECT BIBLIOGRAPHY

Prologue

THE PRESIDENCY

Borden, Morton. *America's Eleven Greatest Presidents*. Chicago: Rand McNally, 1971.

Burns, James McG. *Presidential Government: The Crucible of Leadership*. Boston: Houghton Mifflin, 1966.

Corwin, E. S. *The President, Office and Powers*. New York: New York University Press, 1957.

Cornwell, Elmer. *The American Presidency: Vital Center*. Chicago: Scott, Foresman, 1966.

Hargrove, Erwin C. *The Power of the Modern Presidency*. Philadelphia: Temple University Press, 1974.

Koenig, Louis W. *The Chief Executive*. New York: Harcourt, Brace and World, 1964.

Rossiter, Clinton. *The American Presidency*. New York: Harcourt, Brace, 1956.

THE PERIOD

Commager, H. S. *The Empire of Reason*. Garden City, N.Y.: Anchor Press/ Doubleday, 1977.

May, Henry F. *The Enlightenment in America*. New York: Oxford University Press, 1976.

Meyer, Donald H. *The Democratic Enlightenment*. New York: Putnam, 1976.

Parrington, V. L. *Main Currents in American Thought*. 3 vols., volume 1 *The Colonial Mind 1620–1800,* New York: Harcourt, Brace and Company, 1927).

Savelle, Max. *Seeds of Liberty*. New York and London: A. A. Knopf, 1948.

Wills, Garry. *Inventing America*. New York: Doubleday, 1978.

———. *Explaining America*. New York: Doubleday, 1981.

JOHN ADAMS

Allison, John M. *Adams and Jefferson*. Norman: University of Oklahoma Press, 1966.

Bowen, Catherine Drinker. *John Adams and the American Revolution.* New York and Boston: Little, Brown, 1950.

Brown, Ralph. *The Presidency of John Adams.* Lawrence: University Press of Kansas, 1975.

Chinard, Gilbert. *Honest John Adams.* Boston: Little, Brown, 1964.

Haraszti, Zoltan. *John Adams and the Prophets of Progress.* Cambridge: Harvard University Press, 1952.

Shaw, Peter. *The Character of John Adams.* Chapel Hill: University of North Carolina Press, 1976.

THOMAS JEFFERSON

Adams, William H., ed. *Jefferson and the Arts.* Charlottesville: University Press of Virginia, 1976.

Beloff, Max. *Thomas Jefferson and American Democracy.* New York: Macmillan, 1949.

Binger, Carl. *Thomas Jefferson: A Well-Tempered Mind.* New York: Norton, 1970.

Dumbauld, Edward. *Thomas Jefferson and the Law.* Norman: University of Oklahoma Press, 1978.

Koch, Adrienne. *Jefferson and Madison: The Great Collaboration.* New York: Knopf, 1950.

———. *The Philosophy of Thomas Jefferson.* New York: Columbia University Press, 1943.

Malone, Dumas. *Thomas Jefferson and His Times.* 7 volumes Boston: Little, Brown, 1948–86.

Peterson, Merrill. *Thomas Jefferson and the New Nation: A Biography.* New York: Oxford University Press, 1970.

———. *The Jeffersonian Image in the American Mind.* New York: Oxford University Press, 1960.

JAMES MADISON

Brant, Irving. *The Fourth President: A Life of James Madison.* Indianapolis, Ind.: Bobbs-Merrill, 1970.

Burns, Edward McN. *James Madison: Philosopher of the Constitution.* New Brunswick, N.J.: Rutgers University Press, 1938.

Ketcham, Ralph L. *James Madison.* New York: Macmillan, 1971.

Koch, Adrienne. *Madison's Advice to My Country.* Princeton: Princeton University Press, 1966.

Meyers, Marvin. *The Mind of the Founder: The Source of the Political Thought of James Madison.* Indianapolis, Ind.: Bobbs-Merrill, 1973.

Schultz, Harold S. *James Madison.* New York: Twayne Publishers, 1970.

Theodore Roosevelt

Beale, Howard K. *Theodore Roosevelt and the Rise of America to World Power.* Baltimore: Johns Hopkins University Press, 1956.

Blum, John M. *The Republican Roosevelt.* 2d rev. ed. Cambridge: Harvard University Press, 1977.

Burton, David H. *Theodore Roosevelt Confident Imperialist*. Philadelphia: University of Pennsylvania Press, 1968.

Collin, Richard H. *Theodore Roosevelt, Culture, Diplomacy, and Expansion*. Baton Rouge: Louisiana State University Press, 1985.

Cooper, John. *The Warrior and the Priest*. Cambridge: Harvard University Press, Belknap Press, 1983.

Cutright, P. R. *Theodore Roosevelt the Naturalist*. New York: Harper, 1956.

Dyer, Thomas G. *Theodore Roosevelt and the Idea of Race*. Baton Rouge: Louisiana State University Press, 1981.

Einstein, Lewis. *Roosevelt, His Mind In Action*. Boston: Houghton Mifflin, 1950.

Gatewood, Willard. *Theodore Roosevelt and the Art of Controversy*. Baton Rouge: Louisiana State University Press, 1970.

Harbaugh, William H. *The Life and Times of Theodore Roosevelt*. New York: Collier Books, 1963.

Morris, Edmund. *The Rise of Theodore Roosevelt*. New York: Coward, McCann & Geoghegan, 1979.

Pringle, Henry F. *Theodore Roosevelt: A Biography*. New York: Harcourt, Brace, 1931.

Putnam, Carleton. *Theodore Roosevelt: The Formative Years, 1858–1884*. New York: Charles Scribner's Sons, 1958.

Wagenknecht, Edwin. *The Seven Worlds of Theodore Roosevelt*. New York: Longmans, Green, 1958.

William Howard Taft

Anderson, Donald F. *William Howard Taft: A Conservative's Conception of the Presidency*. Ithaca: Cornell University Press, 1968).

Anderson, Judith I. *William Howard Taft, An Intimate History*. New York: Norton, 1981.

Butt, Archibald Willingham. *Taft and Roosevelt, The Intimate Letters of Archie Butt*. 2 vols. Garden City, N.Y.: Doubleday, Doran & Co., 1930.

Coletta, Paolo E. *The Presidency of William Howard Taft*. Lawrence: University Press of Kansas, 1973.

Duffy, Herbert S. *William Howard Taft*. New York: Minton Balch, 1930.

Hicks, Frederick, C. *William Howard Taft, Yale Law Professor and New Haven Citizen*. New Haven: Yale University Press, 1945.

Manners, William. *TR and Will: a Friendship that Split the Republican Party*. New York: Harcourt Brace and World, 1969.

Mason, Alpheus T. *William Howard Taft: Chief Justice*. New York: Simon & Schuster, 1965.

Minger, Ralph E. *William Howard Taft and United States Foreign Policy: The Apprenticeship Years 1900–1908*. Urbana: University of Illinois Press, 1975.

Pringle, Henry F. *The Life and Times of William Howard Taft*. 2 vols. New York: Farrar & Rinehart, 1939.

Scholes, Walter V. and Maria V. *The Foreign Policies of the Taft Administration*. Columbia: University of Missouri Press, 1970.

Taft, Helen H. *Recollection of Full Years*. New York: Dodd, Mead and Company, 1917.

Woodrow Wilson

Blum, John M. *Woodrow Wilson and the Politics of Morality*. Boston: Little, Brown, 1956.

Bragdon, Henry W. *Woodrow Wilson: The Academic Years*. Cambridge: Harvard University Press, 1967.

Craig, Hardin. *Woodrow Wilson at Princeton*. Norman: University of Oklahoma Press, 1960.

Diamond, William. *The Economic Thought of Woodrow Wilson*. Baltimore: Johns Hopkins University Press, 1943.

Elletson, D. H. *Roosevelt and Wilson, A Comparative Study*. London: J. Murray, 1965.

Freud, Sigmund, and Bullitt, William C. *Thomas Woodrow Wilson: A Psychological Study*. New York: Houghton, 1967.

George, Alexander and Juliette. *Woodrow Wilson and Colonel House: A Personality Study*. New York: J. Day and Company, 1956.

Grayson, Cary T. *Woodrow Wilson: An Intimate Memoir*. New York: Holt, Reinhart, & Winston, 1960.

Link, Arthur S. *Woodrow Wilson*. 5 vols. Princeton: Princeton University Press, 1947–.

————. *Wilson the Diplomatist: A Look at His Major Foreign Policies*. Baltimore: Johns Hopkins University Press, 1957.

Mulder, John M. *Woodrow Wilson: The Years of Preparation*. Princeton, Princeton University Press, 1978.

Weinstein, Edwin A. *Woodrow Wilson: A Medical and Psychological Biography*. Princeton: Princeton University Press, 1981.

Epilogue

THE PRESIDENCY AGAIN

Cronin, Thomas R. *The State of the Presidency*. Boston: Little, Brown, 1975.

Cunliffe, Marcus. *American Presidents and the Presidency*. New York: American Heritage Press, 1976.

Pious, Richard M. *The American Presidency*. New York: Basic Books, 1979.

Reedy, George E. *The Twilight of the Presidency*. New York: World Publishing Company, 1970.

Schlesinger, A. M., Jr. *The Imperial Presidency*. New York: Houghton Mifflin, 1973.

Thompson, Kenneth. *The President and the Public Philosophy*. Baton Rouge: Louisiana State University Press, 1981.

HERBERT HOOVER

Best, Gary D. *The Politics of American Individualism*. Westport, Conn.: Greenwood Press, 1975.

Burner, David. *Herbert Hoover*. New York: Knopf, 1979.

Eckley, Wilton. *Herbert Hoover*. Boston: Twayne Publishers, 1980.

Fausold, Martin, and Mazuzan, George. *The Hoover Presidency: A Reappraisal.* Albany, N.Y.: State University Press, 1974.

Nash, George H. *The Life of Herbert Hoover.* New York: Norton, 1983.

Robinson, Eugene, and Bornet, Vaughan. *Herbert Hoover, President of the United States.* Stanford: Hoover Institute Press, 1975.

Wilson, Joan H. *Herbert Hoover.* Boston: Little, Brown, 1975.

INDEX